PENGUIN BOOKS

THE LAST SEASON

Phil Jackson is one of the greatest coaches in the history of the NBA. In his fourteen seasons as a head coach, he is 832–316, the best winning percentage in NBA history. He also holds NBA coaching records for the most playoff wins and playoff winning percentage. Prior to coaching, he played for thirteen years in the NBA, primarily with the New York Knicks. He is also the author of *Maverick*, *Sacred Hoops*, and, with his friend Charley Rosen, *More Than a Game*.

Michael Arkush, an award-winning sportswriter, has written eight books, including *Rush!*, a *New York Times* bestselling unauthorized biography of Rush Limbaugh. Arkush lives in Oak View, California, with his wife, Pauletta, and daughter, Jade.

PENGUIN BOOKS

THE LAST SEASON

A TEAM IN SEARCH OF ITS SOUL

PHIL JACKSON

WITH MICHAEL ARKUSH

PENGUIN BOOKS

Published by the Penguin Group
Penguin Group (USA) Inc., 375 Hudson Street, New York, New York 10014, U.S.A.
Penguin Group (Canada), 90 Eglinton Avenue East, Suite 700, Ontario, Canada M4P 2Y3
(a division of Pearson Penguin Canada Inc.)
Penguin Books Ltd, 80 Strand, London WC2R 0RL, England
Penguin Ireland, 25 St Stephen's Green, Dublin 2, Ireland (a division of Penguin Books Ltd)
Penguin Group (Australia), 250 Camberwell Road, Camberwell, Victoria 3124, Australia
(a division of Pearson Australia Group Pty Ltd)
Penguin Books India Pvt Ltd, 11 Community Centre, Panchsheel Park, New Delhi – 110 017, India
Penguin Group (NZ), cnr Airborne and Rosedale Roads, Albany, Auckland 1310, New Zealand
(a division of Pearson New Zealand Ltd)
Penguin Books (South Africa) (Pty) Ltd, 24 Sturdee Avenue, Rosebank, Johannesburg 2196, South Africa

Penguin Books Ltd, Registered Offices:
80 Strand, London WC2R 0RL, England

First published in the United States of America by The Penguin Press,
a member of Penguin Group (USA) Inc. 2004
Published in Penguin Books 2005

10 9 8 7 6 5 4 3 2 1

Photo insert pages 1, 4, 8, 9 (bottom), 10, 13: © Andrew D. Bernstein/Getty Images
2: © Getty Images   3, 5: © Catherine Steenkeste/Getty Images   6: © NBA Photos/Getty Images
7: Lucy Nicholson/Getty Images   9 (top): Copyright 2003 Los Angeles Times. Reprinted with
permission.   11: © Noah Graham/Getty Images   12: © Stephen Dunn/Getty Images
14: © Garrett Ellwood/Getty Images 15 (top): © Lisa Blumenfeld/Getty Images
15 (bottom): © Sam Forencich/Getty Images   16: © Chris Ivey/Getty Images

THE LIBRARY OF CONGRESS HAS CATALOGED THE HARDCOVER EDITION AS FOLLOWS:
Jackson, Phil.
The last season : a team in search of its soul / Phil Jackson with Michael Arkush.
p.   cm.
ISBN 1-59420-035-1 (hc.)
ISBN 0 14 30.3587 8 (pbk.)
    1. Los Angeles Lakers (Basketball team)   I. Arkush, Michael.   II. Title.
GV885.52.L67J33 2004
796.323'64'0979494—dc22
2004057260

Printed in the United States of America
Designed by Amanda Dewey

CONTENTS

THE
LAST
SEASON

PROLOGUE

The writing of a book about something as personal as a basketball team runs the risk of sounding like talking out of school. I didn't want this book to be about the small petty gossip that makes up a lot of the NBA world. We have plenty of reporters who fill that bill. I did want to develop a story about a season that was built around a team of stars—a couple of them past their prime and a couple who have all the problems that the modern sports world can bring to bear. These are young men with too much money and too much fame for something as relatively inconsequential as sports, but this is entertainment. Teamwork is a nebulous thing. It is as ephemeral as love, disappearing at the latest insult. My coaching style over the years has been one that has accommodated stars in a system of basketball that encourages a great deal of team play. The experiment of joining older stars with an established team would be a remarkable opportunity to exhibit teamwork, or it could self-destruct and be a bust. In any case, I was willing to write about the effects of working with these young men. I am grateful to these professional basketball players for their effort. They gave me blood, sweat, and tears, and my thanks goes to each one of them. I'm also indebted to all my coaches, who did everything I asked and more.

This book has been in the works for fifteen years. I have written in journals all of the seasons I have been a head coach in the NBA. Some years those entries have been sporadic, but this season loomed as the one for which I wanted to have a complete record. Jennifer Walsh of the William Morris Agency encouraged me to develop this as a book. She has been a constant supporter, and I thank her for her unbridled enthusiasm. She helped find a cowriter in Michael Arkush who could help me develop a story line and pattern for this book. Michael really kept after me during the pressures of the playoffs to make this book happen and without his effort, it wouldn't have any legs. We spent many days after the season in taping sessions to help color the bare bones of many of my entries. If there was a coauthor of this book, it would be him. Thanks.

I want to thank Scott Moyers, my editor at Penguin, and his assistant, Jane Fleming, for keeping us on the beam, and Jay Mandel and Liza Gennatiempo at William Morris. I am also grateful for the support I've received from my counselor and friend, Todd Musburger, and his son, Brian, and from Kristen Luken, my longtime assistant with the Lakers.

I've had great support from my family. Brooke and Ben have lived with me in LA the past five and three years, respectively. They have gone to all of the games. They are happy that I have laid my mantle down. Charley, Chelsea, and Elizabeth, my other three children, attended as many playoff games as possible over the last five years. I've often said they feel that the NBA throws a party for them every spring when they get to go to the championships. It's been a joy to have them with me in times of winning and losing. My former wife, June, called me after the final game in Detroit and started crying about how sad it was, but how glad she is that I was going to retire. She's the original cheerleader.

Jeanie Buss took me in like a lost dog and nurtured and loved me. It hasn't been easy having a relationship that is so tenuous in her position, but she's been honest from day one and balanced that teeter-tatter love affair between the executive vice president and her partner, the coach. We've had many good laughs and too many dinners together. She encouraged me to write this book in the most honest way I can. I've tried to let the story tell itself.

Thanks to the Laker fans. You have been most generous. In my last game, I wanted to walk off the court and shake your hands and applaud you for your support. Shaking hands with Jack is something I can do again, but I especially want to thank those people who sit up in the bowl or at the rim. I can't begin to tell all the times I've been stopped and thanked by the fans for the years I've spent in LA. You have been most gracious and kind.

ONE

ONE MOUNTAIN
AT A TIME

JULY 11, 2003
Flathead Lake, Montana

I'm going eighty miles per hour, just my bike and my thoughts. I
embark on a journey like this every summer, heading from one
distinct world to another, from Los Angeles, and the high stakes
and high stress that come with coaching in the National Basketball
Association, to the small, secluded spot I call home, Flathead Lake.
I planned to take my time, visiting friends I hadn't seen in years,
places I haven't seen at all. This summer's journey, like the ones before, is the way I make the transition between the two worlds. I
can't fly in from LA, pick out a fishing pole from the garage, and

immediately segue into Tranquility 101. That is not my rhythm. I need to decelerate, allowing the natural beauty of the landscape to usher in serenity. Before me, I saw forever, nothing and every-thing—mountain ranges, canyons, sagebrush, the simple life at last. There was not a single vehicle in sight, and miles and miles between towns with names I won't remember. I was free, happy.

But this year's journey was not like the ones before. Typically during the ride I examine the past, the season behind me, won or lost. A montage of moments springs up, some glorious, some not so glorious, stops along another adventure, one I've taken almost every year since my high school days in North Dakota, when I be-came infatuated with the game of basketball. This journey was dif-ferent because I was already focusing on the season ahead, with its tremendous possibilities—and suddenly, with the alarming news from Colorado, its tremendous pitfalls.

So much has transpired since May, when the San Antonio Spurs beat us in the Western Conference Semifinals, halting our run of three straight championships. A week later, I flew to Honolulu to meet with Dr. Jerry Buss, the Lakers' owner. He asked if I would be interested in coaching the team for another two years beyond the upcoming season, the final one guaranteed under the terms of the original five-year contract I signed in June 1999. "I'd like to win two more championships," Dr. Buss told me. "That would tie us with the Celtics," who have captured sixteen. "Gee, I don't know, Jerry," I said. "Two's a tough order. One is tough enough." Before our visit, I was ambivalent about extending my coaching career beyond the 2003–04 season. During last year's playoffs, I underwent an an-gioplasty to repair a blocked artery. Now that I'm nearing the age of sixty, I recognize how every season, championship or not, exacts a heavy toll. Can I make it through two more years? I wondered.

Do I *want* to make it through two more years? But as I listened to Dr. Buss, my doubts began to dissipate. I thrive on challenges, and there is no more imposing challenge for someone in my profession than winning an NBA title. As long as I received the official go-ahead from my cardiologist, I told Dr. Buss, I would give it a try.

We discussed ways to reload immediately, to plug the major holes exposed in the six-game series against the Spurs: a power forward with strength in the post and a defensive-minded guard who could stick with San Antonio's speedster, Tony Parker; Sacramento's Mike Bibby; and other fearless penetrators. Dr. Buss will never be confused with Dallas owner Mark Cuban—Jerry maintains a low profile, thank goodness—but he cares deeply about the franchise he purchased from Jack Kent Cooke in 1979. "My idea is to pursue Gary Payton," he said. "Gary is a player who can get the ball to people. Teams will not be able to double-team Shaq as easily." I was more excited by the difference that Payton, a.k.a. The Glove, would make at the other end of the court. "We really need someone who is decisive, a defensive leader," I said. "We haven't had a lot of leadership there since we lost Ron Harper." Harper retired in 2001.

Another familiar veteran who popped up on our radar screen was my old cohort from Chicago, Scottie Pippen, the most intelligent defensive player I've ever coached. But I heard rumors that Scottie, underpaid for much of his career, would not be willing to come to LA for the relatively modest $4.9 million midlevel exception we could afford, and with his nagging injuries he was unlikely to be available for more than about sixty games. We let it go. (This was the second time I tried to bring Scottie to Los Angeles. In 1999, two months after joining the Lakers, I made a strong pitch to Dr. Buss. The Houston Rockets were trying to dump Scottie's big salary, and it was my contention that he was exactly the type of battle-tested competitor who, as the third scoring option behind Kobe and Shaq, could propel this very young, very immature group to its first championship. Dr. Buss put an end to my plan in a hurry. "Phil, this is what the organization has for money and this is what I own," he said. "Scottie Pippen would put our salary cap at this number and this is the penalty we would have to pay." Failing to land Scottie almost backfired when he signed instead with Portland, which nearly knocked us out in Game 7 of the 2000 Western Conference Finals.)

In June 2003, the other prominent free agent to surface was Karl Malone, finally prepared to bolt from Utah for what would be in all likelihood his last opportunity to snare a ring. When Dr. Buss had brought up Karl's name to me two years earlier as someone we might pursue, I must confess I hadn't been overly enthused about the concept. His game had dropped off since the mid-1990s, when he was arguably the most talented power forward in the league. I was also concerned that Karl would focus too intently on attempting to surpass Kareem Abdul-Jabbar's all-time scoring record. With Shaq and Kobe, there was no room for a third player who would demand the ball. After we were eliminated by the Spurs, I received the first indication of how serious Karl Malone was about becoming a Laker. His agent, Dwight Manley, called to see if I wanted to attend a Pearl Jam concert. "Yes," I answered, "but we can't do this if this is about Karl Malone." Under league rules, teams are not permitted to discuss with agents the prospect of signing their clients until July 1. "No, no, no," insisted Manley, who formerly had represented Dennis Rodman. "This is about old times. Remember when Eddie Vedder used to come to the games with Dennis?" Sure enough, Manley crossed the line during the concert. "Karl would really like to come here," he said. "We really can't talk about this," I reiterated. He understood the game. He snuck in one final point. "Karl is not going to try to break the record," Manley said. "He just wants to win a championship."

First things first. Before determining which free agents we might be able to acquire, the Lakers had to prepare for the NBA Draft in late June. Picking as far down as we normally do, one major drawback of success, did not leave us with many attractive options. Each winter, in the weeks before the All-Star break, I inform the staff of the specific needs I anticipate for the following season. This past winter, I perceived the need for more athletic players. What transpired a few months later against San Antonio reinforced my original perception. Knowing the unlikelihood of re-signing our own free agents, Robert Horry and Samaki Walker, we also began the search for a big man from the college ranks. Ultimately, we selected Brian Cook, a six-foot-ten, 240-pound forward from Illinois, with the twenty-fourth pick in the first round, and Arizona's Luke Walton, a six-foot-eight forward, with a high pick in the second. Cook, we figured, would be an effective post-up player, while Walton, a pass-first-shoot-later player—a rarity in today's game—would be an ideal fit in our pass-oriented triangle offense. Days later, when it became clear that we stood a good chance to snag both Malone, thirty-nine, and Payton, thirty-four, in what will turn out to be essentially a package deal for an incredibly cheap price, it felt as if the pieces were all coming together.

"Do you feel you've still got that defensive killer instinct?" I asked Gary the other day.

"Yeah, I'm still there," he assured me.

"Do you think you've slowed down, that perhaps you've lost a step?" I continued. "Can you still play a forty-minute game?"

"I can do that," he said.

I tracked down Karl at his ranch in Arkansas. "Coach," he said, "I know I would have to average like twelve points a game for two seasons to break the record. That's doable." He was animated, relaying a recent conversation with Shaquille. "I told him that he better get himself in shape," Karl said, "because if any forty-year-old man comes out there and kicks his butt running up and down the court, he ought to be embarrassed."

There is one final piece to assemble. I've asked Mitch Kupchak, our general manager, to locate Horace Grant, the power forward during the first three championships in Chicago. Horace told me he wanted to come back after sitting out almost all of the previous season. He is exactly what the Lakers lack, a dependable backup to Shaquille and Karl and someone who is very familiar with my system. Horace and I have gone through our share of clashes in the past, but that was a lifetime ago. He has grown, and so have I.

I was at a motel in Williston, North Dakota, when the call came from Mitch. "You're not going to believe this," he said, telling me about Kobe and the rape allegations in Colorado. Was I surprised? Yes, but not entirely. Kobe can be consumed with surprising anger, which he's displayed toward me and toward his teammates. Yet despite our recurring conflicts during our four years together, I was genuinely concerned for him, concerned about how this young man could, in the soul-consuming NBA world, become a mature adult.

Knowing Kobe, I recognized how easily the whole situation might escalate. He rebels against authority. With the new, powerful authority figures in his life—the police, the prosecutors, etc.— I was quite certain he would look for a way to rebel more than ever, doing and saying things that would not be in his interest. The fact that the alleged incident took place in Colorado heightened my level of concern. Here was one state in the Union in which the word "no" definitely meant no. I also began to worry about my team. Just as we were making the moves to set up a season of great promise, along came a scenario that threatened to sabotage our hard work. This dark cloud will hang around us all year long, in the headlines and, I fear, in the locker room. I have no idea how we'll overcome it, *if* we'll overcome it.

As I approached Flathead Lake, these thoughts drifted back and forth, thoughts with no answers, just thoughts. I tried not to judge, only to take notice. One mountain at a time, I told myself.

JULY 19
Flathead Lake

I've been home for more than a week, my mind centered, finally, on this world. My days are occupied with boating, fishing, reading, and hanging out with my daughter Elizabeth who, like me, came to the woods to take a break from life. But the other world is never far from my consciousness. Several days ago, I called Kobe for the first time. His machine picked up. "I'm sorry to hear about what happened," I said. "Call me." I saw the press conference at the Staples Center, in which Kobe, accompanied by his wife, Vanessa, declared his innocence. The whole scene was very difficult to watch. Usually I'm in the huddle, calling plays. I was nowhere near the huddle this time, and hoped that Kobe and his other coaches were calling the right plays. I phoned Kobe a second time and got the machine once more. "I'm sure you've been inundated with calls,"

I told him. "I'm in Montana for a while. Here's my land line number. Call whenever you can."

My brother, Joe, a therapist in Virginia, was here recently for a visit. I asked him for suggestions on how I might improve my relationship with Kobe. To be completely fair, there were a couple things I did over the years to alienate Kobe. The most glaring example was the interview I gave in 2001 to Rick Telander, a writer I knew in Chicago. Rick asked if I believed Kobe was the heir apparent to Michael Jordan. Assuming, naively in retrospect, that a conversation after the official interview was off the record, I mentioned to Rick that I had been told that in high school Kobe "sabotaged" games to keep them close enough for him to dominate at the end. Needless to say, the quotes appeared verbatim in Rick's story, sparking a major uproar. (Kobe has never forgiven me. Last spring, during a particularly acrimonious team meeting, Rick Fox complained to Kobe and Shaq. "The thing that hurts us about this season," Fox said, "is that both of you have acted like you're apart from us, and that we're not any good. We have won championships for each other, sacrificing, and all of a sudden, you turn your backs on us." Shaq, clearly affected, began to respond when Kobe cut him off. "Quit your crying," Kobe said. I then jumped in. "Kobe, you're as much to blame as Shaq is, if not more." "You're the one who should fucking talk," he said. "You said I sabotaged games.")

I think I represent a father figure. He consistently plays out a similar dynamic to how he's interacted with his dad, former NBA player Joe "Jellybean" Bryant. From what I understand, the defining characteristic of Kobe's childhood was his anger. Yet whatever theories I might toss out as an amateur shrink, my brother, the professional in the family, advised me to share with Kobe my own culpability in the relationship, apologizing, for example, for how I wronged him with the sabotage accusation. The point was well taken, and one I will bring up when the right moment comes this fall.

Meanwhile, there's plenty to do around here. My main project will be to lay out plans for a new house on the same grounds where my parents, both deceased, once resided. I want a home spacious enough for my kids and their kids. My family has been spending summers in Montana for more than thirty years. I guess I am, in a way, taking the first significant step to set up my next life, my post-NBA life. I don't have a handle yet on exactly what that will entail, although I imagine trying a little yoga, a limited amount of public speaking, and perhaps some mentoring in basketball. I have no desire to venture into the broadcasting field. After thirty-five years, I think I've seen enough arenas. Maybe I'll head overseas for a year or two to get the NBA out of my system. One option might be Australia, where Luc Longley, who played for the Bulls, has invited me to watch his team. Maybe I'll pick up golf, an act of heresy, I'm sure, for those who still peg me as a counterculture figure, an image that's been overblown from the start.

August 16
Los Angeles

I usually prefer to stay away from Los Angeles for about two months, a substantial enough break to recharge for the upcoming season. Not this summer. After the recent arrival in Montana of my ex-wife June, I flew back to California for two weeks, giving her some space and me a chance to take care of some important business. One high priority was to check out, for the first time, the tape of Game 6, when the Spurs clinched the series by humiliating us, 110 to 82, on our home court. I watch in our video room, as usual, with assistant coach Tex Winter, the innovator of the triangle, or the triple-post offense, as it was originally labeled. Tex, in his early eighties, rarely travels with the team anymore, but he sits in the row behind me at home games. We dissect the tape, a process that proves argumentative, enjoyable, and most of all, enormously productive. We roll it from the beginning, observing each possession, keeping track of the opponent's strategy at both ends of the court. Many coaches experiment with a series of designated options early to determine which ones work and which adjustments will be necessary. On certain occasions, we'll freeze a play four, maybe five, times to figure out how we might better execute it in the next game. Tex, who coached at Kansas State and several other Division I schools, brings a vast amount of knowledge to how he breaks down every sequence. "This is what happened in 1951 when we were coaching against Kentucky in the Final Four," he'll say, as if the game took place weeks, not decades, ago. "Don't stop me, because I'll lose my train of thought." Tex, an unapologetic purist, gives credit to players, but concentrates more intently on adhering to the game's enduring fundamental principles: Are we moving the basketball? If we take something away from our opponent, what will they attempt as a counterattack? The two of us don't always come to the same conclusions, but in assessing Game 6, Tex and I were definitely in agreement. We were amazed at the lack of discipline shown by a three-time defending NBA champion, more glaring on tape than even I remembered. We were completely befuddled by San Antonio's screen rolls, which allowed Parker to roam freely.

Lacking the home-court advantage for that second-round series was a pivotal handicap, along with our not-ready-for-prime-time mental approach. After investing so much of ourselves in three successive championship runs, it seems there was nothing left in the tank. The team assumed that despite its spotty play during the regular season, everything would suddenly, magically, come together once the playoffs arrived. The only thing that was sudden was the end of our season.

August 26
Los Angeles

In the first six weeks after the Colorado story broke, I did not speak to Kobe. I called for a third and final time from Montana, but again the machine answered. He never returned my calls. Imagining the anxieties in his new life, I was not offended. Kobe will confide only with the people he trusts, and I certainly have never been a card-carrying member of that group. Mitch and I wondered whether Kobe, as some people have suggested, might elect to sit out the entire season. We also talked about perhaps offering him a leave of absence. No professional athlete, I believe, has ever tried to perform at the top level of his sport for any extended length of time while fighting to keep his freedom. We didn't wonder for too long: we recently received word from Kobe's people that he intended to treat the upcoming season like any other. He must be in denial. This season, if nothing else, cannot possibly be like any other.

Finally, earlier this week, Kobe came into my office at our training facility in El Segundo. He looked weak and gaunt, down to maybe a little more than two hundred pounds, ten or fifteen less than his standard playing weight. Most NBA players participate in pick-up games during the off-season and work out daily to maintain the conditioning they'll need to compete in top form. Many use the time to develop another move or facet of their game, something, anything, to provide them with an edge over their opponents. Kobe has been playing basketball since he was three years old. He loves the game more than anything else. To realize that he hadn't been doing much physically was quite a shock.

"We really want you to survive this thing," I told him.

He smiled.

"Are you getting any help?" I asked. "Do you have anybody to talk to?"

"No."

"Kobe, you've got to have someone to talk to."

"We have a minister."

"That's a start."

We didn't rehash our old conflicts. I thought of what my brother had told me in July about admitting my own degree of fault for the quality of our relationship but sensed this was not the appropriate moment. We were here to talk about this year, this team, and the necessary adjustments to make this coming season successful. We didn't go over his case. We discussed how he was recuperating from the injuries to his knee and shoulder. The conversation was fairly harmless. Until out of nowhere it became anything but harmless.

"I'm not going to take any shit from Shaq this year," Kobe blurted out. "If he starts saying things in the press, I'll fire back. I'm not afraid to go up against him. I've had it."

I tried to calm him down as quickly as possible. "Kobe, we'll watch what's being said," I assured him. "We'll make allowances this year so you'll be able to do what you have to do and then come back to the team. Don't worry. We're hoping for the best."

I looked him right in the eye and gave him a hug. No matter what had gone on between us in the past, he is a member of the Laker family, and families stick together in difficult times. I was sure that at least for the moment, the anger he flashed toward Shaquille was neutralized. After we wrapped up, Kobe headed straight to see Mitch, who later informed me that nothing had been neutralized.

"Shaq didn't call me this summer," Kobe told Mitch.

"Kobe, I gave you a message from him," Mitch responded. "He invited you to Orlando to get away from everything."

"Shaq didn't have to leave a message through *you*," he said. "He knew how to reach me."

The exchange with Mitch revealed the underlying contradiction in Kobe's attitude toward Shaquille, a symbol, in fact, of a much broader dichotomy in his psyche. On the one hand, he insists that he doesn't "give a shit what the big guy does," but on the other, he shows he cares a great deal about what the big guy does. The meeting with Kobe reinforced an idea I had been contemplating since July, since Colorado, since everything changed. I decided to enlist a therapist to help me cope with what will surely be the most turbulent season of my coaching career. I recalled how much a psychologist helped the Bulls deal with Dennis Rodman. (The psychologist didn't put Dennis on the couch, hoping to fix everything in fifty-five minutes. Nobody fixes Dennis Rodman in fifty-five minutes. Instead, he met with Dennis on Dennis's terms, watching him party, watching him vent. Believe me, allowing Dennis Rodman to vent *away* from the court was surely better than the alternative.) I consulted only a couple of people about this idea, including Mitch. After receiving a few recommendations, I selected a therapist who has dealt with narcissistic behavior in the Los Angeles public school system. He'll be right at home here.

SEPTEMBER 9
Los Angeles

I talked to Shaquille recently for the first time since the exit interviews, which we conduct with our players to evaluate their performances in the just-concluded season and lay out the groundwork for the one ahead. This particular exit interview had attracted more attention than usual because Shaq had skipped his first appointment two weeks earlier. I told the media that Shaq's behavior demonstrated a lack of respect toward our staff and what we're trying to accomplish. To his credit, when he did sit down for the interview, he assumed full responsibility for missing the first meeting. He recently participated in a charity event at our training center. I could tell he was still a little upset with me, probably because I have insisted he report in better shape this year. His decision to delay toe surgery until last September was one of the reasons we didn't win another championship. We staggered at the start, losing nineteen of thirty games, and with them any chance to clinch home-court advantage for the entire playoffs. The statement he made publicly—"I got hurt on company time, so I'll recover on company time"—was outrageous. By not being healthy when the season started in October, he was on the injured list during company time.

I kept my distance during the controversy over his operation. With the amount of negative feedback I give him *during* the season, the last thing I could afford to do was get on his case *before* the season. There are only so many corrective comments I'm allowed before I risk causing serious, perhaps irrevocable, damage to our relationship. As it is, there have been several occasions when I've come dangerously close to crossing that invisible line, whether referring to his weight, attitude, lack of defensive aggressiveness, or woeful free-throw shooting. Fortunately, Shaq has responded in a positive manner on almost every occasion, raising his game to an even higher standard. Shaq looked slimmer, quicker, closer to the old Shaq. He seemed determined to wrest away from Tim Duncan the MVP trophy that, if he competes hard at both ends, should be awarded to him every year. Nobody in the NBA can defend him. With the inevitable distractions that will arise from the Kobe situation, the Lakers will need the old Shaq this season more than ever.

TWO

WHATEVER IT TAKES

October 5
Honolulu

We arrived in training camp only a week ago, and already it feels like an eternity. Most basketball pundits are convinced that with four future Hall of Famers on the same roster, the Lakers should begin preparations for the parade in downtown Los Angeles right now. I am not one of those pundits. As a matter of fact, I'm extremely apprehensive about how this whole experiment is going to work. Given the complicated nature of the triangle offense, the system I've followed since I took over the Bulls in 1989, it will require more than talent. It will require discipline and sacrifice. If a player tries to score every time he touches the ball, the system will break down. Success depends on everyone, at one time or another, accepting, if not embracing, the role of playmaker. I'm also apprehensive about the age of our team, and our lack of athleticism. By drafting Brian Cook and Luke Walton, we received some much-needed help up front, but did very little to upgrade our running and jumping skills, the most basic actions in basketball. I worry about how we will fare against quicker, younger teams, especially on the second night of back-to-backs. If that wasn't daunting enough, there is also the Kobe matter, with its potential for combustibility. If this week was any indication, a major confrontation between the two of us appears unavoidable.

He failed to show up for the opening day of camp, passing word through his agent, Rob Pelinka, that he was too ill to make the trip. When Mitch relayed this information, I asked him to reach Kobe. He tried, but the woman who answered the phone at his home in Newport Beach said he was "resting." Privately, the Laker organization, which includes myself, was furious. This was not the way for a professional athlete to behave. If Kobe was sick, he needed to visit a doctor. Publicly, we put out a different message, telling reporters that with his knowledge of the system, Kobe would easily make up any missed time. We had made the decision, after all, to be very flexible with him this season, the less risky of two risky options. If we were to hold Kobe to the usual standards and rules, he might resist, straining his relationship with the club. As one of his harshest critics, I must also soften my approach. He's dealing with enough pressure without having his coach, yet another authority figure, on his back. When Kobe finally showed up, he didn't seek me out to clear the air, much less apologize, nor did I look for him.

Before Kobe arrived, we held our first official team meeting. Traditionally, I like to use this opening session to articulate a theme for the upcoming season. Of the themes from previous squads, the most memorable was "The Last Dance," the rallying cry for the 1997–98 Chicago Bulls, the last of our six championship seasons. "I don't care if you're 82–0," Bulls' general manager Jerry Krause told me, "this is the last year." I told Krause in response, "I certainly don't want to come back here." For the current Laker contingent, the theme is obvious: sacrifice. No clearer example is needed than the millions of dollars sacrificed by Karl Malone and Gary Payton in pursuit of the elusive first ring. I asked the players to offer their own thoughts, which never proves to be an easy exercise. On the court it is nearly impossible to shut players up; trash-talking's a contest the NBA ought to consider putting in the All-Star festivities. But in a private forum, in front of their teammates, the words don't flow naturally. There have been some notable exceptions. In 1998, before the playoffs began, I asked the players to contribute a poem or a section of prose related to their experiences together, which we then burned. "I couldn't do it without you, Michael," Scottie said. Michael cried. This time, Karl, the oldest in the group, was the most inspiring. "I just want to win a championship," Karl said. "Whatever it takes."

OCTOBER 11
Honolulu

With eight new faces in camp this fall, I've spent more time than ever teaching the fundamental principles of the triangle. Over the years, many players, after only a few practices, have insisted, "Yeah, coach, I know how it works." Well, in almost every single instance, they did not know how it works. The system is far too intricate to be mastered in a short period of time, which is why repetition, from the first day of camp until the last day of the playoffs, is essential. Once a player goes through a physical routine seven times, he starts to ingrain the habit, forming a muscle memory. The body will begin to respond instinctively. On average, players need a couple of years to grasp the triangle's complexities. Making the learning curve even slower is the fact that many of today's players find the triangle offense boring, limited, a waste of their immense individual skills. My answer to their complaint is simple: championships are secured by team, not individual, performances. Michael Jordan, as superb as he was, did not win a ring until he and his teammates discovered how to excel consistently within the parameters of the triangle. Only then were the Bulls able to dethrone the Pistons, our chief nemesis, thwarting Detroit's strategy, known as the Jordan Rules, of deploying three or more defenders to hound Michael every time he drove toward the basket.

Unfortunately, bringing players to this level of team awareness remains a very challenging assignment in today's me-first NBA. Many feel pressured by their families, friends, girlfriends, and agents to concentrate on individual achievement, the surest path to "max out," to land the big-money contract that will enrich everyone in their privileged inner circle. Anything or anyone that stands in the way of that potential windfall is perceived as an impediment. The question becomes: is there enough value for me to notch an assist instead of a basket? Sadly, the answer too often is no. Just as in baseball, where the home run hitters earn the big bucks, the scorers in basketball profit the most as well. An acrobatic dunk will make it onto *SportsCenter*. A simple, unspectacular bounce pass in the rhythm of the offense will not. System basketball has been replaced by players who want to *be* the system.

Granted, every player would like to win a title, but only if it doesn't threaten his more pressing individual needs. In the 1960s and '70s, players asked: "Where do I fit in? How can I help this team win?" Now they ask: "How do I get what *I* want?" Given this selfish mind-set, it is remarkable, actually, that teams play with any cohesiveness. I can't help but believe that for both the players and the fans, the purity of this wonderful game has been compromised in the process, perhaps for good. I was fortunate to be a member of two New York Knicks championship squads (1970 and 1973). We didn't possess the most outstanding individual talent in the league, but we blended perfectly as a team, *because* we were a team, and our fans were knowledgeable enough to appreciate the selflessness. Our coach, Red Holzman, made the game simple. "Just hit the open man," he said.

Ironically, in Los Angeles I have chosen perhaps the most incompatible environment in America for promoting the concept of team play. This isn't Chicago or New York. This is Hollywood, the land of stars, where top billing means everything. Fans, spoiled by the Magic Johnson–led Showtime squads from the 1980s, have been conditioned to prefer entertainment, a Kobe slash to the hoop over a Shaq turnaround in the lane. They don't appreciate the degree of difficulty in a Gary Payton left-handed layup from twelve feet away or a Karl Malone fallaway. They only appreciate Kobe's degree of difficulty. Many root fiercely for their favorites, in a manner that reminds me of Beatles fans in the 1960s who didn't feel a concert was of great value until John, Paul, George, or Ringo performed their favorite song. The same attitude pervades Laker upper management. Dr. Buss wants to see Kobe and Shaq on the All-Star team every year, which is fine with me. But, as the coach, I want to see my team succeed, even if that in some way diminishes the contributions from the two superstars. I was never comfortable when the press referred to the Bulls as Michael and the Jordanaires. My first priority is not to entertain. My first priority is to win.

I've often pointed out that the triangle is designed to enhance the experience for everyone on the floor. It was dubbed "the equal opportunity offense" by Michael. If executed with commitment and energy, it stretches the defense and ensures that there will be plenty of good looks to go around. A fully engaged player will become a happier—and more successful—player. Even so, I've constantly had to give lectures about the need to move the ball to the open man. The system remains alien to players who, as their team's top performer at every level since grade school, assume it is their divine right to dominate games. Shaq complains about sharing the rock too much with his teammates, but as I've explained numerous times, "this is the way we have to play basketball." The quality that sets good players apart, their single-minded willfulness, also can work to their detriment. They drive down the lane over and over, assuming that at worst they will get to the free-throw line. They don't take into account that their stubbornness will result in more charges or turnovers.

In Hawaii we've worked extensively on proper spacing, an integral part of the triangle offense. If players drift too far from one another, or become bunched up too closely together, the offense will sputter. The triangle depends on effective dribble penetration, everyone moving in rhythm with a clearly designated purpose, like members of an orchestra. I wasn't surprised to see a few players struggle, failing to make good passes because for perhaps the first time in their careers, they were *thinking* about making good passes. For Gary and Karl, the transition has been especially difficult. Veteran players with deeply ingrained habits need more time to become acclimated to a new program. I've worked with players whose games were so deeply entrenched—Mitch Richmond and Dennis Hopson come to mind—that they were never able to conform to the cadences of the triangle offense. Consequently, Richmond, who signed with the Lakers near the end of his career for one last chance at a ring, much like Malone and Payton, was replaced in the rotation by Brian Shaw. Conversely, Ron Harper learned how to alter his game. Earlier in his career, Harp was a slasher. With the Bulls and eventually the Lakers he evolved into a dependable spot-up shooter.

Entering a new season, every player starts with a clean slate in my view. I'm thrilled to be afforded the opportunity to coach four future Hall of Famers at one time, but what matters is how they perform now, how willful they are, how much stamina, courage, and intelligence they demonstrate on a consistent basis. Since we started camp, I've been extremely encouraged. Karl, for a veteran player with his credentials, has shown a remarkable willingness to learn. During a recent practice, he asked one question after another related to his positioning in the offense. He's never played on the wing, always the high post in a two-post offense. Before camp started, I was concerned about how he and Gary might respond to rigorous, twice-a-day practices. That concern did not last long: each displayed tremendous energy. I've been impressed as well with their commitment to the passing game. The key will be how they interpret the various actions in the triangle. Their only frustration, which I share, has been the absence of any practice time with Kobe, who is still recovering from his injuries.

The rest of the roster is also taking shape. At the small forward, I plan to go with Devean George, the only non–Hall of Famer in the starting lineup. The rap on Devean, our first pick in the 1999 draft, has been a perceived lack of mental toughness, ascribed to the fact that, emerging from tiny Augsburg College in Minnesota, a Division III school, he didn't compete against college basketball's finest. Personally, I don't approve when players are saddled with this type of rap, and for another matter, anybody who makes the leap from Division III to the NBA, believe me, possesses a sufficient degree of mental toughness. Nonetheless, Devean remains unproven as a starter.

I'm starting Devean because Rick Fox, the incumbent at the 3 position, is rehabbing from a devastating foot injury he suffered during last year's Minnesota playoff series. Fox, overshadowed by Shaq and Kobe, hasn't garnered enough recognition for the contribution he's made to our reign, both on and off the court. He gave an impassioned speech during halftime of Game 6 against Portland in the 2000 Western Conference Finals. "Here you guys go again," said Fox, a mainstay on the squad swept in prior playoffs by San Antonio and Utah. "Are we just going to go passively? We're not going to fight this out?" Tex asked me to shut him up. No way, I told him. "He's the conscience of this team." Fox is the quintessential system player, placing the group ahead of any individual goals. He throws the precise entry pass to Shaq, and can be counted on down the stretch to make the defensive stop we need. Our most optimistic forecast is that he will be ready by Christmas, but as insurance we've signed free agent Bryon Russell, who played in Utah for many years with Karl.

With our aging squad, bench play will prove more significant than ever, especially on the road. Anchoring the second unit will be Derek Fisher. Fish, like Fox, is too often overlooked, but the job he did in the spring of 2001 will never be forgotten by Lakers fans. Sidelined for the first sixty-two games with a stress fracture in his right foot, he provided the spark that helped us secure our second championship, taking charges and hitting clutch three-pointers. Fish also puts the team first. This season, I'm asking for his biggest sacrifice yet. For Fish, a starter the last two years, going back to the bench will feel like a demotion, which, unfortunately, comes at the most inopportune time, the option year of his contract. I know what he's going through. I was a starter on the 1974–75 Knicks squad that lost Dave DeBusschere, Willis Reed, Jerry Lucas, and Dean Meminger. We developed an impressive flow early in the season, but we lacked any real scoring presence in the post—our center was John Gianelli—and we finished 40–42, prompting a trade for All-Star power forward Spencer Haywood. The following year, I was back on the pine. The transition can be difficult, but if a player fully commits to his revised role, he can be very effective. I'm convinced Fish will make it work. Fish is aware of his limitations, which for players at this level is not a given. Many try to do too much, and their teams absorb the consequences. Fish finds it difficult to get around picks and often misses layups when pressured by a shotblocker.

I'm looking for a contribution as well from Slava Medvedenko, a six-foot-ten forward from Ukraine we signed as a free agent in 2001. Slava possesses a wonderful shooting touch but is beaten too frequently at the defensive end. For him to log significant minutes, he'll have to prove capable of making the proper adjustments. There are also question marks surrounding second-year guard Kareem Rush, the product of Quin Snyder's program at the University of Missouri. Kareem, the second-best athlete on the team behind Kobe, has the potential to be an excellent three-point shooter, but he must learn to treat basketball as a serious profession. His older brother, JaRon, a former UCLA star who failed to make it in the league, has been living in Kareem's house. Coming home late, often with friends, he's kept Kareem from the preparation he needs to elevate his game. Kareem also doesn't look like a guard, yet is too small to play as a wing. On the day of the 2002 NBA Draft, when we acquired his rights in a trade with Toronto, I knew his name, but that was the only thing I knew. I make it a point to watch video of potential picks to be part of the decision-making process, but Kareem was one player whom I overlooked. "Who is this guy, Mitch?" I asked. "We didn't try this guy out." Mitch explained Kareem was, in the view of some experts, a possible lottery pick, who'd dropped unexpectedly. The Lakers would be making a mistake, he said, to let him slip by.

As for Walton and Cook, who is recuperating from a broken finger, I don't expect too much this season. I'm not generally in favor of giving rookies a ton of minutes. In a rotation primarily with second-unit players, they will not be placed in a strong enough position to succeed. They won't receive the calls the veterans, especially the stars, acquire and won't be familiar with the opposition. Some players on this team have squared off against a Damon

Stoudamire or a Derek Anderson forty, perhaps fifty, times. I'll put Walton and Cook in sparingly, gradually boosting their confidence and experience for what I hope will be long and lucrative careers in the years ahead. Too many young players lose a fundamental belief in themselves, and never capture it again.

Yet at the same time I know I can't afford to run our starters into the ground. In camp I've begun to gain a clearer sense of the specific role I anticipate for each player. Aiming to conserve their energy for the playoffs, I'll limit Gary to about thirty-four minutes, Karl to thirty-three. Fish will receive between eighteen and twenty-two, enough to maintain his shooting rhythm. At first I don't share my vision with the players, primarily because I wouldn't dare to stifle the creativity that makes them unique. They must be given enough room to explore their potential without interference. Once they've participated in a few practices or games, I'll carefully approach them with ideas for how they might improve without compromising their distinctive styles. Gary Payton is an excellent cutter, but doesn't utilize the skill nearly enough. I'll show him a few moves to make from the corner that might free him in the lane for an easy bucket.

I don't concern myself with the score in exhibition games, playing the starters no more than about twenty-five minutes apiece. My staff told me I've probably lost more exhibition games than any coach in history because I don't place any value on them. Actually, I place a great deal of value on exhibition games, looking for ways to make everyone comfortable on the court together, mainly the new players. I'm curious to see how effectively the second unit will compete in the fourth quarter. At some point during the long season, with the inevitable injuries, they will be need to come through in critical moments.

OCTOBER 21
Los Angeles

I wonder what Kobe is thinking. Yesterday he reiterated his intention to opt out of his contract and become an unrestricted free agent at the end of the season. I would never oppose a player's desire to explore his true market value—if only the players in my era had been granted a similar freedom—but I do question his sense of timing. Since the charges were made, Kobe has been treated remarkably well by the Lakers organization and the fans. He gave his press conference at Staples with our blessing, and we have agreed—once we attained permission from the league to make sure the funds wouldn't be applied to the salary cap—to cover a percentage of his private plane expenses to and from Colorado for court hearings. This will cost thousands of dollars. Kobe was unhappy with the type of plane that was selected; he wanted one with higher status. He should feel fortunate he's not footing the whole bill himself. Not every organization in professional sports would make that kind of commitment. Frankly, I can't understand why Kobe is even contemplating leaving Los Angeles.

On the issue of contracts, I probably shouldn't be too critical. I'm dealing with my own problems. Back in May, when I visited with Dr. Buss in Hawaii, I assumed the negotiations would proceed very smoothly. A month later, after receiving a positive report from my cardiologist, I went to Jerry's house in Los Angeles. He was about to leave for Venice, and I was preparing for my journey to Montana. We made plans to talk again in September. But in the interim, Tim Brown, the beat writer for the *Los Angeles Times,* revealed, according to "source on the ball club," the terms of a new deal that was under consideration. Dr. Buss, I found out through his daughter, Jeanie, who is also my girlfriend, was very unhappy that I was negotiating through the newspaper. In truth, the source was most definitely not me, nor my agent, Todd Musburger. In a loose organization like the Lakers', there are a zillion sources. I told Todd to pass the word to Mitch that we're just as anxious to keep this issue out of the papers. Since then Dr. Buss and I have not met.

The uncertainty has caused some friction between Jeanie and myself. Jeanie is the team's executive vice president of business operations, and as such she's caught in a very awkward position between an attachment to me and her unswerving loyalty to the organization and her father. "Get it done," she implored, "so the season can start and we can have things in place, so Gary and Karl can feel comfortable about coming back next year, and so that one year isn't the end of this thing." Her primary fear, and it's a very legitimate one, is that if I were to leave the Lakers after this season, it would mean the end of our relationship. "I'll be in LA," she said. "You're only here as an American tourist." Generally, this is why, although I share my thoughts with her on other team-related issues, the matter of contract negotiations is one topic we try to avoid as much as possible.

I harbor no ill feelings toward Tim Brown, or other members of the fourth estate. I recognize they have a job to do, and most of them do it quite well. In fact, in many ways, I have more in common with reporters than with my own players. We maintain an on-going dialogue about subjects other than basketball. But in Los Angeles, unlike Chicago, their agenda is different, more dangerous. In Chicago, the vibe I received from the press was one of adoration for Michael, for the team, everyone reveling in the success we generated for a franchise that until this new era arrived, never hung a championship banner from its rafters. In LA, which has fourteen banners, reporters want to know: what can I write that advances the drama for one more day?

From this vantage point, they pose the most leading questions, designed to produce the story they've already framed in their minds, needing only the right quotes to fill in the blanks. Players, especially ones who aren't media savvy, too often fall for this trap. I don't, copping, in many cases, a plea of ignorance by making it a point not to be up to date on every single development. In this high-stress job, in this city, if I were to read every word, I would go insane. The only section I read regularly is the letters to the editor on Saturday mornings in the *Times,* because I find that fans provide the goofiest but, on occasion, the most provocative analysis. At times my strategy of willful ignorance has backfired and caused me and the organization to appear as if we're on different pages. More often I've afforded myself a legitimate out, forcing the pack to search elsewhere for its daily diet of dirt. I can't always cop the ignorance plea. If there is something I absolutely need to be informed about before addressing the media in a pregame conference, or following practices, the PR staff, headed by John Black, will hand me a stack of the day's newspaper clippings. I prepare the sort of pithy, unrevealing responses, that, ideally will disarm the hordes for at least another twenty-four hours. The other day offered a perfect example. Shaq told the press, "I had two Phils in my life," referring to his stepfather, Phil Harrison, and myself, and "I only got one now." When the reporters came to me for a response, I said: "I thought it was me, but that's how selfish I am about it." I don't understand the whole exercise of pregame comments. The league forced these mandatory sessions on us about five years ago, trying,

I imagine, to generate more stories, more buzz. But what I am supposed to tell the press? "Oh, yes, guys, this is what we'll do against Golden State today. We'll try more isolations with Gary, move Shaq over to the wing, and show them that we can't play pick-and-roll." Give me a break!

October 28
Los Angeles

After going 3–5 during the exhibition season—maybe the staff was right about my record—we started serious preparations a few days ago for, at long last, tonight's opener at Staples against the Dallas Mavericks. While we put together probably only one decent half in eight games, this is a veteran group that will know how to perform when everything matters. This being the Lakers, the longest-running soap opera in professional sports, there has been plenty of intrigue off the court over the last seventy-two hours. The stars of the newest episode? Why, Kobe Bryant and Shaquille O'Neal, of course. Their most recent feud had taken place in early 2001. After a two-year hiatus, the duo have reunited—wrong word, I suppose—for a sequel. I heard the news while checking out video of the Mavericks, trying to devise a game plan to disrupt their highly explosive attack. There was a knock at the door. Kobe walked in, anxious to talk about another highly explosive attack.

"He popped off," Kobe said. I did not have to ask who "he" was.

"You're kidding me," I said. "What did he say?"

"Did you read the paper? It's in the paper," he said.

It was in the paper, all right, Shaq suggesting that for the Lakers to be successful this season, Kobe, who played in only two exhibition contests, needed to rely more on his teammates until he regained his full strength.

"Is this what you're talking about?" I asked Kobe.

"Yeah," he said.

"Kobe, what's wrong with this?" I said. "Shaq is right. This is *exactly* what we want you to do."

"Maybe," Kobe admitted, "but it's not *his* business to say that. He can't be talking about my game, about what I should be doing."

"You're not going to take offense at something like that, are you?" I said. "It doesn't make any sense."

"Yeah, I am."

What now? We needed to contain this situation right away. Fortunately, Horace Grant was in the room. Horace is exactly the person a team needs during these moments, a player who has been through his share of feuds. "Horace, have you been listening to this?" I asked him.

"Be patient, Kobe," Horace said. "You're way off base on this one."

Kobe suddenly grew silent, and the anger began to disappear. We had managed, for the time being, to avoid another civil war in Lakerland. I've grown to expect one every season. I just don't expect one *before* the season.

But the anger did not disappear. After practice, Kobe fired back at Shaquille, through the press, exactly as he promised he would in August. "I definitely don't need advice on how to play my game," he said. "I know how to play my guard spot. He can worry about the low post." The war was on.

"He doesn't need advice on how to play his position," Shaquille said, "but he needs advice on how to play team ball. If it's going to be my team, I'll voice my opinion. If he don't like it, he can opt out."

On and on it went, the two protagonists in top form. Why don't the two get along? I have my theories, one of which is that Shaquille is making the type of money—about $25 million a year—that Kobe will never earn due to the changes in the league's collective bargaining agreement. No matter how many MVP trophies Kobe might collect in the decade ahead, there is nothing he can do about this discrepancy. In fact, the word I got was that Kobe was the only player in the entire league who voted against the agreement because of the cap it put on salaries.

How players deal with one another *off* the court, I've always believed, will play itself out *on* the court. Unlike Malone-Stockton, Kareem-Magic, and other superstar tandems, this duo, after seven years together, still doesn't know how to consistently execute the all-important two-man game. Each looks awkward, tentative, without trust in the other regarding how to read screen rolls, give and go, dribble weaves, and other two-man games.

The newspapers, needless to say, have treated the Kobe-Shaq feud as if it were the second coming of Cain versus Abel. IT'S THE RETURN OF STAR WARS was the headline in the *Times*. The story was destined to last for days and days, every basketball reporter in the city, maybe the nation, on a scavenger hunt for the next insult or innuendo to filter through the grapevine. There was only so much the Lakers could do to try to tame the beast, and whatever we were going to do, we had to act fast. I placed a call to the therapist. "Get them apart," he recommended. "Tell them that what they're saying about each other is not doing anybody any good." He mentioned a psychological term for this damage-control strategy: suppression. I took Shaq aside, and Mitch found Kobe.

"We can't have this," I told Shaq. "This isn't right. We're on a mission, and we want nothing more in the press." Shaq was not in the mood to suppress anything. "Phil, I have a stepbrother," he explained, "and when I was young, I was the outcast. Everything I did was wrong and everything he did was okay even though he did stuff that I could never get away with. If I tried to do it, they would have beaten the heck out of me. It's the same situation with Kobe. He ends up getting an operation from some doctor, who knows where, and I end up getting an operation and I'm the one criticized for it. I end up looking like crap in this thing, and he can do whatever he wants. I'd like to pound the chump." I empathized with Shaq but I told him the team needed to put the feud behind it as soon as possible. He agreed to keep quiet. This was another example of the basic difference between him and Kobe. Ask Shaq to do something and he'll say: "No, I don't want to do that." But after a little pouting, he will do it. Ask Kobe, and he'll say, "okay," and then he will do whatever he wants. Against our instructions, Kobe did an interview with ESPN, vowing that if he were to leave the Lakers at the end of the season, it would be due to Shaq's "childlike selfishness and jealousy." So much for suppression.

With only hours remaining before opening night, I've decided to look at the bright side, my standard approach in adverse times. Kobe and Shaq venting in public is not the worst thing in the world. If there's going to be a nasty exchange, this might as well be the moment to get it out in the open. The venting, in fact, motivates Shaq and Kobe in ways that nothing else does. With the tremendous scrutiny—from the media, the fans, teammates, everybody—they realize they must be on their best behavior or else the criticism will become even more intense. Neither wants to be blamed for dragging the whole franchise down. I'll go back to prepping for the Mavericks, a part of this job I can control. There's already enough I can't control.

THREE

AN OPENING STATEMENT

OCTOBER 30
Los Angeles

Opening night took place a few days ago, at last. With the months of hype—some dared to suggest the Lakers might even surpass the single-season record of seventy-two wins set by the 1995–96 Bulls—and the days of histrionics, we finally took to the floor, ready to do what we do best, yes, believe it or not, better than bickering. Of course, opening night wouldn't be the same around here without another plot development in the soap opera. This one took place, mercifully, behind the scenes and away from the press. I was in my car on the way to Staples when a call came from John Black.

"We'd like you to do the meet-and-greet thing," he said, referring to the words of appreciation that a player from the home team delivers to the crowd on opening night. Every club stages one these days, a ritual initiated after the 1998 lockout for teams to regain the support of the fans. Derek Fisher, a very thoughtful spokesman, was asked to do the honors, until, at the last minute, Shaq's representatives, Perry Rogers and Mike Parris, called to put in a formal request. "Why not?" I asked John Black. "What better way to welcome in the new season than with a few words from the big guy?" The Lakers did not share my sentiments, wondering whether, given what had transpired over the last few days, it might be a little risky to offer Shaq the podium. He wouldn't dare to criticize Kobe, but his charming demeanor would certainly go over well with the fans, and this was no time, according to Mitch and John Black, to give either superstar an edge over the other on the ever-critical PR front. "I ran the idea by Kobe," Black said, "and he wasn't too keen on it." The Lakers, to be sure, are determined to do anything to make Kobe happy, to keep him in Los Angeles. A Kobe who stays in Los Angeles is a Kobe who sells season tickets and tons of merchandise, building the Lakers brand. I agreed, in this case, to be the compromise solution. I told the crowd that we were not accustomed to staging opening night without a ring ceremony.

As for the game itself, we were motivated. There's nothing like the Mavericks, except maybe the Kings, to fire us up. Exhibit A: owner Mark Cuban. In 2000, shortly after we captured our first title in the Shaq-Kobe era, Cuban, who is always stepping out of his bounds, criticized the Lakers organization for not rewarding our free-agent forward, Glen Rice, with a lucrative long-term contract. Instead, we'd pulled off a sign and trade, acquiring Horace Grant for his first stint here. What Cuban failed to realize was that Rice's physical capabilities were rapidly diminishing. He has played, in fact, about only eighty games over the last two seasons, averaging less than nine points. Then in August, Cuban said that from a "business perspective," the Kobe rape case was "great for the NBA. It's reality television, people love train wreck television and you hate to admit it, but that is the truth." True or not, this was a remarkably insensitive comment to make in a situation where two youngsters—Kobe and the alleged victim—have been deeply harmed, however the trial turns out. In addition, the case has inflicted more damage on the image of a league that has seen too many players implicated in criminal activities. Later on, Cuban would weigh in on the Kobe-Shaq feud, charging that "If the president and the CEO of a corporation were speaking publicly like that, you'd have to say the board of directors was doing something wrong." The Lakers organization chose not to make an official response. Last time we fought back, in the Rice matter, we only kept the story alive longer.

Exhibit B: Coach Don "Nellie" Nelson, architect of the Hack-a-Shaq strategy. There have been suggestions that the NBA make the practice illegal. When I played for the Knicks, we adopted the same strategy with Wilt Chamberlain, who was just as abysmal from the line, and that was in the days when players were given three opportunities to make two points. I have nothing personally against Nellie, and actually admire how everyone on his team is empowered at the offensive end. However, in the spirit of the game, one should not profit from committing a foul, and as aggressively as the Mavs foul Shaq, the referees need to do a better job of calling flagrants.

The game went as well as we could have hoped, Gary pushing the ball up court, and Karl playing the type of aggressive, physical defense we lacked at the power forward spot last year. Each nearly finished with a triple-double, Karl with fifteen points, ten rebounds, nine assists, while Gary recorded twenty-one points, nine assists and seven boards. We won, 109–93. The only negative in the entire evening revolved around Kobe, who sat out, claiming he didn't want to risk further injury and possibly miss more games. Gary Vitti, our trainer, viewed the situation much differently, telling us that Kobe could play thirty minutes and it wouldn't set him back in the least. Then why the reluctance? Perhaps with the trial and the feud, he simply wasn't mentally prepared to suit up. He may be an awesome athlete, but he is also a very vulnerable human being, especially now. None of us can begin to imagine the anguish he must be experiencing every day. In normal times, we would have told him: "Kobe, there is no reason why you can't play," and Kobe would have played. These are not normal times, and as far as we can tell, they will not be normal for a long time. One particular moment on opening night was most symbolic. Before the game, our players formed a circle on the floor. Kobe, who didn't appear on the bench until the third quarter, did not join the circle. A part of him wants desperately to be in the group, to enjoy the camaraderie of his teammates, basketball serving as his only true escape. But there is another part of Kobe, which often wins out, a part that wants, perhaps needs, to be isolated from the group. To have it both ways is simply not possible. One can be the leader of the group but one must be *inside* the circle. With Kobe, how this internal tug-of-war plays out in the months ahead will go a long way toward determining whether we march toward a title . . . or march toward a breakup.

NOVEMBER 10
Memphis

Over the last two games, our first losses of the young season, on the road to the New Orleans Hornets and the Memphis Grizzlies, we displayed the deficiencies that could easily haunt us come May. Most disconcerting was our performance on the defensive end, which, as the cliché goes, in basketball as in football, decides who wins championships. For all of Michael Jordan's acrobatic exploits and fierce leadership, we prevailed in Chicago because we shut down opponents for prolonged stretches, especially in the fourth quarter. Our quarterback on defense was Scottie Pippen. "Go get him, Luc," he'd yell to center Luc Longley. "Bring some help." All I needed to do was whistle, and Scottie would know instinctively how our defense should react. On the occasions when I signaled a player toward the bench to ask why he suddenly changed his defensive position, the standard reply was: "Scottie sent me." Which is why, when I met Dr. Buss in Hawaii last May, Scottie was my first choice among the prospective free agents. Against Utah in the NBA Finals, John Stockton was killing us on the screen roll with Karl. Scottie went over to double team Stockton, trapping him at half-court. The extra pressure forced Stockton to give the ball up too quickly, taking valuable time off the twenty-four-second clock. When the ball came back to Stockton, there were usually less than ten seconds left, not long enough to develop any rhythm in the possession. In a playoff game against Orlando, after Shaq put up close to thirty points in the first half, Scottie trapped Penny Hardaway on the opposite side of the floor.

The Magic offense sputtered. We took teams away from what they liked to do.

These current Lakers rarely take teams away from what they like to do, screen rolls, up tempo, isolations, you name it. We may engage in tough, energized defense—getting in people's faces, contesting every shot, chasing every loose ball—for the first six minutes of the game and the last six minutes. But in between, and that's thirty-six minutes, we've been unable to sustain the same intensity. Last week we were lit up by Milwaukee's Michael Redd (36 points) and San Antonio's Manu Ginobili (33, a career high), yet found a way to prevail on both occasions, edging the Spurs, who were playing without Duncan and Parker, in double overtime. Our good fortune—we started 5–0—could not possibly last. It didn't. In New Orleans, we gave up 114 points, Baron Davis, one of the quickest guards in the league, going off for 23 points and dishing out twelve assists. Tonight in Memphis we surrendered 105, six Grizzlies scoring in double figures.

I was not surprised. Last May, after the San Antonio debacle, I started to map out strategies to upgrade our defense. During the exit interview with Kobe, I asked for suggestions. "I think I should take the guys who are on ball," he volunteered, referring to the lead guards. "Without Shaq helping out a lot on screen roll, maybe we can get some pressure on the ball and stop teams from over-penetrating against us." The suggestion was the exact adjustment I had been contemplating, but I was gratified Kobe was the first to mention it. I always prefer when players come up with a new wrinkle on their own. Feeling a greater degree of ownership, they will invest more effort in the strategy's outcome. Kobe's defense, to be accurate, has faltered in recent years, despite his presence on the league's all-defensive team. The voters have been seduced by his remarkable athleticism and spectacular steals, but he hasn't played sound, fundamental defense. Mesmerized by the ball, he's gambled too frequently, putting us out of position, forcing rotations that leave a man wide open, and doesn't keep his feet on the ground. By picking up Payton, who could play off ball, we figured the problem was solved. Unfortunately, Kobe, with his knee problems, hasn't possessed the stamina required to chase point guards all over the floor. Whatever energy he does possess must be conserved for offense.

The other major impediment is Shaquille. I once asked him: "What would be more important, that you play defense and rebound or that you play offense?" His answer was most telling: "I've always been an offensive player. I've never been a defensive player." To understand his mind-set, one has to remember that from the time he became dominant in grade school, Shaq was told over and over by his coaches: "Do not foul! Do not foul!" Fouling out meant then, as it does today, that he would squander the opportunity to help his team the way he feels is best, on offense. Without denigrating Shaq's contributions in that department, especially in the playoffs, when he has consistently deflated the opposition with thirty-point, twenty-rebound nights, the simple truth is that big men affect the outcome of the game more on defense than offense. The elite centers in the game's past—Bill Russell, Wilt Chamberlain, Kareem Abdul-Jabbar, Patrick Ewing, Hakeem Olajuwon—made it extremely difficult for other teams to score in the paint. I constantly have to remind Shaq: "If the other players are playing pressure defense, *you* have to play pressure defense. Because if your man steps up and receives the pass, it takes all the pressure off the ball. Everyone's on the ball, and now your man steps into the gap, you don't go out with him, and our defense is compromised." Four active defenders isn't enough. Each of the Bulls' centers during our reign was extremely active. I will say this: when Shaq wants to elevate his game, he can play defense as well as anyone. Although he has paid more attention to his conditioning, it remains to be seen how hard he's prepared to work at that end of the floor.

So much of playing effective team defense is linked to what happens at the other end, a point we made repeatedly in Hawaii. If the triangle offense is properly executed, our players will be in position for a balanced defensive retreat. Two players in addition to the shooter will, ideally, have the opportunity to rebound any misses, forcing the defense to stay home until the ball is secured. Consequently, often teams possessing quicker, younger legs won't be able to run as freely on us. But if we're out of sync on offense, as was the case tonight in Memphis—we committed twenty-three turnovers!—we won't drop back in transition to stop anybody. More than anything else, playing inspired defense is a matter of will: What are you *will*ing to do as a group to help each other out? What are you *will*ing to do as an individual to put the clamps on the opponent you're guarding? In Game 6 of the 1973 playoffs, Dean Meminger, the Knicks guard, kept complaining about the half-court picks the Celtics were using to free Jo Jo White. Finally Red Holzman said, "You've just got to get through it. It's as simple as that." Meminger persevered, leading us to a lopsided victory in Game 7 at Boston Garden. The Knicks went on to beat the Lakers in five games to win another championship. For this Lakers team, the will is often not apparent. We do not have many players who will take charges—Fish, Fox, Karl, maybe Gary. One reason we're struggling is that by focusing in Hawaii on the complexities of the triangle, there was little time left to work on our defensive principles.

Finally, tonight's loss in Memphis exposed another problem that could keep us from any June celebrations. With us down sixteen points in the fourth quarter, Kobe took eight shots, missing five of them. There are nights when Kobe, like Michael Jordan, will ditch the triangle and take over a game to try to help us win. Tonight, however, was not a night he should have been so assertive, and his teammates knew it. I was not surprised to see them dejected in the locker room afterward. Nothing alienates a player more than the sense that he is being ignored. These are the best players in the whole world, and are not accustomed to being ignored by *anybody*. Kobe knows how to play basketball the right way. So why does he persist in playing the game *his* way? My theory—I clearly have no shortage of theories—is that every time a fearless defender, such as Portland's Ruben Patterson or San Antonio's Bruce Bowen, vows to shut him down, Kobe needs to prove him wrong, as if his manhood was on the line. I don't mind his taking on challenges and against the less talented teams, he will often be successful playing his way. He'll make everything in sight or draw fouls. But what happens when he doesn't draw fouls? I used to believe Michael was fouled on almost every shot, but there were countless occasions when he didn't get the call, and the same applies to Kobe. I would prefer that Kobe step to the edge of the precipice, draw the requisite double-team, and then find the open man for a much better look. In almost every possession, an open shot is the highest-percentage shot. That's where he and Fish, who have played together for seven years, hook up extremely well. Kobe knows exactly where on the floor Fish prefers to spot up, ready to drill his jumper.

At times it seems difficult to decipher whether Kobe is *causing* the lack of initiative in his teammates or *responding* to it. If other players become the least bit tentative, he will not hesitate to step into the void. If the game is on the verge of getting out of hand, Kobe will feel there is no other choice and on certain occasions, he will be right. Kobe recognizes the true purpose of regular-season games: to entertain. Once the playoffs roll around, he alters his mind-set, aware that the risk that comes with trying to dominate is too severe in a high-stakes game. I only wish he would arrive at this conclusion earlier. He has to rise above his ego, above the individual challenge to meet the larger, more important team challenge. I encountered similar stubbornness from Michael in the early stages of his career. He changed in the 1990–1991 season, and not coincidentally the Bulls finally broke through. Michael gave his teammates clearance to make the most of their specific talents. If he hadn't granted permission, I can safely assume John Paxson wouldn't have made the jumper to defeat Phoenix in Game 6 of the 1993 Finals, and Steve Kerr wouldn't have nailed his buzzer shot in Game 6 against Utah in 1997. Even so there were instances when Michael didn't follow the program. During one game in the 1991 Finals against the Lakers, I called time-out to reinforce the point. "Michael," I said, "all you have to do is penetrate and pass the ball to Paxson. He'll hit the shots we need." When he complied, possession after possession fit the same pattern: pass, jump shot, bang, pass, jump shot, bang. Michael once explained to Kobe his formula for how to sufficiently feed teammates while still staying ready to do what's necessary to win the game in the fourth.

In my postgame address to the troops tonight, I was very careful. I showed them I was firmly on their side but in sticking to my preseason pledge, I didn't single out Kobe for criticism. "We didn't play as a team," I said. "We have to move the ball more and include everybody in the offense." I am sure Kobe got the message. I am also sure it will not be the last time I have to deliver it.

NOVEMBER 19
New York

Last night in Detroit, there was another message to deliver, this one to the whole squad. Without belittling the talents of Larry Brown, one of the brightest minds in our business, Detroit is simply not a very good basketball team, and they won because they worked harder than us. I've seen this type of lackluster effort too often during my four-plus years in Los Angeles. The experts say it keeps happening because we've proven that we can coast through the regular season and still get our act together by April. To a certain extent, I buy into that argument. In 2001 we won eight in a row to close the regular season, and fifteen of sixteen in the playoffs. Perhaps I should assume the blame. From the beginning of the season, I pace the players for the long haul. I told them this year in Hawaii: "We're a good enough team that we can make ourselves get into the playoffs in good shape. So I'm not going to drag you through long film sessions and long practices. We'll make the playoffs, and then once we do, I'm going to put you under extreme duress because that's the money time in this game. In the regular season, you'll learn how to play together, but in the playoffs, I'll be inside your heads. You'll have more control during the season, but I'll have more control in the playoffs." I don't second-guess this approach. Otherwise, if players were to burn themselves out, they would snap and not have the legs for April, May, and June. Steve Kerr has always harped to me about Shaq's lackadaisical attitude. "I can't stand that he lays around all season," Kerr says, "and wants to turn it on in the playoffs." I've told Kerr there's absolutely nothing wrong with this mind-set. Shaq is a unique individual, and that uniqueness must be tolerated for him to flourish. When the playoffs come, he'll be focused. There is no mystery about why Kerr holds this opinion. The Chicago teams he played on treated the regular season with a sense of urgency, an unwillingness to lose, ever. No sacrifice in the pursuit of winning was too much to expect. Coaching the Lakers, who have never carried that attitude, has required some adjustment on my part. I gaze at the mantra I keep on my desk: "Unceasing change turns the wheel of life, and so reality is shown in all its many forms." If one accepts this credo, one can live in peace. If one doesn't, one will not find peace anywhere. At the same time, I do expect from my team, as professionals, a certain degree of effort and I didn't feel that they gave it last night against the Pistons. The regular season does matter. As we discovered last year, going into the playoffs without home-court advantage against the Spurs hurt us. The Western Conference, with the roster moves made by Sacramento (Brad Miller), Minnesota (Latrell Sprewell, Sam Cassell, Michael Olowokandi), San Antonio (Rasho Nesterovic, Hedo Turkoglu, Robert Horry), and Dallas (Anton Jamison, Antoine Walker), should be more hotly contested than ever.

I saw this performance coming. During our noon shootaround at the Palace of Auburn Hills, the guys were sleepwalking, trying to adjust to the change in time zones. They'll earn no pity from this corner. I've coached in the CBA, where we traveled all day to the next city . . . by car. In the locker room, after the Pistons dictated the tempo at both ends of the court, after we allowed Chauncey Billups to look like an All-Star, I let my team have it. I may seem out of control in mid-rant but believe me, I'm very much in control; I think of coaches' tirades in the same category as timeouts—you're only allocated a limited amount. If I were to turn the outbursts into a habit, and there are obviously some coaches in this league who do, they would gradually lose their effectiveness. I'm often reminded of what Johnny Bach, my former assistant in Chicago, used to say: "You only throw your team off the court once a season." The risk is that by demeaning their players, coaches build an animosity that will be almost impossible to reverse, which is how they lose their jobs. They reach a point at which everything they say is negative: "You're never going to wake up. Are you always going to be a horse's ass?" Etc. etc.

I've never reached that point, although in the minds of several people I picked on, I probably came closer than I thought. Stacey King, a highly touted forward/center from Oklahoma, was one player I drove extremely hard. I envisioned Stacey as a better player than he turned out to be, and wondered if some of his inability to tap that potential was my fault. Regardless, I don't beat myself up about it. If I don't try to squeeze the most out of these players, what good am I? Better yet, what good are *they*? Generally, when I reprimand them, I try to balance two positives with every negative. Sounds like a scientific formula, I suppose, and in a way, it is. If you're going to bruise their egos—because as talented as they are, believe me, their egos are easily bruised—any message will get through much more effectively if you pump up those egos at the same time. I might preface any criticism with comments such as: "You're hustling really well," or "We appreciate your effort." I'll then ease into the real purpose of my address: "I don't know if you're not feeling good today or not able to give as much energy, but you don't look like you're playing up to your usual standards. Looks to me like you're not moving as well. Is something wrong? You feeling okay? Are you hurt?" According to the Positive Coaching Alliance, which trains coaches in youth sports, the ideal is a 5–1 ratio of praise to criticism. I'm the national spokesman for the alliance, but I can tell you that at the professional level it can be nearly impossible sometimes to come up with five positives for every negative. What possible reinforcement can I offer to a player who committed five turnovers in the fourth quarter and failed to guard his man? "Way to make that layup?"

Choosing my words carefully, I try to make players understand that I'm criticizing their *performance,* not their *personality.* If, for example, a player has begun to lose sight of his teammates, I don't tell him, "You're being selfish by shooting the ball too much." The use of the word "selfish" would indicate something fundamentally wrong with him as an individual, which would only cause resentment. Instead I'll say, "You were a little thirsty out there, weren't you?" Being "thirsty" for individual glory is why he abandoned the concept of team ball. The player is much more likely to absorb the criticism and modify his behavior. In basketball if one makes positive moves *half* the time, one is doing extremely well, whether it relates to any aspect—shooting, passing, rebounding, etc. All we as a coaching staff ask for is a chance to correct the mistakes that are correctable. If players become brittle or defensive, the mistakes will not be corrected.

After addressing the players, I met with the media. I usually can't wait to finish this useless exercise but last night I was willing to extend the session. There was an important point to make. The Pistons were successful in their game plan of luring Shaquille into fouls, a strategy that works much better on the road, where the fans are able to influence the calls, than it does at Staples. Referees, after all, are human—most are, anyway—and susceptible to human influences, human pressures. As a result Shaquille spent too many minutes on the bench, which impeded our ability to win the game, but the damage extended beyond the fortune of the Los Angeles Lakers. There will be other games on other nights in other cities. But this night, due to the logistics of the NBA schedule, was the only opportunity this season for Detroit fans to see Shaquille O'Neal.

Fouling out certainly wasn't what Dr. James Naismith had in mind when he invented the game in the 1890s. According to one of the original thirteen rules Naismith devised, the player responsible for committing a second infraction left the court until the opposing squad scored a goal. When I coached in the CBA during the early 1980s, there was a no-foul-out provision. After the sixth personal foul, the other team shot two free throws and was awarded possession. I wouldn't be opposed to increasing the amount of free throws as the fouls accumulate—any adjustment to keep the stars on the court as long as possible. For those who counter that changing the rule would enable players to play too aggressively without the risk of any consequence, I can assure them: giving a team free throws *and* the ball is a huge consequence. Changing the rule, if anything, would allow referees to call the game more honestly without being wary of eliminating a star. Coaches wouldn't be able to tailor their strategy toward enticing a player to foul out, which is precisely what many opponents—exhibits A, B, and C: Vlade "The Flopper" Divac—attempt with Shaq. Teams should triumph from the pure ability of their players, nothing else.

NOVEMBER 22
Los Angeles

The past and present collided last night. The Bulls were in town, coached by one of my former players, Bill Cartwright, and run by another, general manager John Paxson. I remain very friendly with both, which is why things are a bit awkward these days. With the team going nowhere again, its highly regarded draft choices more bust than boon, word is that John might fire Bill, believing, according to insiders, that he isn't enough of a disciplinarian. That may be true, but next to Michael, Bill was the toughest player on the Bulls in the early '90s. In that unforgettable 1994 Eastern Conference Finals game against the Knicks, when Scottie Pippen refused to go on the floor for the last 1.8 seconds because the final shot was set up for Toni Kukoc—Michael was playing professional baseball—it was Bill who confronted Scottie in the locker room.

When Bill stopped by my office after last night's game, he put on a brave face, though it was quite obvious how much pressure he's going through. I tried to offer some words of encouragement, but as we both know, in this precarious profession, victory is the only real encouragement. Talking to Bill causes me to reflect, for probably the billionth time, on how fortunate I've been in my coaching career. I was fired only once, and that was in Puerto Rico, when

Raymond Dalmau, the team's star, did not approve of my offensive system. Sound familiar? I don't suppose it really counts, especially since I was picked up by another squad within days. Today coaches work on a shorter leash than ever. I'm hoping Bill, who lost last night's game, can somehow turn things around in time.

For three of my assistants, Tex, Frank Hamblen, and Jim Cleamons, who worked with me in Chicago, there is no satisfaction in watching the Bulls struggle. The roster has been revamped, but there are still many familiar faces—equipment manager John Ligmanowski, radio announcer Neil Funk, ticket manager Joe O'Neil, and others. The bonds that are established do not suddenly evaporate when a coaching staff moves to another city.

There is no way to overemphasize how much Frank, Jim, and my other assistant, Kurt Rambis, contribute to our success. In addition to their assignments of scouting nine opposing teams apiece during the course of the season, each has his own special role. Jim, a former guard in the league, works with the smalls on offense and defense. Kurt assists the players with their shooting, which many may find ironic. During the Showtime era in the 1980s, he was probably the Lakers' *last* option on offense. Truth is that he can shoot. During a game he shouts: "You're leaning back," or "You short-armed that one." He chronicles every possession. If, for example, we're in the middle of a drought, he will tell me how we scored our most recent bucket. Frank keeps track of the opposition's "needs" or "criticals," as we refer to them in a game's closing minutes. He pulls out a folder with a detailed account of plays the other team tends to run in crunch time. Tex focuses on principles and fundamentals. We call him the voice of the basketball gods.

DECEMBER 1
Los Angeles

The Indiana Pacers came into Staples last night with the best record (14–2) in the league, including 7–0 on the road. We told the players that if we take care of business, this is a team we may very well meet in June. The not-so-subtle message: make a statement. For this team there is no more powerful, deflating statement to the opposition than to pound the ball inside to Shaquille. There's a reason he leads the league almost every year in shooting percentage— most of his field-goal attempts are four or five feet away from the basket. Indiana, like most victims, has no answer except, obviously, to foul him. Feeding the ball to Shaq is not as elementary a matter as the experts tend to assume, especially with rules that sanction double-teams. I'm always irritated when the Lakers are criticized for forgetting about Shaquille for long stretches of a game. Let me clear this up right now: we rarely forget about Shaquille! The opposition often is able to dictate what you can do offensively, and can make it enormously difficult to get Shaq the ball in prime post-up position. Many teams will hound the player trying to make the entry pass, attacking his arms, putting a hand in his chest, anything to force him to turn and pivot away from the passing angle. There is an art to the entry pass, which is why we work on it over and over in drills. There are very few people on this team who throw it properly, and nobody better than Rick Fox. When the passing angle isn't there, he proceeds with the next best option, resetting the offense with a replacement dribble away from the basket. On many occasions, after Shaq receives the ball in the lane, he passes it back once the inevitable double-team arrives. The second entry pass in the same possession, once he has maneuvered closer to the hoop, is the one that often leads to a score.

Against Indiana, in only two minutes, their center, Jeff Foster, picked up two fouls. Early in the third, their coach, Rick Carlisle, called two timeouts within two minutes of each other. Carlisle subscribes to the Lenny Wilkens philosophy of using timeouts as a defensive weapon to halt the opponent's momentum. I don't subscribe to that philosophy and I know it's one of my unconventional tendencies that infuriates my critics to no end. They see a run by the other team, and figure I'm the one who ought to stop it. I figure that my players are the ones who ought to stop it. Only by stewing in the mess that *they* created can they be subjected to its full, embarrassing outcome, and only by discovering on their own how to extricate themselves can they be adequately prepared for the next time they lose their rhythm. I suppose the situation is akin to the father who refuses to bail his son out of jail, teaching him a valuable lesson. I've coached players—Fish and Ron Harper come to mind—who took the initiative to call timeout on their own. If they want to submit and call a truce, I'm fine with that, but I am not going to save their hides. Of course, once the playoffs get under way, I call timeouts more readily. Winning games takes precedence over teaching lessons. I save one timeout to stop the clock in the last five or ten seconds of the game.

We won easily, which only provided more ammunition to those who harp on about the wide discrepancy in talent level, both among individuals and teams, between the two conferences. I'm not about to dispute that fact, not when the West can boast the likes of Shaquille, Kobe, Tim Duncan, Chris Webber, Steve Nash, Kevin Garnett, and others. Nonetheless I don't view this gap as a sign of the apocalypse. I actually view it as a wonderful opportunity for teams in the East, who can exploit the underdog status to their advantage. In theory I would be in favor of reseeding the teams after the first round of the playoffs, but I recognize what a logistical nightmare that would create. The playoffs already last long enough. Besides, everything is cyclical. Not too long ago, the Pistons and Bulls won every title.

December 5
Open skies

We're cruising in our chartered plane at roughly 35,000 feet, somewhere over the Southwest, not far from the journey I took on my bike in July, when I visited Tuba City and Monument Valley in Arizona on the way to Flathead Lake. So much is clearer now on this other journey, the victories piling up, the doubts diminishing, the troops sacrificing just as they promised in Hawaii. The triangle comes and goes—Gary prefers a faster pace—and Kobe's game, with all his distractions, also comes and goes. But we're 16–3, fresh from back-to-back road wins in San Antonio and Dallas, two of the league's toughest foes, and I'm confident that over time, Gary will learn the system.

Two nights ago in San Antonio, we dispatched the team we expect to face again come May, outscoring them 28–15 in the fourth to prevail by four. Shaq was awesome, with fifteen points, sixteen boards, and nine blocks. Most significantly, with Karl's aggressiveness, we held Tim Duncan without a field goal in the fourth. Before that performance, I hadn't seen a way we could beat the Spurs. Hours ago in Dallas, our effort was even more outstanding, especially coming on the second night of a back-to-back sequence. When I received my first copy of this year's schedule, one of the initial things I checked out were the back-to-back dates. We're slated for nineteen, which is on the high end. Usually in the first game, I try to squeeze ten minutes out of the reserves in the second quarter, as opposed to six or seven. In the second half, I adhere more to my traditional rotation, taking whatever steps necessary to win *that* game. I can't afford to worry about the next game. Fortunately, only Kobe played more than forty minutes against the Spurs, leaving us sufficiently fresh to keep up with the high-energy Mavs. We won handily, benefiting from the absence of their dangerous big man, Dirk Nowitzki. Up here in the clouds, I'm still savoring the victory, although there is one tiny dark cloud on the horizon. Karl, I'm certain, will be suspended for an incident involving Steve Nash.

Early in the third quarter, trying to knock a rebound out of Karl's hands, Nash was met with an elbow to the chops. I leaped off the bench immediately, which for me in a regular season contest is about as frequent an occurrence as a Shaquille three-pointer. I was screaming for a foul on Nash, so when the official called it on Karl, I picked up a technical foul, my second of the year, normally about my limit for an entire season. I used to acquire Ts more routinely but then it dawned on me that all I was doing was giving free points to the opposition. Sure, maybe you'll get a call at some point later in the game, and I can see occasions when a technical might send an important message to your team, but there's a manipulative aspect to such outbursts that offends an old-fashioned purist like myself. I will argue for calls that should have gone our way, but there is a line I will not cross. The game, whatever else it may signify, is just that, a game. Many coaches adopt a much different view. Nellie, for instance, when his team was stinking up the joint, used to tell the refs: "Throw me out of this game. I'm going to call you a cocksucker and a motherfucker. Now throw me out. I can't stand my team." The refs didn't always submit. "I'm not throwing you out," one might say. "You're going to have to stay and watch this shit yourself." Nellie would still find a way to get thrown out, jump in a cab, and be in his hotel room before the game was over.

For me the turning point came in 1995, when Dennis Rodman joined the Bulls. I noticed that whenever I became animated, Dennis, who did not need much to be provoked, would almost duplicate my reactions. He was dealing with enough authority problems already without being further incited. I started to behave more stoically, which did not mean I wasn't as involved in the game. If there is any major misconception about me, or any coach, for that matter, it's that we're not as engaged if we don't scream at the refs or pace along the sidelines. Such antics only serve to distract the team from the game plan. I also believe the majority of coaching is done *before* the game. Timeouts and substitutions obviously play an extremely important role, but the strategy, which principles should be followed, is put in place many hours before tip-off.

DECEMBER 7
Los Angeles

We escaped with the "W" tonight, but escaping is not exactly what I had in mind with this unique collection of talent, even without Karl, who was indeed suspended for one game. Karl did nothing wrong. According to the rules, a player is allowed to pivot with the ball "chinned" and the elbows extended. If contact is made, he's not in violation unless he swings his elbows. Nash is the one who initiated the contact. We took a fifteen-point lead at the half but allowed the Jazz to outscore us 28–27 in the third quarter, which, given our sizable advantage, may not seem like such a big deal. But winning a quarter, even by a point, is a very big deal on the psychological front. Teams often start to control a game long before it is reflected on the scoreboard. In the huddle before starting the fourth quarter, I exhorted my guys: "Get back the momentum." Apparently my exhortation did little good. The Jazz, picked by many to be among the worst teams in the conference, kept clawing away, finally assuming the lead in the last minute of the game. We prevailed when Devean George hit a three-pointer with twenty-four seconds left for our ninth straight win, our longest streak in two years. The fans were thrilled. I was not. Our familiar inability to display, pardon the cliché, a killer instinct is very troubling. We must find one, and soon.

FOUR

LOSING OUR WAY

DECEMBER 13
Portland

For weeks, I was concerned about how this team, which coasted to an 18–3 start, would respond the first time it encountered adversity. I'm about to find out. The last two nights have been dreadful, especially on the defensive end. We've yielded a total of 222 points, a complete breakdown in this age of low scoring. First, against the Mavs in Los Angeles, Devean couldn't handle the much taller Dirk Nowitzki in the post, while Nash ran us all over the court. I called an early timeout—this was one instance in which I was not going to let them stew in their own mess—urging the guys to match up immediately on misses and play the closest man until we stopped their break opportunities. When we fell into a deeper hole in the third quarter, I put Kobe on Nash, but he picked up several fouls. At the other end we were stymied by Nellie's 1–1–3 zone, which kept us from feeding the ball into Shaq on a consistent basis. When we were able to find Shaq in deep position, they fouled him before he could deliver the slam, and the Hack-a-Shaq strategy worked to near perfection. Shaq was seven for seven from the field, but only eleven for twenty-four from the line.

My attitude toward Shaq's struggles at the line has evolved considerably since I first arrived in Los Angeles. Early on I twitched so nervously on the bench—"Gosh, he's going to miss his free throws and it's going to really hurt us!"—that I probably wore a hole in my pants. These days I assume he's going to miss them, and when he proves me wrong, I consider the points to be a bonus. I've urged him repeatedly to consult a hypnotist, who could provide him with some kind of mantra he could say to himself on the line, but he always resists. Typical Shaq. As much as he's embarrassed by his inept free-throw shooting, he's determined to fix the problem his way. Only his way doesn't work. People have demonstrated to him what a substantial difference greater success at the charity stripe would make in his overall numbers—if he shot 70 percent instead of 50 or 60. "If you miss two free throws," we explain over and over, "it's just like committing a turnover. It kills the team." I don't go along with his contention that he'll "make them when they matter." Every single one matters. Until he demonstrates significant improvement, and that appears doubtful, he won't be the dangerous option he should be in the later stages of a game. I'll use him as a decoy.

In the Dallas game, Gary Payton was tossed out by referee Steve

Javie. Only a few minutes earlier, Javie called a technical on Devean over a relatively minor dispute. The warning was clear: Javie was jacked up tonight. Leave him alone. This came as no shock. In the locker room, a member of the staff informed me that in the wake of the Malone-Nash elbow incident a week earlier, Javie had let it be known that he wasn't going to tolerate any shenanigans this time around. There are some refs, and Javie is one of them, who will not hesitate to become control freaks. Gary, who has a reputation for pushing officials to the edge, didn't heed the warning. Because officials are generally more reluctant to eject a team's top player, Gary might have been able to get away with it in Seattle but given his diminished role on this team, he's lost the layer of protection the stars receive. The first technical came when he complained, the second when he rolled the ball the length of the floor.

The initial five or six minutes of a game, until the first television timeout, typically present a rough blueprint of how the action on the floor is likely to be judged. Are the refs soft or hard? Are they calling reaches or over the back? What about post-up defending fouls? Are they letting charges go? How physical are they allowing players to be with screens? When the coaching staff detects the pattern for the night, we make sure the players adjust accordingly. "They're not calling ticky-tack fouls," I might say, "so don't come over to the bench and complain about getting fouled. Don't be stopping your play because you think you were fouled. Just play through it." The simple truth is that a player is fouled about 90 percent of the time, defenders bumping the shooter, coming across his arm. All I ask for, and I'm far from alone, is consistency, for the refs to call it the same way at both ends. In any case Gary's dismissal evened the score with the Mavs, who were playing without their superb swingman, Michael Finley. I try, as usual, to find the bright side of the loss, our first to the Mavs in Los Angeles since 1990, an amazing span of twenty-seven games. The streak was bound to end, and better, I suppose, that it ends in December than in May. But I'm having trouble finding the bright side of tonight's loss to the Blazers. Unable to box them out, we surrendered twenty-nine second-chance points.

Upon our arrival in Portland, the Blazers were making headlines off the court, a fairly common occurrence for a franchise once referred to as the Jail Blazers. In recent years, their players have been charged with drug possession, sexual assault, drunk driving, and speeding. This time the uproar was caused by Rasheed Wallace, their talented, if volatile, power forward, who was accusing the league of going after black athletes because "we're dumb n---s. It's as if we're going to shut up, sign for the money and do what they tell us. . . . That's why they're drafting all these high school cats, because they come into the league . . . and don't know the real business and don't see behind the charade." The league wasted no time firing back at Wallace. Commissioner David Stern claimed that "Mr. Wallace's hateful diatribe was ignorant and offensive to all NBA players." I can understand the league's indignation, especially when the commissioner has favored an age minimum of twenty years. Wallace was also out of line to introduce the race card where it clearly doesn't belong. Yet his basic argument, that owners disrespect players, the labor force, is hardly revolutionary. We felt exactly the same way in the '60s. But when you're earning $17 million, as Wallace is, compared with the $40,000 or $50,000 or so we pocketed, it becomes impossible to convince Joe Public you're being disrespected. To me the most fascinating aspect of the whole episode was the urgency with which the NBA reacted, proving how threatening it can be when somebody dares to question the all-important product. Too many people own a stake in that product to allow any threat to go unchallenged.

DECEMBER 19
Los Angeles

I gave the players two full days off after the game in Portland. I was concerned about their recent lack of execution, but they desperately needed some rest. Since July, actually, everyone had been pointing to this fortunate break in the schedule—five days between games. I've always believed that if you can afford players two days in a row away from the court, they will return with a freshness in their legs and in their minds. No doubt in another week or two their legs will be dead again. The NBA season is one long grind.

There is another grind under way, one whose resolution means so much more: the Kobe case. Since camp started back in October, we had made sure to give Kobe the space he needed, not allowing the press to badger him and us with trial-related questions. We've gone about our business every day as professionals. Even so, the case is never far from our prayers, especially on a day like today. Kobe, instead of attending the shootaround with his teammates, was attending a hearing in Eagle County with his new teammates, the ones who wear suits. Our thoughts were with him, but also on our opponents, the Denver Nuggets, a split focus that for us, and even more for Kobe, is sure to produce consequences we can't begin to anticipate. No wonder some suggested he sit out the whole season. How he manages to compartmentalize is beyond me. For myself and, I'm speculating, Kobe's teammates, it is too difficult to keep track of every detail regarding his case. I don't know which motions have been filed by the prosecutors or which ones by the defense team. The only details I need to know are: when is the next hearing and how will it affect Kobe's availability for practice or a game?

Tonight Kobe arrived on the bench moments before the start of the second quarter. When I inserted him into the lineup, he was anxious to show the fans that he could spend an entire day in one court and yet be his usual self at night in the other. But he wasn't his usual self, missing a series of shots down the stretch, allowing the Nuggets, with two Carmelo Anthony free throws, to tie the game at ninety-nine with 2.5 seconds left. Which is why I designed a play for Gary, with Kobe as the second option. Even if he were on his game, I wouldn't automatically designate Kobe for the final shot. I prefer to keep the opposition off balance and discover how other players will respond under that kind of pressure. I might need to call on them again later in the season, when the pressure will be more intense. Michael didn't always take the last shot, even in critical games.

In tonight's game I called for "starburst," a set in which players come together and then, like a series of comets shooting out from the sky, abruptly break apart. Two players at the top of the floor make diagonal cuts around the high post while another player most likely occupies the high post, setting a pick on the guard stationed right under him. Starburst, like many of our plays, has been around the game forever.

Digger Phelps, the former Notre Dame coach, once approached Red Holzman during a 1972 holiday tournament at Madison Square Garden. "I see we're running a play that's similar to what you run with the Knicks," Digger said.

Red smiled. "There are no such things as new plays in this

game," he told Digger. "All these things have been done over and over again at YMCAs."

Basketball wasn't complicated for Red. He didn't diagram plays, use chalk, or move salt shakers around during breakfast. There was one play Red liked to run, but since he couldn't remember its name, he kept saying in the huddle: "What the fuck was that play?" So we started calling it "what the fuck," and ran it for years. Once, against the Rockets in 1974, I inbounded the ball but it was promptly intercepted. "I guess we're not going to let you be the take-out man again," Red told me. Tonight, when Gary didn't break clear in the corner because the Nuggets played the baseline side, the inbounds pass went near the top of the key to Kobe, who nailed the winning twenty-foot jumper at the buzzer. He was his usual self after all.

DECEMBER 25
Los Angeles

I've lost the holiday spirit, and apparently, so has my team. Everything started to go downhill during last Sunday night's game against the Suns. The seemingly indestructible Karl Malone sprained his knee when Scottie Williams landed on him in front of our bench. When I saw Karl tumble, I did not think he was severely injured. Then I heard Scottie's voice. "Get to him," he told us. We commiserated with Karl in the locker room, confident that with his incredible work ethic he would soon be back in the lineup. I coached against Karl for about fifteen years, but it wasn't until I started observing him day after day on the practice floor and in the weight room that I fully appreciated the extent of his dedication.

The first sign came one day last summer when I called his house, and was told he was riding his mountain bike. "How long will that take?" I asked. Four hours, I was told.

The team is struggling without Karl. Two nights after the injury, we were outscored 38–15 in the second quarter at Golden State and lost by nine points. This afternoon, we fell meekly to the Rockets at Staples, and on national TV, where the camera-conscious Lakers normally shine. I don't have any magical solutions. All I know is that the troops are not playing as a unit, which I attribute to December doldrums, the stretch of the season when, distracted by family holiday gatherings, they have trouble finding motivation for every game. In response, I must be careful not to drive them too hard. There is a limit to how much they are prepared to give, mentally and physically. I've talked to many people in this organization who would prefer I adopt a tougher stance, but at what point does the team spend so much energy on the practice floor that there is little left for the game? At what point do I risk taking years off a player's career? A prime example was James Worthy, the Hall of Fame forward for the championship Lakers teams in the '80s. Worthy retired at the age of thirty-three, and he probably should have played till he was at least thirty-five.

Today also illustrated once again the tendency of this organization to send mixed signals. Before I left the house, John Black called to say that Karl wasn't planning on coming to the game. His knee hurt and he was depressed about spending the first Christmas without his mother, who had died in late summer. I told Black I understood Karl's reasoning, but he still needed to call me directly. He didn't call. When I was asked about his absence in the pregame press conference, I mentioned he had not been officially excused. Only later did I find out that in an interview with ABC, Mitch said

Karl was indeed excused for missing the game. It sure would be nice if we were all on the same page around here.

JANUARY 1, 2004
Los Angeles

Jeanie and I ushered in the new year together with good food, a bottle of champagne, and as usual, a little shop talk. An ally from day one, telling me who I could trust and more important, who I couldn't, Jeanie is remarkably helpful whenever I discuss the problems of the team. I trust she will not divulge anything I say about Kobe, Shaq, or any player to her father. On the occasions when I lean toward being too rigid, she will present a logical argument to help me come around. She was there for me again yesterday. Shaq didn't show up for work. There was no word of his whereabouts until Gary Vitti informed me he was home complaining about a bad back. Nonetheless, by not phoning ahead, bad back or not, Shaq violated one of our rules. I will have to rein him in somehow, but after running it by Jeanie, I realized once again the need to avoid provoking Shaq with a harsh punishment. The fine for missing practice the first time is $250; it then goes up to $1,000 and maxes out at $2,500. But taking money out of their pockets, I've always believed, is not the most effective way to keep players in line. Far more threatening is the loss of my approval. Despite their tremendous talent, they are still, by and large, young adults, seeking validation from an authority figure, and there is no greater authority figure on a team than the coach. Needless to say, in today's warped, self-indulgent climate, too many players couldn't care less about appeasing the coach. So how do I combat those forces? Well, one way is to take away playing time. The loss of playing time means the loss of precious stats, and most threatening, perhaps, the loss of potential income. Being ostracized from the group also brings shame and embarrassment.

I've been occupied lately with scouting our next opponent, the Seattle SuperSonics. Each season while my assistants divide the rest of the league, I pick one team to evaluate on my own. I selected the Sonics this year largely due to their success against us in recent seasons; they run the screen roll, our most glaring defensive weakness, to near perfection. Part of the problem has been that we don't want Shaq to rotate to a guard in the corner to contest three-point attempts. We prefer Shaq to stay parked near the lane, where he can do the most damage, as an intimidator, contesting dribble penetration and blocking shots. The only exceptions may arise during critical possessions at the end of games, when we can't afford to allow any open looks.

As a science, scouting has progressed tremendously since I entered the league. The NBA provides tapes of the games, although I wish the television producers were a little more concerned with fundamentals than flair. Too often, by showing replays of spectacular individual achievements, they miss critical, if less glamorous, sequences. A player will take a shot and I'll wonder: How did he get the ball in *that* position? Where on the floor did the pass come from? The pass that *leads* to an assist, after all, is frequently the most important pass of the possession, the pass that begins to stretch the defense out of position. In my early coaching days, I watched video for hours and hours, searching almost frantically for every possible nuance that could give my team an edge. Finally, to gain some sleep—and sanity—I learned how to delegate more work to my assistants, to incorporate the most useful advice I ever received about coaching, which came from Al McGuire, the late Marquette leader and TV analyst. "Remember, if it can't be done in eight hours," said McGuire, whose brother, Dick, was my first coach with the Knicks, "it can't be done." Coaches become engrossed in their own world, losing any sense of balance or perspective. They think only of the most recent game or the game tomorrow. Of course, come playoff time, I'll break down, along with Tex, possession after possession, game after game; on those days, eight hours will not be enough.

JANUARY 2
Seattle

Midway through tonight's second quarter, the scouting reports were paying off. We were up by six, hoping to keep the Sonics' top scoring threat, Ray Allen, from having a huge night. But then Shaq waved to me, asking to come out of the game. He limped off the floor and headed for the locker room. The lead began to evaporate. While I was pacing the sidelines, which I rarely do—knowing the plays the Sonics prefer to run, I was communicating with our defense—Vitti told me Shaq was done for the night. "Don't tell me that shit," I yelled back. With Karl still sidelined with the knee injury, losing Shaquille was not a scenario I was willing to accept. At halftime, seeing him on the training table, I grabbed his ankle to let him know I was concerned, which is always important with Shaquille.

For all his bravado, Shaq is a very sensitive, fragile soul who appreciates any sign of tenderness. He's often maligned for his lack of durability, his unwillingness to play with severe physical discomfort, yet the critics have no clue to what he must regularly overcome to compete at this level. Nobody can begin to understand what it must feel like to haul a 340-pound body around, stopping and starting, stopping and starting. There are players in this league who can't play with a hangnail, but Shaquille O'Neal is definitely not one of them. Besides, there's a discernible advantage to his sitting out fifteen or twenty games a year. The reduced wear and tear will help preserve his knees for May and June when we will need him for forty-plus minutes a night. I see an analogy between Shaq and a 1972 220SL Mercedes. In 2004 one is not going to race this car at one hundred miles per hour down Sunset Boulevard because it would risk damaging the vehicle. How many times do you expect Shaq to run up and down the floor before something goes wrong? Shaq plays with an orthopedic device in each shoe that weighs about three pounds, forcing him to wear a size twenty-five instead of twenty-two. When he jumps or runs, he pushes off the outside of his foot instead of his big toe.

Nobody will admit it, but it seems obvious he injured his calf because he tried to compensate for his toe problems. Watching his body begin to break down, he fears how it might affect his future. His current contract, which he hopes to extend, expires after the 2005–6 season. Already the difference between his game today and that of two or three years ago is quite noticeable. He remains the most dominant force in the game, only not as dominant as he once was. When he was younger, he bounced off the floor with amazing quickness for a big man. Now he has to bend down and load up before he jumps. I'm concerned about him. If we don't win it this year, with such high expectations, he will be the first blamed, not Kobe, not Karl, not Gary, not me. I don't think that is necessarily fair, but that is the perception around here. When the fans see him at his best, he is such an overpowering presence that they automatically wonder: how come the Lakers don't win *every* game? Therefore when we lose, they assume it must be because Shaq didn't play hard enough. Even members of our inner circle put the pressure on his shoulders. I asked Tex recently about an upcoming game. We stand a chance, Tex responded, if "Shaq plays at the level he is supposed to play at." Shaq? What if, I counter, Kobe plays up to his standard? No matter, Tex said. "Everything depends on Shaq." That is a huge burden. For some reason, which we've never figured out, Shaq always seems to be in a funk between Christmas and his birthday, March 6. The staff has joked that we should ask him to take off the whole month of January. Tex grows especially agitated when Shaq won't pay attention when we're watching video. I don't worry about his focus. When the playoffs start, he will be focused.

Tonight's game was tight down the stretch, Ray Allen driving down the lane to put Seattle up by a bucket with 5.8 seconds left. I called for Horace to set a screen for Kobe, but when the play got busted, Devean inbounded the ball directly to Kobe, who missed a three-pointer that would have won the game. After the gun sounded, Kobe went over to Devean, berating him for not calling timeout when the play broke down. Kobe was right but he was wrong to reprimand his teammate on the court, in front of the crowd and the cameras. Players must be very delicate in how they interact with each other, especially in public. The wrong word may destroy another player's confidence, or worse yet, sow resentment that will not be easy to erase. When I call timeouts, for instance, I allow the players about forty-five seconds alone on the bench. I expect them to work things out together, to make suggestions but as

I've made very clear from day one, I do not expect them to coach. That's my job.

JANUARY 8
Los Angeles

I never pictured this team losing four straight. Of course, I never pictured this team without Karl, without Shaq, down suddenly from four future Hall of Famers to two. The last two setbacks, on the road to the Timberwolves and the Nuggets, weren't close. Since the 18–3 start, which raised expectations even further, we've gone 3–8, and our chance for home-court advantage throughout the playoffs is slipping away. There is no way to predict when Karl will be back, or Shaquille, or, for that matter, the rhythm that left us somewhere along the journey. We figured that yesterday's game in Denver would be difficult, staged in the state where Kobe stands accused, and that many fans would not wait for an official verdict before rendering their own—guilty. When Gary Vitti informed me of Kobe's request to skip the morning shootaround at the arena, I agreed immediately. The last thing he or we needed was more press. Kobe was more emotional than usual in the locker room before the game. "I want this one, guys," he told us.

In reviewing video from the matchup a few weeks ago in Los Angeles, we realized the Nuggets were able to erase a double-digit deficit with screen rolls and defensive gambles that took us out of our half-court offense. Our game plan this time would be to establish a slower tempo, *our* tempo, confident that if we passed the ball four or five times, the Nuggets would not be able to rotate quickly enough. So what happened? On our first possession Kobe raced upcourt, missing a twenty-footer. On our second Gary drove the length of the floor, missing a jumper. On our fourth Gary went to the hoop and was knocked down without a call, and the Nuggets scored easily in transition. "How's that for setting a slow tempo?" Frank Hamblen said. Establishing the proper tempo, I should point out, is no easy task. When the other team applies pressure, the tendency is to take shots too early in the shot clock, assuming it will be the best shot available in that possession. Rushing down the court plays right into the other team's hands. At halftime, I moved Kobe to the 3. Kobe likes to attack the hoop from there; most small forwards are too slow to chase him. The switch also put Kobe on Carmelo Anthony, who went off for sixteen in the first half. Asking Kobe to work hard on defense always runs the risk of sapping his energy for the other end, but trailing by fifteen, it was worth the risk. We narrowed the deficit to twelve, but couldn't creep any closer, losing 113–91. Worse yet, Kobe and I had gotten into it earlier in the game after he threw a poor pass that Anthony stole, resulting in a Denver layup. "You can't make that pass," I told Kobe when he came off the floor in the next timeout.

"Well, you better teach those motherfuckers how to run the offense," he said.

I sat him down on the spot. "Watch your mouth," I said.

The last few days have been difficult off the court as well. The organization has decided to put Jannero Pargo, a reserve guard, on waivers. There are a lot of things I love about this job, but one thing I absolutely hate is cutting someone, telling a young man that his dream has come to an end, at least for the time being. Any way you try to spin it, it's full, outright rejection. With Jannero, popular with all the players, the task was especially wrenching. The kid was the first on the court in practice, showing a wonderful capacity to learn. He saw only limited action, but when he did play, he usually made an impact. Most memorable was last year's Game 5 in the San Antonio series, when we nearly overcame a twenty-five-point deficit to assume a 3–2 lead. Pargo, extremely quick, stayed close to Parker and pushed the ball. Nonetheless, the bottom line is . . . well, the bottom line. Being over the salary cap, every dollar we would pay Jannero would cost us an equivalent amount in luxury tax penalties.

The video session before the Denver game was excruciating. I had to go in the room and look at Jannero, who didn't have a clue about his fate. No wonder I was testy. Afterward I pulled him aside. "We're not going to guarantee your contract," I said. "You can either take a flight home now or wait until after the game and fly back with us. But you can't go to the game and sit on the bench because you're not part of the team anymore." He flew to Los Angeles. There is no doubt that, in retrospect, it was a mistake to take him to Minnesota. We could have spared him the agony of flying home alone, a Laker no longer. The next morning he arrived at our training facility early to clean out his locker. When I saw him, he was walking out of Mitch's office, tears in his eyes. I asked Jannero to step into my office, grabbed a few tissues, and closed the door. I told Kurt Rambis, who coached him in the summer league, to join us. Jannero needed some reassurance that while his dream may end here, it doesn't have to die here. Kurt outlined the aspects of his game he needed to upgrade, which Jannero took extremely well. I was also concerned about the effect that cutting Jannero might have on the guys. They are professionals who have been around long enough to understand that, as the cliché goes, basketball is a business but the bonds they establish within their circle become very tight. We spend an inordinate amount of time around each other's spaces. When a member of the circle is forced to leave, the others also feel a sense of loss. For the Denver game they put his name and number on their shoes.

Given Jannero's departure and our recent mediocre play, I concluded that the time was as good as any for a team meeting. I'm generally not a big believer in team meetings, which rarely produce any earth-shattering changes. I can't recall a single instance when I felt better afterward. I did hear of one meeting that made quite an impression on players. Disgusted with his team's performance during a West Coast trip, Jack McMahon, who coached the Cincinnati Royals in the 1960s, called a meeting in the hotel to restore order. The players dreaded it, but according to my former Knicks teammate, Jerry Lucas, they were greeted with two cases of beer, four quarts of whiskey, and three hookers. "Guys, you figure this out," McMahon said before leaving the room. The Royals figured it out, all right, going on a long winning streak.

In our case holding a team meeting I called was surely better than if the players were to call one on their own. In that situation the coach will always be the scapegoat. I hoped that allowing the players an opportunity to vent in an appropriate forum, toward me or toward their teammates, without repercussions, might be precisely what they needed. We convened in the locker room, everyone on time except for Kobe, who, when he did arrive, began to fiddle with the mobile phone in his locker. If venting was what I expected, I was not disappointed. When I asked Kobe to stop his habit of screaming at his teammates on the court because it creates insecurity, he came right back at me. "That's bullshit," he said. "You're the one that's causing them to be anxious. They're afraid to make a mistake."

Instead of reacting in an angry manner (the therapist would be pleased) I patiently polled the younger players—Kareem, Devean, Luke, Brian—to see who was more accurate, Kobe or myself. "Are you nervous because you might miss a shot?" I asked. "I want you to be able to play with freedom out there." With their manhood on the line, and perhaps not wanting to alienate me or Kobe, they insisted they weren't affected by any harsh comments. I'm sure Kobe wasn't too crazy about my questioning, but that wasn't my concern.

I asked the coaching staff to offer a few observations, aware that the troops were probably sick of hearing only one voice, mine. Too many coaches have lost their players, and subsequently their jobs, by not recognizing when they need to step back. Tex, the Xs and Os man, spoke about running the offense with poise and control. Kurt talked about the need for everyone to help their teammates execute better at both ends. Jim brought up the importance of more efficient practices. But it was Frank who really seized everyone's attention. "You all know what to do as players," he said. "Yet you punked out last night. We made a pact in training camp not to take shortcuts, to pay attention to the basketball gods. Shaq, it isn't right that you missed practice, and Kobe, it isn't right that you were late today. We just need to quit feeling sorry for ourselves, and go out and play ball. You know what's really pathetic? Jannero Pargo was released yesterday. He came to play every day and he paid his dues to the basketball gods." By "the basketball gods," Frank was referring to the game's irrefutable principles: Hit the open man. Help each other out on defense. Box your man out. Play inside the system. Don't break off plays. Don't force the action if you're being doubled. Etc. etc. Unfortunately the players I've coached in Los

Angeles have never adhered to those principles the way the players did in Chicago.

Frank's words hit home. A few minutes later the coaches assembled in the video room where Kobe, and then Shaq, paid brief visits. There would be no official apologies, but each sounded somewhat contrite, embarrassed about being singled out in front of the group. I only hope Frank's words will still hit home in a week or two. As he pointed out in a similar meeting last year, "Great things are being said here, but the actions are what matter."

JANUARY 16
Sacramento

We lost to the Kings tonight, again without Karl and Shaq, and as if that wasn't overwhelming enough, without Kobe. He sprained his right shoulder a few days ago against the Cavaliers, and will be out for at least another week. In the Cleveland game, I was impressed with LeBron James, who has made strides since we played the Cavs during the exhibition season. Yet as talented as this kid definitely appears to be, I don't believe he or any nineteen-year-old should be playing in the NBA. These young men grow so dependent on their posses, who fetch their cars and their girls, that they can't possibly develop into mature, self-sufficient human beings. One day, I'm convinced, we'll find out the true extent of the psychological damage that's being caused. I consider the age of twenty-eight to be about the time most people become fully mature. Until then they don't know how to read their emotions and are still trying to come to terms with the perplexities of life, death, and love. Spurs coach Gregg Popovich told his former player Steve Kerr, *If I ever talk about drafting a high school player, please slap me in the face and tell me how stupid I am.*

Tonight's defeat was to be expected, yet as well as Sacramento is playing, leading the division, I wonder how the team will fare when Chris Webber returns to the lineup. Webber is a bona fide star, but like Kobe, tends to hold on to the ball longer than necessary, causing the offense to stagnate. The brightest part of the evening was the performance of Kareem Rush, who scored thirty points in thirty-four minutes. Our preseason concerns that Kareem would not be serious about his profession have been put to rest. With help from his grandmother, who monitored the housing situation, Kareem has come through and should be a productive player in this league for a long time.

I love coaching the kids on this team. After dealing extensively with players with ingrained habits, to work with youngsters eager to soak up every ounce of basketball knowledge is very refreshing. The first rule of learning is the desire to learn, which veteran players often lose. They begin to believe their clippings, assuming they know everything about this game. I have news for them. They don't and never will.

The minutes the kids are logging, due to our injuries, are invaluable. They may dissect all the video in the world, but only on the hardwood, where the banging is real, can developing players truly begin to understand the mentality and will required to succeed in this league night after night. They may scrutinize an opponent's moves over and over—Does he prefer going to his right every time? Where on the block does he like to receive the entry pass?—but until the opponent has beaten them, discovering *their* weakness, they cannot fully appreciate the challenge, and know how to approach it the next time. With this unit I've been calling more timeouts than usual, hoping to provide it with a sense of relief when it gets into jeopardy. The players may need to stop and refocus. If Kareem, Brian, and Luke maintain this level of growth, I won't hesitate to use them in critical spots come playoff time. As for Karl, who was placed on the injured list for the first time in his career, we must be patient. "Whatever it takes, don't worry about it," I told him the other day. "We don't expect you to come back in two weeks. If it takes you two months, if it takes you three months, we'll be here and the game will still be going on. We'll make it up in the playoffs and find a way to win anyway."

JANUARY 23
Dallas

During the season I dream about basketball almost every night. In last night's dream my players couldn't convert a single jump shot. No matter what plays I tried to run, they threw up brick after brick. I woke up and couldn't get back to sleep. Friends suggest I take medication to rest more easily but I suppose I do not want to lose these intrusions. They provide inspiration and on occasion concrete ideas for improving the team. We've dropped four of the last five, not exactly the way to prepare for an upcoming seven-city road trip, our longest in several seasons. In last night's loss to the Mavericks, I went with my tenth different starting lineup in forty games, putting Luke at the 3, but nothing worked. Finley scored thirty-one, and Antawn Jamison came off the bench to put in twenty-six. Cuban was also on last night. During the game he instructed a member of the public-address staff to turn up the noise volume. "It's as loud as it's supposed to go," the man said, reminding Cuban he would incur a league fine if the sound rose above a certain decibel limit. "I don't give a shit if we get fined," Cuban said.

The Mavs do a lot of things over the top. Several weeks ago, when I was dining at the Ritz Carlton in Marina del Rey, the hotel staff told me that the Mavs, after ending their thirteen-year drought in Los Angeles, celebrated into the early morning hours. The tips alone, the bartender said, paid for his entire Christmas shopping. Well, there's nothing wrong with a little celebrating now and then, but to go to that extreme after a victory in December shows a lack of perspective. Any real celebrating should wait till June.

JANUARY 29
Los Angeles

Jeanie and I lunched in her office today, often our best place and time to catch up. When I arrived, waiting for me was a chicken Caesar salad and the printout of a story claiming Kobe hit on a room service attendant in Portland. We were waiting for stories like this to surface. The woman, according to the article, refused the overture, saying that Kobe accepted the rejection "like a gentleman." This was bound to create trouble at the Bryant home in Newport Beach.

In the evening Jeanie and I attended a concert given by the Scottish group Travis. We ducked out before the encore, heading to our separate homes even though we live only about a hundred steps apart. "The secret to a good relationship," Katharine Hepburn said, "is to live close and visit often." We enjoy what I call a dependent-independent relationship. Each of us gives the other plenty of space, yet Jeanie is always there when I make the late-night call from the road. Being around the sport for most of her life, she understands the insane existence an NBA coach leads. Yet that doesn't make the situation any more palatable. The long road trip, which starts in two days, means yet another good-bye, and too many good-byes cause damage even to the most stable romances. The person left behind is the more affected, as the other goes off to another new place. Only rarely does Jeanie join me.

The road, glamorous or not, is tough, lonely. I was walking through the training room recently when the players stopped me, seeking my thoughts about something more important than the triangle. "Coach, coach," they said, "tell the rookie, tell the rookie." The rookie was Brian Cook, and they wanted me to tell him that he would be making a big mistake by getting married. "I can't tell you, Cookie, that you're making a mistake," I said, "but this NBA life is difficult enough. Are you ready to be monogamous?"

"Yes," he answered. My job in this department is to let the players know that I'm not going to endorse irresponsible behavior, yet at the same time I won't sit in judgment. They are human beings, with human frailties. I usually advise players that if they harbor even the slightest doubts about whether they can be true to their sweethearts, they might want to hold off on any marriage plans. The temptations in the unreal world they occupy are too prevalent and, with today's salaries and perks, aren't likely to go away any time soon.

FIVE

ON THE ROAD

JANUARY 31
Open skies

We're headed toward Toronto, the first stop of the long trip. I've challenged the team to win at least four of the seven games. On the road the idea is to win at least 50 percent of the time. Giving goals is not a practice I followed with the Bulls, who were sufficiently self-motivated from Michael down to the twelfth man, watching countless games on television to scout their opponents. When I arrived in Los Angeles, I sensed that this team needed a measurable target to advance its cause. The players weren't nearly as driven. During the first year here, I tried some psychology on them. "I think we can win five out of six," I told them, referring to an upcoming string of games, "but I don't think you guys can do it, so I'll say four out of six." Of course, by that point I had already put the higher number in their minds. Determined to prove themselves to me, the new coach with the six rings, they consistently met the challenge, laying the groundwork for our first title. Once they became more familiar with my tricks, the psychology didn't work as well. "Oh, Phil, he's just tweaking us," they said, "trying to get us to rise to the occasion." I plead guilty.

The key to achieving success on the road is to enter the fourth quarter with a lead, any lead. That way, the home-crowd hysteria can be kept to a minimum. Against some of the inferior teams, it is possible to trail the entire game and steal it at the end, but that formula is not one I recommend for this group. A sizable cushion is necessary unless a team is dominant from the free-throw line, which we are not. The road team must also not try to outrun the opponent on its own floor. That strategy may be effective in November but it won't work later in the season. Feeding off the crowd's energy, the home team will run the floor with more abandon, attempting to establish a wild, frenzied pace, a trap that must be avoided. On the road I constantly remind the troops: "Be careful of the shots you take from out of the corner. That is a fast-break shot. Miss it, and you will be a defender in jeopardy." I coach differently on the road, calling more timeouts, always seeking to be more protective. I suppose the gap between how well a team performs at home versus on the road seems wider than it should reasonably be. If the ball, the dimensions of the court, and the personnel stay relatively the same, why is there such a discrepancy in results? There may be numerous explanations. A player's eating habits might be different. He might have trouble going to sleep without companionship, without sex. He might not be able to stay alone in his room. Any change in routine may take the player out of his comfortable rhythm.

On this particular trip, I had another goal I didn't share with the players—to maintain my sanity. This strange season of injuries has claimed one more, and it was the strangest one to date. I found out about it yesterday at around nine A.M. when the coaching staff was watching video of the night's opponent, the Minnesota Timberwolves. Gary Vitti took a seat. Usually Tex asks Vitti for an injury update. "Okay, what bad news do you have to tell us today?" he'll say. Then there'll be laughs all around. Only Vitti didn't wait this time, and there were no laughs. "You won't believe this," he said. "It's Kobe. He can't play tonight." Vitti explained that Kobe apparently gashed his hand when moving some boxes in the garage, requiring ten stitches in his index finger. When I informed the team before the video session, one player placed a Styrofoam cup in my hand and then knocked it away to illustrate what he thought really happened to Kobe. The others laughed. I needed to stop the growing suspicions immediately. "I want you guys to suspend judgment," I told them. "We don't know the details." To me the incident illustrated how Kobe's life continues to spiral out of control. Only days after he had returned to the lineup, we lost him again.

On the subject of losing Kobe, I wonder once again whether our relationship has deteriorated beyond repair. Earlier this week at El Segundo there was an incident at practice. On the way to the court, I asked Kobe, still nursing a sore shoulder, if he was up to doing a little running. Sure, he responded, as soon as he finished his treatment. Almost an hour went by, and there was no Kobe sighting. Finally, with an ice pack on his shoulder, he took a seat on the sideline. It began to dawn on me that contrary to what he had told me, Kobe had no intention of running. After practice I followed Kobe to the training room, asking him why he lied to me. He was being sarcastic, he said. Wrong answer. I told him that he needed to treat me with respect, not sarcasm. I turned and walked away, heading to the coaches' locker room. A minute later I heard him cursing in the training room in front of the players, though I couldn't make out the exact words. After I showered and addressed the media, I asked Vitti, one of the few people Kobe trusts, what the cursing was about. Vitti didn't know . . . or perhaps wasn't willing to admit he knew. Kobe's going through another hard time, Vitti tried to explain. I wasn't in the mood. Believe me, I can't begin to imagine how difficult this whole ordeal has been for Kobe, but that doesn't mean I will allow myself to be the recipient of his displaced anger, especially when I've been firmly on his side since the Colorado story broke.

Now I was the one who was angry. I went upstairs to see Mitch in his office. Wasting no time, I went off on a tirade about the need to deal Kobe before the trading deadline in mid-February. "I won't coach this team next year if he is still here," I said emphatically. "He won't listen to anyone. I've had it with this kid." My monologue— Mitch barely said a word at first—reminded me of a similar eruption in the middle of my first year when I presented what I thought was a very logical argument for trading Kobe at that time. "Everyone says what a mature person this kid is," I said. "He's not mature at all." The deal I had in mind was Kobe to Phoenix for Jason Kidd and Shawn Marion. Jerry West, the general manager, said there was no way Dr. Buss would trade Kobe, a sentiment Mitch reiterated this time. In 2000 Jeanie put everything in perspective. "Phil," she said, "Kobe has fourteen years left as a player. You don't understand what this means to ownership. That's money in the bank. We can sell season tickets every year because we have a superstar that will be coming back." Maybe so, but I remain convinced that the Lakers would have been as successful, and less divided, with Jason Kidd running the show. With his selflessness, his ability to find the open man, coupled with Marion's athleticism and defensive intensity, we might be gunning for our fifth straight championship. No names were obviously considered this time, although, as I casually pointed out to Mitch, Tracy McGrady, the player closest to matching Kobe in pure individual ability, was "no picnic to deal with, either. I heard that every time someone says 'get back on defense,' his back hurts."

FEBRUARY 2
Indianapolis

With the acrobatic Vince Carter finding space to hit jumpers, the sizable advantage we enjoyed through much of yesterday's game against the Raptors was starting to dwindle late in the fourth quarter. The home-crowd hysteria was no longer at a mininum. I gave significant minutes to Rick Fox, making only his third appearance since coming off the injured list. I felt that Rick, who played a total of only fifteen minutes in his first two games, would do a good job of containing Carter. He knows how to keep his feet on the ground, and his body between the attacker and the hoop. Once a defender leaves his feet, he immediately puts himself in a vulnerable position, unless, like Kobe, he's athletic enough to make a quick recovery. In addition, with Shaquille primed to dominate against Toronto's undersized front line, I felt Rick would help us rotate the ball more easily into the post. Ahead by one point with a few seconds left, Rick was involved in the biggest play of the game. He forced Carter to his left, where help came from Gary Payton, who knocked the ball out of Carter's hands to secure the game. The victory was no cause for exuberance—we almost blew a sixteen-point lead against a below .500 team—yet with more formidable challenges in the days ahead, surviving this first test was essential.

If only we could have survived the fourth estate. During a postgame interview with a Los Angeles–based television station, Shaq, still fuming over the fifty-five fouls that were called, went off. "David Stern wonders why the league is losing money," he said. "That's why. People pay good money to come watch these athletes play. They [the officials] try to take over the [bleep] game." That wasn't even the worst part. When informed by the interviewer that he was on live TV, Shaq saw no reason to modify his language. "I don't give a [bleep]," he said.

This morning after our shootaround, we learned Shaq would be suspended for the game against Indiana. The second comment is the one that sealed his punishment. I couldn't believe it. Fining him for his profanity would be understandable, but to deprive the Indianapolis fans of seeing one of the game's marquee attractions in our only visit here this year, as I told the press, was another example of the league's "vindictiveness." Especially galling was the fact that Shaq's behavior was far less offensive than that of Latrell Sprewell, who was fined $25,000 but not suspended, after shouting profanities toward the fans and Knicks officials at Madison Square Garden earlier this season. Without Shaquille, down again to one future Hall of Famer, Payton, we were crushed by the Pacers, one of the Eastern Conference's elite teams. If that weren't upsetting enough, we lost Kareem Rush with an ankle injury. I'm beginning to wonder whether maybe this truly is a cursed season.

FEBRUARY 5
Philadelphia

The flight from Cleveland to Philly normally takes about fifty minutes. This one, delayed because the plane was deiced twice, took three torturous hours. We didn't arrive at our downtown hotel until around four A.M., putting everyone in a major funk. I canceled the morning shootaround, preferring that the players try to rest as much as possible. Though we had adjusted to the three-hour difference in the time zone, we would now be facing the second game of a back-to-back that was certain to deplete our energy. The road trip was becoming longer with every hour. I can't blame the league for the poor weather and the deicing. Can I? They seem to control everything else related to the game. But I sure wish they could move the eight P.M. starts for national TV games to seven-thirty. A game on TNT or ESPN takes forever, usually starting about five minutes late, and running an extra twenty minutes with the commercial interruptions. Last night's contest, which we won in overtime, thanks to a retro performance from Shaquille—thirty-seven points and twelve rebounds—didn't wrap up till after eleven P.M. If the tip-off was thirty minutes sooner, we might have been able to escape Cleveland before the weather worsened. I don't expect to win this battle. I'm a lone voice against powerful interests: the cable networks, who generate millions for the league's coffers. Yet I can't help but pose this question: if the games started a half hour earlier, does the league really believe it would lose a significant share of its viewing audience? There is no way. Pro basketball fans are incredibly dedicated, many arranging their lives around the games.

Sleep wasn't the only thing I lost. I was notified this afternoon that I would be fined fifty big ones for my comments against the league, and so would the Lakers. The league called Jeanie with the news because she is the team's executive vice president. Usually, protocol would dictate passing the word through Mitch. It seemed like the league was going out of its way to embarrass the organization. I was tempted to laugh at the amount, which seemed excessive, but I knew that Dr. Buss would not think there was anything amusing about forking over that much dough to the league. The Lakers may be worth a fortune, but $50,000 is $50,000. Fans are led by the media to believe that with the obscene amount of money professional athletes and coaches earn, fines don't make the slightest impact. I'm here to report that isn't the case. This fine stings plenty, and because I don't have sufficient funds in my checking account to cover the amount, I will need to take them from my savings. On occasion the league will funnel the money back, if I behave for the rest of the season. I still keep a receipt from a $5,000 check the league sent to reimburse me for a fine seven or eight years ago.

In tonight's contest the officials who, determined to make us pay on the court for Shaq's maligning their brethren, missed one call after another. Of course, they would never admit it, but believe me, that type of retribution is common in the NBA. Nine minutes into the game, the lead official, Joey Crawford, signaled Gary Payton for a second technical for laughing about a previous call. Without Gary and Kobe we didn't have anyone to block Iverson's path to the hoop. He burned us with thirty-nine.

"You took the guy [Gary] out of the game," I complained to Joey.

"I can't help that, Phil," he said. "He crossed the line."

The line? What line? I tried to explain that Gary and referee Bennie Adams had resolved their differences. "Were you aware that the ref admitted that he made a mistake?" I asked Joey. Joey was not aware, but it didn't matter. I looked over at Steve Kerr, doing the broadcast for TNT, and shrugged my shoulders. I tried to remain calm and absorb the customary abuse the fans dish out in Philadelphia, the so-called City of Brotherly Love, but one idiot in the row behind me became a little too obnoxious. "It looks like you guys can't win without Kobe," he said, "just like you couldn't win without Jordan." I told this model citizen to kiss my ass and immediately regretted it. I'm usually more immune to any heckling.

FEBRUARY 8
Orlando

I'm always amazed when I come to this town and experience how far the Magic have fallen since the mid-1990s when, anchored by Shaquille and Penny Hardaway, they were supposed to be the dynasty of the future. In 1995, the year Michael came out of retirement to play the last seventeen games, they beat us in the Eastern Conference Semifinals, highlighted by Nick Anderson's memorable steal from MJ in Game 1. For the 1995–96 season we retooled our club, among other things by acquiring Dennis Rodman, specifically to counter Orlando's strengths. But weeks after we returned the favor in that year's playoffs, Shaq bolted for Los Angeles, a loss the Magic has never overcome. Hardaway was slowed down by a series of injuries and in 1999 signed with Phoenix. In the summer of 2000, when Orlando signed free agent Tracy McGrady and acquired Grant Hill from Detroit, they seemed finally on their way back to prominence, but Hill was sidelined with an ankle injury that has yet to heal. Since he joined the Magic, he's played in only forty-seven games. Their misfortune illustrates how in this sport talent alone isn't enough to sustain a high level of success. The Bulls were extremely lucky, rarely suffering a major injury. Even during "The Last Dance," when Scottie was sidelined for almost half the season, he made it back in time for the playoffs. This year notwithstanding, the Lakers have been just as fortunate. During our three championship runs, Shaq didn't miss a single postseason game, and Kobe missed only one.

Without Kobe, who can bend his finger only about 35 percent of the way, we struggled again, trailing by fourteen heading into the fourth. I inserted a second unit of Horace, Luke, Devean, Kareem, and Fish. I've been criticized in the past for going with reserves in critical situations. The most notable example was during Game 6 of the 1992 NBA Finals against Portland, when, down by fifteen points, our bench ignited a 14–2 run to start the fourth quarter, leading to a 97–93 triumph that secured our second straight championship. The dismayed Chicago partisans kept yelling for me to put Michael back in, but I was very comfortable with the group on the floor. Often when the bench players enter a game, the other team tends to relax, giving the substitutes less due than they deserve. But in basketball momentum can shift dramatically, in the span of two or three possessions. Then once the starters rejoin the fray, they feed off the energy provided by the second unit.

In the early going of the game, the Magic was very effective in keeping the ball out of Shaquille's hands. When teams devote their entire game plans toward that objective, it usually leaves open dribble penetration. Luke was able to enter the lane with consistency and, with his passing ability, locate the smalls on the perimeter. Luke is definitely a liability on defense, but the guys love playing with him. They know he will pass the ball to them in prime shooting position. As a result they work extra hard to provide him with help on the defensive end. Suddenly we started knocking down shots, clawing our way back into the game. Midway through the quarter, I reinserted Shaq and a couple minutes later, Gary. Tied with about ten seconds left, the Magic called timeout. With a foul to give, I instructed the guys to go for the steal. There are times when having a foul in the bank can backfire because it will take away valuable seconds when I would prefer to put a team on the line. But more often teams will have license to play more aggressively. Fish swiped the ball from Rod Strickland, feeding Gary for the winning layup. The win put us one shy of the magical four.

FEBRUARY 10
Miami

This afternoon I did something I almost never do. When Shaquille and Rick stepped off the bus at our hotel in Coconut Grove, an upscale Miami suburb, I asked them to enter my suite for a brief chat. From the puzzled expressions on their faces, I could tell they were extremely curious, perhaps alarmed. I believe the time on the road between practice and the tip-off is almost sacred; the players should be allowed to prepare in their own ways for the challenge awaiting them. But this time I was facing my own challenge, and it had nothing to do with the Miami Heat. Recognizing that my relationship with Kobe was becoming more acrimonious by the day, I decided that a conversation with Shaq and Fox could not wait any longer. At practice the day before Kobe, who told Vitti that his finger hadn't healed sufficiently for him to play in the Miami game, was taking a few shots left-handed when I asked him not to be a distraction. I needed to work with the players who would be suiting up. *"Distraction,"* he said, mockingly, unable to resist taking one more shot. A few hours later, during dinner in Key Biscayne with the staff, Vitti told us that Kobe has been threatening again to opt out of his contract, vowing "to take Slava with me." *Slava?* Was this an indication of Kobe's being totally out of touch with reality? If Kobe was interested in taking along a player who would defer to him, Slava Medvedenko was the worst choice imaginable. He hasn't passed up a shot since November.

Shaq and Rick took a seat in my room. Inviting Rick, I felt, would keep the discussion at a high level. I got right to the point. "What would you guys think if I were to offer Kobe a leave of absence?" They wasted no time, either. Kobe, they promised, would contribute to the team in a positive manner once he recovered from his finger injury. I was gratified to note the genuine sense of compassion, especially coming from Kobe's supposed enemy, Shaquille. The press, I have long believed, with its sensationalistic, insult-to-insult coverage, has captured only one component in a rather complicated relationship between two proud, if emotionally fragile, superstars. Shaq and Kobe will never be buddies, but they remain linked together by a common goal, perhaps destiny, each aware that they can't win championships here without the other. With Rick and Shaquille opposed, along with Mitch, I filed the leave of absence idea away for good. "What happens if he won't accept it?" Mitch asked. In that case, I replied, I would tell Kobe that we would suspend him with pay regardless, but for PR purposes call it a "leave of absence." The choice would belong to him. I knew precisely what I would say: "Kobe, you're not a positive element with the team anymore. You can't have these kind of anger situations in front of your teammates because it's destructive to the balance that has to be maintained."

The conversation with Shaquille and Rick, which lasted about twenty minutes, also touched on an interview I had given two weeks earlier with Howard Beck, the beat reporter for the *Los Angeles Daily News.* Every season I agree to separate, exclusive sessions with both the *Daily News* and the *Times,* making sure to feed each beast roughly the same amount, while not divulging anything of real consequence. In the *Daily News* interview, I stressed the point that whether Kobe stays or leaves after this season, "Shaq's going to be the focal point." Figuring into the equation, I explained, was the substantial financial commitment the Lakers have made to him, more than $50 million over the next two years. I also mentioned that I encouraged Kobe to model his play after Magic Johnson, who deferred in his early years to Kareem Abdul-Jabbar. "That's Magic. That's not me," Kobe once told me. "You're right," I said. "It's not you. But it's a good example to emulate." Magic was patient, young, willing to wait. Kobe's agent, Rob Pelinka, called Mitch soon after the *Daily News* article appeared. Kobe, he made sure to mention, would take notice that I referred to the Lakers as Shaq's team. I told Mitch I never used those exact words. The exact words I used were "focal point." The story's headline writer, not me, was the one who created the problem: PHIL ON KOBE: IT'S SHAQ'S TEAM.

In tonight's game, with us ahead by three points midway through the third quarter, Shaq and the Heat's Malik Allen engaged in a war of words, and both drew technicals. During a timeout in the fourth, Kobe came over to the coaches' huddle, suggesting I run a play for Shaq. "He's motivated," Kobe said. Adopting his suggestion, I charted a little sequence for Shaq to receive the ball in the center of the lane, and sure enough, he powered through the defense for a dunk and was fouled. Shaq was indeed motivated, scoring fourteen of his twenty-five points after the altercation. As we used to say about Wilt Chamberlain: "Don't ever get him angry." I'm not about to suggest that Shaq isn't sufficently motivated the rest of the time— another knock on him he doesn't deserve. But there is no doubt he elevates his play in games that mean something extra. The reality is that he's played in more than seven hundred regular season games. We won handily against the Heat, reaching our goal of four victories for the trip, with one game remaining in Houston.

I was very encouraged by how Devean and Fish performed. Devean, an integral contributor before the rash of injuries, had lost his shooting touch and become despondent. I was afraid I might lose him for the whole season. Maybe the rap on him being not tough enough was on target after all. Fish was encountering more trouble than I imagined with his diminished role, playing on the second unit with youngsters not as familiar with the triangle. Since he's not receiving the ball in good position, he hasn't been knocking down the outside shots with his usual consistency. After the game I was most struck by Kobe's selflessness, the flip side, I suppose, of the dichotomy that never ceases to confound me. I was preoccupied for much of the day about how his presence had become such a disruptive force, and then, after being away from the team for a week, he was totally into the game and tried to help the staff. I've coached other players who displayed that type of involvement—Ron Harper comes to mind—but this was the first time I could recall a non-playing Kobe becoming so engaged.

FEBRUARY 11
Houston

I was relaxing in my hotel room this afternoon when Todd Musburger, my agent, told me the Lakers were about to go public with the news that negotiations over my contract extension would be put on indefinite hold. I was perplexed. Why today, on the eve of our last game before the five-day All-Star break, did the Lakers feel compelled to release this information? Why, given that the talks officially broke down last weekend, couldn't they have waited one more day? I would be at my beach house in Playa del Rey by then, pleasantly inaccessible. Instead I knew I'd be inundated with questions from the press during my routine session before tonight's game.

I immediately called the therapist. Could there be a connection, he wondered, between my recent tirade about Kobe in Mitch's office and the sudden halt in talks? Absolutely. Todd told me that Mitch relayed my disparaging comments to Dr. Buss, who was "disappointed." I suppose there is ample justification, as the therapist suggested, to feel that Mitch betrayed me, but he never promised to keep the conversation between us. At the same time, the therapist stressed, "he undermined you to the owner. He could have made you an ally by keeping that information." Maybe, but the way I analyze the situation, as frequently as Mitch and I confer over the makeup and fluid state of the team, he is still part of management, and I am not. Even my references to the organization as "the Lakers," not "us," reveal how I perceive my true status within the hierarchy.

Since I took the job in June 1999, I've been perceived as an outsider, perhaps due to the fact that I didn't rise from within, or perhaps due to the scruffy, maverick image that still persists from my days in New York, not exactly compatible with being a company guy, a team player. No wonder I don't like to see players tagged with raps they can't elude. I was also blamed by some parties for forcing Jerry West, the most inside of insiders, to leave town. That charge was completely unfounded, although I won't argue that with me at the helm, Jerry might have sensed that his role would be less of a challenge, and he is someone who definitely needs challenges. I've never been one to scheme, to pit one person versus another, to move them around like pawns on a human chessboard. Jeanie at first found this lack of office politicking astonishing, assuming that it was how I rose to the top in Chicago, and in time, made enemies with Jerry Krause, leading to the end of my tenure.

That doesn't mean I was hesitant to make necessary changes, both in Chicago and Los Angeles. As the staff prepared for my first draft with the Lakers, there was a gentleman who hung around our facility even though he wasn't an official part of the organization. I was told he was a friend of Jerry West's. "What difference does that make?" I said. "This is *our* draft." He left. A few months later, I kicked him out again when he showed up at training camp. I learned that it was standard procedure for players and other staffers to invite family members and friends to practices. In my reign, as long as it lasted, standard procedure would be different. "We're going to make critical comments here," I told the team.

"I want you to have as much privacy as possible. If we ever fight, I want the fight to be here, so nobody ever sees it." Inheriting a team that failed to fulfill its promise—the Lakers were ousted in the playoffs by Utah in 1998, San Antonio in 1999—I felt changes were definitely in order.

Fast-forward to February 2004. Here I was, despite winning three titles in four years, in a Houston hotel room, a lame-duck coach with a future more uncertain than ever. How did this happen? Why couldn't the Lakers and I get this thing done? Were there any signs I missed from Dr. Buss? In our original offer, we asked for a substantial raise over the first contract, which would include two years as coach, and five as a special consultant. That way the amount of money would not appear outrageous. When the Lakers indicated that seven years was not in their interest, we countered with a two-year offer, to serve only as coach. I am not sure what happened next. Todd has handled the negotiations. Given the awkwardness of Jeanie's position, I felt it would be better if I were not directly involved. I told Todd he didn't need to update me on every detail. I'm also not clear what role Kobe might have played. For a long time I assumed that the Lakers would want to extend my contract to keep intact as many pieces as possible of a successful combination. But I must now consider the much more cynical possibility that Kobe, perhaps through Pelinka, passed word to the highest level that he wouldn't consider signing a new contract with the Lakers if I came back. That might explain the timing of the announcement, a signal to Kobe that the Lakers would surrender to his ultimatum once the season ended. Before concluding our conversation, the therapist reminded me to breathe, a vital part of the meditation process. Exhaling allows a person to let go and accept the next, new impulse of life.

The game against the Rockets was almost secondary. Shaq was outscored by Yao Ming 29–24, and Kobe, back in action for the first time in two weeks, lost the battle with his man, Cuttino Mobley. While we didn't defeat any teams over .500, the long road trip was over, at least. In the locker room after the game, I told the guys to spend time during the mini-vacation thinking about the team, and to return to practice on Monday with a renewed spirit. I was telling myself the same thing.

SIX

THE HERE
AND NOW

FEBRUARY 16
Los Angeles

The All-Star break is usually a slow period around here. But I'm beginning to realize that there will be no such thing as a slow period this year. On Thursday after reviewing video of our fifteen-point loss to the Rockets with Tex, I went to see Mitch, seeking an explanation for the timing of Wednesday's announcement. Mitch wouldn't offer one, referring me to John Black, the public relations man.

"What in the world would make you guys sit down and make this statement now?" I asked Black.

"Your agent was in the meeting, too," he responded. "He obviously agreed with us. The sooner we bring this out in the open, the better."

I was not placated. Black and I could have debated the issue for hours, but there was no point. Besides, there was a much more pressing matter to deal with: Kobe Bryant. Ever since the episode in Miami, I had been looking for the right moment for us to talk. The right moment never came. Right or not, the moment could no longer wait. The two of us needed to reach a level of understanding before the season was lost. The distance between us would drag the whole team down. To be adequately prepared, I discussed my strategy with the therapist. The main point he emphasized was "to not let it get personal." The focus must remain on the welfare of the team.

On Friday morning while I was driving to the office, my assistant called. Shaq was looking for me, she said. When I called him, he asked if I wanted him to respond publicly to "Kobe's comment." *Kobe's comment?* As usual I hadn't read the papers.

Shaq filled me in. Asked if the sudden uncertainty of my coaching status might affect his own plans with the Lakers, Kobe responded: "I don't care." Shaq was angry. "I can't believe this guy," he said. "We've gone to three championships in four years, something we never did before, and he's not willing to stand up for you." I appreciated Shaq's gesture, the way he attaches himself to people he trusts. Nonetheless, I told him I did not need anyone to defend me. The last thing this team needed, after the injuries and losses we could never have anticipated, was another feud. There would be no guarantee that as a group we could overcome this one. We needed to band together, not come apart, and there wasn't much time. Minnesota, Sacramento, Dallas, and San Antonio weren't coming apart. As for Kobe's comment, I wasn't offended. I'm sure he's upset that during this most turbulent period, instead of providing him with unconditional support, I have once again joined the ranks of authority figures daring to question his conduct. I realize now that my decision to be flexible toward him, which I made in Hawaii, has backfired. Given more room to rebel, he took full advantage. Only by holding him to a higher standard, on and off the court, is there a chance he might be compliant.

Finally, after practice today, I asked Kobe to meet in my office. "How soon?" he asked.

"Fifteen minutes," I told him.

He showed up a half hour later. "What's up?" he said.

I shut the door. The time for flexibility was over. "I feel like you've been very vitriolic," I told him. "If you're not capable of taking coaching remarks, then we're not going to have "give and take" anymore and this is simply not going to work. It will break down the team. Some of the comments you've made have been in front of the kids, and that's disrespectful. I know you feel you've been picked on, but I'm not the one who is picking on you. Don't put me in that classification." I closed with one final point. "As of last weekend, the Lakers are not in contract talks with me anymore, which is just fine with me. That makes it for this year only. It liberates me to coach the team without worrying about whether you're coming back or another player is coming back. You and I can work this out, right?" He nodded. I handed him a tape of the Houston contest. If there was one facet of the game in which we desperately needed a contribution from Kobe, it was on the defensive end. Torched in that game by Mobley, Kobe was not playing defense up to his normal standards.

I felt hopeful about our conversation. Of course, a conversation with Kobe often reveals one of his many narcissistic tendencies. After I told him I believed he and Shaquille have proven they can play effectively together, he brought up Sunday's All-Star game, captured by the Western Conference squad 136–132. Shaq led the way with twenty-four points and eleven rebounds. "I got Shaq the most valuable player award last night," Kobe said. "I know how to make Shaq the best player on the floor." No doubt he was right. Nobody, when he is committed, can deliver the ball to Shaq more consistently, in a better spot, than Kobe. Yet if I were to acknowledge this point, I would betray Shaquille and arm Kobe with ammunition he might later exploit for their one-on-one battle that although camouflaged, always simmers under the surface. Kobe then expressed his disapproval of Shaquille's failure to show up for practice today. "That just shows you what kind of a leader he is," he said. "The conversation is about you and me, not Shaq," I said. He was angry about the allowances the Lakers afford Shaq, failing to note the hypocrisy in his accusation. Nobody this year, or in any year I've coached, has received more "allowances" than Kobe Bryant. At times the pettiness between the two of them can be unbelievably juvenile. Shaquille won't allow himself to be taped before a game by Gary Vitti because he's too aligned with Kobe. Kobe won't let Chip Schaefer, Shaq's guy, tape him. Reporters aren't immune from these territorial disputes. If a writer lingers too often around one superstar's locker, he is likely to be shut out by the other.

The media was waiting for me after Kobe and I wrapped up.

Their sense of excitement was impossible to miss, this latest skirmish the best copy the Lakers had provided since the October feud. They were in full probing mode. I was in full disarming mode. I won this one. What about Kobe's "I don't care" statement? What statement? I asked, generating laughs. What about his comment that he doesn't like you as a person but loves you as a coach? No problem, I said. I've always preached to the players that liking one another wasn't mandatory. "You guys have overwhelming egos," the coaching staff has told them. "It's tough to put two or three of you in the same room together for a long period of time without someone getting on someone else's nerves. That's okay. As long as you respect each other for what you do in your work, then you can go out and play the game together." If on the other hand there is too much animosity, if the team is divided into cliques, the chemistry can easily fall apart. Strangely enough, despite the well-documented squabbles, I can recall only one altercation during my four and a half years here, in February 2002, between Kobe and Samaki Walker, that left Samaki with a swollen eye. Even then there was no long-term damage, except perhaps to Samaki's ego.

Preparing for the second half of the season, I feel a deeper sense of peace than I've experienced in a long time. Tossing aside any attachments, I suppose, allows me to do what comes more naturally, focusing on the day-to-day journey that makes life so fascinating. The more attached I become to something, as the Buddhists believe, the more I set myself up for misery, the more I become needy. June, my ex-wife, used to tell me I couldn't enjoy winning, but that wasn't true. I certainly did enjoy winning, except that like everything else in life, the feeling doesn't last. Everything decays. Tex, who is definitely no Buddhist, has a saying that I've grown to love:

"You are only a success at the moment that you do a successful act."
You can't be a success the next moment because you have already
moved on to do something else, even if it's accepting the award for
the succcessful moment that just passed. That is why I've always
told my players the glorification comes from the journey, not the
outcome.

I don't blame the Lakers for putting my contract talks on hold,
given the uncertain status of Kobe and the other free agents. If we
don't win the championship, or even if we do, the organization is
likely to make numerous changes. If that signifies a rebuilding
phase, a different, less costly, coach might be a better fit. What if
Shaq is traded? What if Karl and Gary leave? There are too many
variables to contemplate. Besides, I'm ambivalent about whether I
want to coach again after this season. I'll be fifty-nine in September, and it may finally be time to explore other options. Do I really
need to spend another year of my life thinking about screen rolls?
Another year in more planes, more hotel rooms, more arenas? For
Jeanie the uncertainty has been very frustrating. "You're not ready
to make a commitment to me as a person, or to the Lakers as a
coach," she said the other day. "You want to play on the edge and
coach them from a distance."

FEBRUARY 18
Oakland

Tonight for the second game in a row, Kobe competed with great
energy and looked for his teammates, recording eight assists to go
along with thirty-five points on only sixteen field-goal attempts.
He also played outstanding defense. I wouldn't presume to take

credit for this resurgence—he's healthy for the first time this season—though I believe our talk a few days ago has made a difference. The therapist told me I was smart not to ask Kobe if he watched the Houston tape. By trusting him to respond as a professional, I was affording him proper respect. Yet even with Kobe's exploits, we've struggled the last two nights, escaping with a three-point victory at home against Portland and prevailing by one here. We're still without Karl, who is about a month away from recovery, and without any consistent efficiency in the triangle, which I hope is less than a month away. Tonight we put ourselves in a position to ice the game, but kept missing free throws, allowing Golden State, down by only a point with 1.3 seconds left, one last possession to steal it. We anticipated that Cliff Robinson, their veteran forward, would take the final shot. Robinson was having an excellent night—eight for thirteen from the field—and scored twenty-four against us here in December, the first game after Karl's knee injury. Robinson took the shot, but Shaq blocked it, securing a hard-fought 100–99 triumph. I never hesitate to leave Shaquille in at the end of games, even when teams counter by going small. He becomes very attentive. I can't begin to recall how many key defensive plays he's made in the closing seconds, just when his detractors assume he won't cover screen rolls or rotate to contest the three-point shooter.

February 27
Washington, DC

Shaq approached me in the locker room after last Sunday's game in Phoenix, broadcast on national television. "Did you hear what

Dr. Buss said on TV?" Shaq asked. I had not. "He mentioned something about your contract." Preparing to board the bus for the airport, there was no time to investigate further, but when I reviewed the tape the following day, I couldn't believe what I heard. According to Dr. Buss, who granted an interview to Jim Gray, a formal contract offer had been on the table for six weeks before the Lakers withdrew it. This was news to me, as well as to Todd, whom I phoned immediately. What made the revelation more puzzling was the fact that Dr. Buss has always been extremely up front with me on any matter relating to the team or myself. On the other hand, he doesn't fully grasp the limitations imposed by the salary cap. "What are you going to do with Shaq's contract?" he was asked in an interview last year. Offer him the maximum for the duration of his career, Dr. Buss responded, failing to comprehend that such a substantial financial commitment to Shaquille would leave the Lakers unable to field a team unless every other player signed for the minimum.

With talks suspended I wonder how I will get to the bottom of this situation anytime in the near future. Shaquille, ever the loyal soldier, offered his services once again. "Should I go to bat for you?" he asked. Thanks, I told him, but no thanks. Given the uncertainty over his own contract extension talks—the two sides were about $10 million apart—Shaq feels he and I are bonded these days against management. If so, we cope with the uncertainty in different ways. This week Shaq openly criticized Mitch in the papers. "The general manager we have needs to take notes from me," he said. "Because if I was general manager, with a team like this, there'd be no problems." I discussed the matter with Shaq when the plane landed in DC. "I never volunteered that at all," he said. "That wasn't even part of the conversation. They asked me what I would do if I was the GM. This was not an issue I brought up on my own." I accepted his explanation, aware of how reporters try to lead the witness.

The real controversy this week revolves around Gary Payton, who sacrificed so much to become a Laker—too much, apparently. Payton's agent, Aaron Goodwin, has gone to the press with his client's complaints about the lack of playing time and the stifling nature of the triangle offense. I have no actual evidence but I would not be shocked if Goodwin had acted on his own. Agents have become extremely powerful. The ones who become too powerful believe that everybody—general managers, coaches, reporters, and others—can be easily manipulated. Jerry Krause used to refer to such agents as "the bad guys." I would have preferred that Gary, if he did indeed authorize Goodwin to speak, had approached me directly instead. But then again I was very familiar with Gary's history before he came aboard, his difficult time with anger management. To be fair, he's behaved extremely well this year. I've talked to people who knew him in Seattle who said there were usually two or three eruptions a *month*!

I sensed Gary's frustration as early as November, when we were blown out in Memphis. I lingered near his locker after the game, making it clear I was available in case he wanted to talk, but he chose not to take me up on it. Weeks later, in one rant that received plenty of coverage in Los Angeles, he barked: "I didn't sign up for this." I've tried to accommodate him, within reason. My plan from the start, as I explained to Gary, who is thirty-five, was to save him as much as possible for the playoffs. Unlike Tex, who suggested we might want to scrap the triangle, I haven't lost faith in Gary. I'm hopeful that as the season wears on, he will grasp the system's intricacies. "He's a square block, but I'm going to squeeze him into that round hole," I told Tex. Lately I've taken note of his mounting discontent. In the Denver game two days ago, he was so surprised when Kobe threw him the ball on the last possession that it almost struck him in the face. Last night, against the Kings at Staples, Gary, unable to contain Mike Bibby, wasn't in the flow, physically or mentally.

In the Denver game, trailing by eleven points heading into the fourth, I put in a lineup of Rick at the 3, Luke and Shaquille, and Kareem and Fish in the backcourt. Midway through the quarter, with more proficient ball movement, we stormed back. With less than 30 seconds to go, Denver called its final timeout, clinging to a two-point advantage. We were playing solid team ball, a rarity this season, although, as usual, Kobe seemed intent on taking over. "Get me the fucking ball," he said on his way to the bench, a demand Kobe had never verbalized. I smiled, didn't say a word, and went to chart a play on the clipboard. I sometimes think Kobe is so addicted to being in control that he would rather shoot the ball when guarded, or even double-teamed, than dish it to an open teammate. He is saying to himself: how can I trust anybody else? Well, he should learn to trust Kareem, who nailed the game winner, a three-pointer. Yet while grateful to escape with the victory, I wasn't about to let the guys escape with the feeling that they deserved it. They didn't. Winning covers up a multitude of sins, the saying goes, while losing makes mountains out of molehills. I believe a team should be rewarded for hard work, a strict adherence to fundamentals. We came up short in both areas.

I hung out earlier in the day with several high school cronies, exchanging stories about our former coach, Bob Peterson, none more memorable than the incident involving Dennis Ditzworth, a.k.a. Ditz. It took place during Ditz's senior year in a huge game against Minot High, the defending North Dakota state champions. Minot jumped out to a 15–2 lead. Coach called for Ditz, but still offended that he didn't start the game, Ditz gave him a nasty stare when he approached the scorers' table. Wrong move. Coach ordered him back to the bench. Ditz promptly took off his jersey, threw it to the floor, and walked across the court. He never played for Williston High again, while his father, a member of the board of education, tried unsucessfully for two years to fire Coach. Finally, only a few months ago, Ditz summoned the courage after forty-one years to apologize. He wasted his time. Coach said he had no recollection of the incident.

Coach Peterson was not only a coach. He was a proud, principled educator who strongly believed in nurturing his players. On one road trip, I was in the backseat of the car when he snatched the book I was reading, a pornographic novel. When we arrived at our destination, he took me aside. "I'm not really disappointed," he said, "but I am, kind of. You're a really good person who doesn't need to read this kind of stuff. This is just going to trash your mind." I didn't realize it at the time, but the way he dealt with me was probably the first lesson I learned in how to treat men. He was simultaneously stern and sensitive, showing that he cared for me, and not only as a basketball player. I hope I've relayed the same message to my players over the years. Strangely enough, even though I enjoy the nurturing aspect of my profession, I've never felt an overwhelming desire to coach at the college level. In the early 1980s, before taking a job in the CBA, I pursued several opportunities—Yale, Fairleigh Dickinson, the University of Colorado—but have no regrets that nothing materialized. I was probably too preoccupied with my own needs. Besides, I have five kids, which is enough parenting for one lifetime.

From Denver we flew home to face the Kings, our fiercest rivals. The last time we met, in January, we played without Kobe, Karl, Shaquille, Rick, and Horace, and lost by twenty points. This time, with only Karl on the injured list, we were primed to show the Kings, who are leading the division, that we shouldn't be counted out quite yet. For the second night in a row, the game went down to the final possession. Trailing by two, I signaled to Shaq "fist chest," which means screen roll. But while looking at Shaquille, I didn't catch a confused Kobe glancing over at me. If I had seen his expression, I would have called an immediate timeout. Instead, Kobe went for the win, hitting the rim on a three-pointer. I couldn't blame him. He was in the zone, having just canned a three-pointer in our prior possession. Plus, with Shaq struggling from the line—he had missed his last three— Kobe was clearly our most attractive option. Afterward, we were skewered for not going inside to Shaq in the closing seconds. I don't pay too much attention to the second-guessing, but I was upset about the dance Mike Bibby did after his three-pointer gave the Kings a five-point advantage. Dear Mike: The NBA championship wasn't won with that shot. A *regular season game in March* wasn't won with that shot. No matter. We put the game behind us as quickly as possible, focusing on the next two weeks, which will go a long way toward determining our playoff seeding. Eight of the following ten will be on the road, where we haven't enjoyed much success this season. Somewhere along the way, I'm expecting Karl to come back, and with him, I hope, a sense of urgency.

MARCH 2
Atlanta

There was no sense of urgency tonight, and as I search for a scapegoat for this latest, most embarrassing debacle, losing to the woeful Hawks, I might as well start with the person in the mirror. I pride myself on making sure my team is fully prepared before every game, no matter the quality of the opposition. On this occasion, I didn't do my job. At today's shootaround, I noticed that the team was going through the motions. Whenever I witness such lethargy, I address the problem immediately. In no way does that guarantee a win. I saw the same lackluster attitude during a shootaround a few months ago in Detroit, mentioned it to the guys, and we still lost by double digits. This time, for some reason, I let it go.

That wasn't the only warning sign that I let go. Yesterday at practice I learned that Shaq, as part of a contractual commitment he'd made, was planning to make an appearance at a local nightclub. I try not to control how players spend their free time on the road, but here was one case in which I should have made an exception. This game would be our third road game in four nights, and we would be playing without Kobe, who was attending a court hearing in Colorado. I should have appealed to Shaq: "Do you really think this is a good night to do this? Can you forget about this party? We really need you at one hundred percent." Whether my suggestion would have done any good is impossible to tell, and in fact I never found out for certain if Shaq did indeed make the appearance. I only heard a rumor he showed up. What was not a rumor was that Shaq scored only one basket in the fourth quarter. Overall he posted decent numbers—twenty-three points and fourteen boards—but against an overmatched opponent like Joel Przybilla, this should have been a forty-point, twenty-rebound, night for Shaquille, which we needed without Kobe and Karl on the floor. We fell one point short, coming up empty on a couple of makeable opportunities in the game's final moments.

But it was the prior possession that most disturbed me. With about thirty seconds remaining, Devean posted up his man, a move he never attempts. Not surprisingly, his shot was blocked by Wesley Person. This was unacceptable. A player's responsibility is to execute the type of game he is best designed for, or as I call it, "licensed to play." We tell the players constantly, "don't get out of character." I can understand a player's desire to expand his role. But too often they see themselves only through their own narrow lens, imagining greatness that simply does not exist. Joe "Jellybean" Bryant, Kobe's father, once said that his game was as good as Magic Johnson's, but "they won't let me play that kind of game." Jellybean was a good player, but he was no Magic. B. J. Armstrong, who played for me in Chicago, tried to emulate Isiah Thomas, one of his favorite players. The problem was that B.J. didn't have the quickness and athleticism that Thomas possessed. He was better suited to the supporting role he played on the Bulls. B.J. eventually earned the opportunity to expand his repertoire when he was selected by the Raptors in the expansion draft, though to this day I tend to believe that his most rewarding years were in Chicago.

I would never want to be perceived as a coach who restricts a player's individual growth. Yet at the same time, my job forces me to do whatever I believe is necessary to enhance *the team's* growth, even at the expense of the individual. The pie simply isn't large enough for everyone. Some players will never truly find out how good they might have become. On any team, there are usually one or two stars. Within the pecking order, players three, four, and five must select more restricted roles—playmaking, rebounding, setting picks, etc. Players six, seven, and eight need to be even more selective, while nine, ten, eleven, and twelve become the wild cards; they receive permission to freelance.

I consider myself a good judge of talent but like any coach, I've made mistakes. In the early 1990s a guard named Bobby Phills tried out for the Bulls one summer, but we didn't believe he possessed the skills to help us. He went to Cleveland and then Charlotte, and had compiled a decent career when he died in a car accident at the age of thirty. There are players who, inch by inch, year by year, will grow beyond expectations, discovering what works and what doesn't work. My favorite example was Mike Riordan, my former teammate on the Knicks. In the 1968–69 season, Mike, a rookie, was sent by Red Holzman into the game solely to commit fouls. In the final game of the playoffs, because of injuries, he scored twenty points against the Celtics. Four years later, as a member of the Baltimore Bullets, he ranked third in the league in minutes.

In Devean's case, here was a player the coaching staff had nurtured for five years. He is not a rookie. He knew that posting up was not a move with which he was likely to succeed. I didn't want to be too hard on him, yet I felt that he needed a message. Nothing hurts a player more than sitting down. The following night at Houston, I kept him on the bench until the final nine seconds of the game. "I hope you understand what I was doing with you tonight," I told him. "You lost my faith and trust."

MARCH 8
Salt Lake City

Entering tonight's matchup with the Jazz, there were plenty of reasons to be optimistic. Rebounding from the Atlanta humiliation, we posted solid victories against Houston, Seattle, and New Jersey to go 10–2 since the All-Star break. Despite our difficulties, many self-induced, we are in position to make a run at home-court advantage, with thirteen of our last sixteen games at Staples. Karl, who has missed more than thirty games, will be back any day, and so will Kobe, sidelined since injuring his right shoulder again a few days ago in the Sonics game when he tried to fight through a screen set by Reggie Evans. We were initially told he would miss about four weeks. But moments after we received the doctor's prognosis, Kobe provided his own. "Hey, I think this one isn't as bad as the first one," he said during practice, confidently shooting a twenty-footer. "See? I couldn't do that for five days after the first injury."

Meanwhile the conflict with Gary over playing time and his role in the offense has been resolved for the time being. "The sharks are out for blood," I warned him in the locker room after I met with the press in New Jersey. "Do me a favor, don't talk about it." Gary followed my advice. In Atlanta on our day off, we sat down to chat. I explained that I needed to give Fish his minutes to stay in rhythm, and to give Kareem, our most dangerous three-point shooter, enough experience to play a vital role come May. At the same time, I told Gary I would try to give him a blow earlier in the third quarter, affording him an opportunity to better influence the outcome in the fourth. "We need your defense and I want you to return to the game competitive," I said. He has been criticized in Los Angeles for breaking his promise to sacrifice individual glory in pursuit of a ring, but that perception is too harsh. Nonetheless, I told him he needs to work harder to find creative ways to be more involved in the triangle. The system offers an opportunity for everyone.

Tonight, the Utah Jazz did not present our only challenge. The other was presented by referee Bob Delaney, who has always been very rough on Shaquille. Two years ago he tossed him out of a contest in Seattle. A year before that, he threw me out of a playoff game in San Antonio after I complained about a ridiculous technical he called on Shaq. Tonight with only five minutes to go, he called a technical on Shaq when he hit Andrei Kirilenko in the neck as he was fouled near the basket. Bob whistled him for a second technical when Shaq, coming down from a dunk, accidentally hit Kirilenko again, this time with an elbow to the head. Leading by four when Shaq was ejected, we faltered, eventually losing by five. In the locker room Shaq was livid, and I couldn't blame him. Yet he wasn't entirely innocent, either. "I went out of my way before halftime to talk to you about the fact you have to stay on the floor," I told him, "and then you do your crunch move on the guy when you know Delaney is going to give you a tough call. It didn't make sense. He thinks you're challenging him. That's what's going through his mind."

Meanwhile, going through my mind was the fact that Shaq was

about to go ballistic. He believes he's being unfairly legislated against, railroaded, to the point that he is almost impossible to approach. His perception is perfectly legitimate. With the pounding, the flagrant fouls he's subjected to night after night, year after year, the bulk of which go unpenalized, it's astounding, actually, that he doesn't go ballistic more often. Nonetheless, acting quickly to avoid any inflammatory comments that might cost him a suspension, I told Shaq: "Let me do the talking now. Let me take the heat for this. Don't say anything to the press about this." He agreed. I took the heat, all right, charging Delaney with being "prejudiced" against Shaq. I was pretty certain I would hear it from the league, but the risk was worth it. I've kept Shaq from getting in trouble, possibly missing a game or two, and I've proven that I will go to bat for him. Recently he listed one by one the coaches he's played for over the years who never hestitated to draw technicals defending him. "Fine," I said, "but just remember they didn't love you any more than I love you."

Officiating Shaquille, I admit, is a most challenging assignment. The game has simply never seen anyone with his combination of size and agility. He slides, floats, shedding bodies as he powers his way through the lane. The rule is that a defensive player is not allowed to impede an offensive player's progress, but Shaq can't run where he wants to run or cut where he wants to cut because there's always a body pressed against him, impeding his movement. The powers in New York put forth the myth that this is a big man's league, but once Shaq became dominant, a movement was launched to enforce new ways to defend him. Teams were suddenly given the license to double-team him off the ball without being cited for illegal defense. No wonder he feels slighted, feels that the ground he patrols isn't the same ground that Wilt and Kareem patrolled.

MARCH 11
Minneapolis

This morning, fresh from a victory in Boston, we prepared to go through our standard routine—bags at nine A.M., bus at ten, plane at eleven. According to our rules, a player is allowed a five-minute grace period before he is considered late. At that point the bus or plane will leave without him, and he must find and pay for his own transportation to the next destination, which can be quite costly. This morning Kobe, who returned to action in last night's game, was late for the bus. His security guy insisted he was in the elevator, but I wasn't about to wait. My watch indicated 10:05. I told the bus driver to take us to the airport. Before we disembarked I saw Kobe emerge from a taxi. "I wasn't late," he insisted. "You should get with the rest of the world and set your watch right." When we arrived in Minneapolis, I asked one of my trainers for the exact time. As it turned out, my watch was indeed three minutes fast. Kobe would've made it to the bus with two minutes to spare. At the hotel, I admitted the error, though I reminded him he had no right to talk to me such disrespect. "I wasn't late," he repeated. When the elevator door opened on his floor, Vanessa and their daughter, Natalia, were standing there. The incident illustrated to me how conditioned I am to find fault with this kid, after everything I've gone through with him. I suppose the anger is deeper than I imagined.

MARCH 12
Minneapolis

I found out today that I owe the league another fifty big ones, and so, unfortunately, do the Lakers. After fining me $50,000 last month, I'm sure the league figured that anything less would not teach me the appropriate lesson. Well, if that was their brilliant reasoning, I'm certainly not going to give them the satisfaction of making a scene. I'll write a check and move on. There's no question that I'm a target because I have the audacity to challenge authority. In the league's opinion, the officials are the sacred cows. In my opinion, the league has a growing problem, which endangers the game's credibility. I don't see the shame in them admitting that officiating is the most difficult part of the game, and that everyone together should strive to make it as efficient and responsible as possible.

For the first time since December 21, a span of thirty-nine games in which our record was a mediocre 22–17, Karl Malone returned to the lineup. I held him back for several games, including the Utah contest, in which he desperately wanted to play, concerned he wasn't quite ready to put his body through the pounding. But I couldn't hold him back forever. The Timberwolves would be the perfect test for him, and for us: a rapidly improving team that we will likely meet in the playoffs. Karl would be matched up against Kevin Garnett, the leading candidate for MVP honors. Karl, despite the effort he puts into his workouts and practices, needs to become more familiar with our system, and there isn't much time. No doubt he looked rusty tonight, but he was active, with thirteen points, two rebounds and two assists. He provides this often passive unit with a certain bravado, which not even Shaq and Kobe can provide. We become suddenly full of life, feeding off his energy at both ends. Karl dives to the floor for loose balls, treating every possession as if it were the last. I was under strict instructions to play him about twenty minutes, in two separate spurts. Ultimately, he played twenty-one, and was ready for more, but this was not the time to take a risk. We hung in there most of the night, down only five entering the fourth, but Troy Hudson, their backup point guard, killed us, just as he did in last year's playoffs.

With our full roster finally in place, we can now gear up for the final month of the season. If this is, indeed, the sequel to "The Last Dance," I only hope it will be as successful as the original.

SEVEN

DOWN THE STRETCH

MARCH 13
Chicago

Has it really been six years since my last season with the Bulls? Since Michael's jumper over Bryon Russell, since everyone parted ways, Michael to retirement (the second one), Scottie to Houston, me to Montana? Whatever I accomplish this season, or in seasons beyond, if my coaching career continues, the players here, in Chicago, who put everything on the line for me, for their team-mates, will always occupy a special spot in my consciousness. I keep in touch with Luc Longley, Ron Harper, and Jud Buechler, and re-ceive regular e-mails from Steve Kerr, who has lunched with me twice this season when doing our games for TNT. Michael and I talk every few months. I can safely say that in my thirty-five years in the league, there has been no single group more dedicated to winning.

Today, after the Lakers slogged their way past the current Bulls contingent, I hung out in the hallway with Michael, Scottie, and John Paxson, along with Horace and Chip Schaefer, who were part of our success here before joining me in Los Angeles. We shared some laughs, about Michael and his motorcycle racing, Horace and the money he was stealing by being on the injured list. Never ones to keep their opinions to themselves, they speculated about my coaching future. "PJ, you've got to come back," one said. "He doesn't want to do that," another responded. "Look at the guys he's got to deal with." I wisely stayed mum on the subject.

Before we broke up, I approached Michael. "Have you had a chance to connect with Kobe?" I asked. "I offered my support," he said. "I let him know that I was available if he needed any advice." A few minutes later, Michael went to see Kobe in the locker room. Kobe, fitted by Vitti with a special shirt and shoulder pad, had been spectacular, scoring twelve points in a row to propel us from a precarious 74–72 advantage to a seven-point victory. "Hey, I saw the fourth quarter you had," Michael said. "That's the way to control the game." I'm sure the ever-sensitive Kobe will savor the compliment. Equally important was the contribution from Karl, playing in the second of back-to-back games. With no limitations this time, he was on the floor for thirty-eight minutes, recording ten points, thirteen boards, and seven assists. Sidelined for almost three months, he appears determined to make up for lost time. I was also pleased to see Devean playing under control again. I put him in for the entire fourth quarter to see if he learned his lesson from his irresponsible play two weeks ago in Atlanta. I will need to restore his confidence before the playoffs.

MARCH 20
Los Angeles

ESPN reported yesterday that as recently as a month ago, the Lakers discussed the idea of offering Kobe Bryant a formal leave of absence. Am I surprised someone leaked the story? No. I'm surprised it took so long. Leaks have long been an epidemic in this business, and tracking down the guilty party is almost impossible. I'm sure I will never find out which "source on the ballclub" released the figures for my contract extension to the *Times*'s Tim Brown back in August, in the article that infuriated Dr. Buss. In Chicago, whenever there was a leak, Jerry Krause went nuts, his natural paranoia rising to record levels. "If I find out who let that story out, I'm going to have their neck," he'd say. "Mr. Reinsdorf is really unhappy about that." The owner of the Bulls, many of us knew, was not the least bit "unhappy." Krause imagined he was in the CIA. In 1992 he sent covert operatives to sneak Toni Kukoc into the Mayo Clinic for a physical. On another occasion, to obtain exclusive information on George Muresan, the seven-foot-seven giant from Romania, he dispatched a scout to ride on the Romanian team bus. In 1993, when the Bulls missed out on the chance to draft Muresan, who was plucked early in the second round by the Washington Bullets, Jerry accused assistant coach Johnny Bach of giving away the company secret even though Washington's personnel director stated that at a European Cup game he saw Krause in the stands in his Inspector Clouseau hat and raincoat.

Today the *Times* ran a follow-up column, lending more credence to the ESPN story, reported by David Aldridge, their NBA guy. During practice I asked the *Times* columnist J. A. Adande why he backed up Aldridge's account. "I thought the story didn't have legs," I told him. At first, Adande, who writes frequently about the Lakers, said his prime motive was to support Aldridge, a friend, whom he considers a very responsible reporter. He then admitted another reason. "I really didn't have anything else to write," he said. I understood. The extent of coverage the Lakers receive in this town is unprecedented, more extensive, amazingly enough, than what the Bulls, featuring the most popular athlete in the world, were able to generate. This year, with the two new future Hall of Famers, the spotlight is more intense than ever. In any case the leave of absence report put me in a tough spot. I prefer to be as candid as possible with the writers, whom I generally like and respect. But if I were to admit that the Lakers considered offering a leave of absence in February, it would be devastating to my relationship with Kobe. He and I have come too far since our post-All-Star-game conversation, and have too much yet to accomplish, in probably our last few months together, for me to jeopardize everything with one ill-advised comment. I told the press that, yes, indeed, the Lakers discussed the possibility during the summer, but it was only one of numerous possibilities, dismissed for good when Kobe notified us he would treat this season as if it were any other. Did I lie? Some might say so. I prefer to say I equivocated. When asked for his view of the matter, Mitch, according to the *Times,* called the story "ridiculous." Mitch, like any general manager, must on occasion overstate or understate news reports that are often pretty close to being right on target. The organization comes first. Who leaked the story to Aldridge? If it wasn't me and it wasn't Mitch, that left only Shaquille and Rick. Nobody else knew. I'm not upset. If I assumed the risk of disclosing, I must bear the consequences.

MARCH 21
Los Angeles

We won our fifth in a row tonight against the Bucks, but this game, like the four preceding it, was another struggle most of the way, and this is not the time of year when we can afford to be struggling on a nightly basis. We prevailed by one in OT, and were very fortunate that the refs didn't put Keith Van Horn on the line with a chance to probably win it. From my vantage point at the far end of the court, it appeared he was hacked when he misfired on a runner, though the officials have always been reluctant to blow the whistle at the end of a game. I was encouraged by the play of Shaquille, a flashback to 2000: he finished with thirty-one points, twenty-six rebounds, and seven blocked shots. Even so, we still were unable to put away a team that had slipped to .500, losing seven of their last eight. Kobe was out of sync, going seven for seventeen with five turnovers, which I think might have been caused by Shaq's dominance. At times, it seems, when one superstar elevates his game, the other loses focus. Under our system, on nights when Shaq becomes unstoppable, it makes little sense for us to feed the ball into anywhere else. Consequently, the other players will tend to let down, and that includes Kobe.

The prior three victories at Staples were equally unimpressive.

First, on Monday against the Orlando Magic, perhaps the worst team in the league, we trailed by eleven points at the half, Tracy McGrady going off for twenty-one. "Let me take McGrady," Kobe said in the locker room. I was tempted. Nobody on our team, when inspired, can lock down an opponent as efficiently as Kobe, and there was no doubt McGrady needed to be locked down. I often assign Kobe, in limited stretches of eight, maybe ten, minutes to cover the other team's most dangerous scorer. But at first I vetoed the idea. "We need your scoring," I told him. "I don't need you to go out and get yourself worn out." In the third quarter, with McGrady scoring another eleven, the Magic extended their advantage to fifteen. I could no longer object. Kobe did a marvelous job, stopping McGrady, and, incredibly, using the challenge to get into his offense, scoring twenty-four of our twenty-nine points in the fourth to force overtime.

I can, to some extent, justify the poor effort against Orlando. The first game home after a road trip is always an adjustment, with players torn between their personal and professional responsibilities. They must meet the needs of a wife or a child, who have been waiting anxiously for their return. On the road teammates are always a few doors away, the bond between them continuing to grow, but at home, after practice, they usually go their separate ways.

I offer no justification, however, for two other lackluster efforts, both against the Clippers. In the first, we nearly squandered a fifteen-point halftime lead. As punishment, I made the players watch video the next day instead of having a regular practice, which, for them, is complete drudgery. Even so, the following night, they were inconsistent again, beating the Clips by six.

So what is our problem? Some experts, including a few of the players, have blamed me, which is nothing new, suggesting that as the playoffs approach the time has come to develop tighter rotations. Even the fans have joined in, making criticial comments when I leave the court. I ignore the second-guessers, strongly believing in bolstering our bench—Fish, Kareem, Luke, Brian, Slava—for the contributions we will most assuredly need at some point in May and, I hope, June. This group, highly receptive to coaching, grew very comfortable on the court when Karl and Kobe were sidelined with injuries, advancing much more rapidly than I originally intended. I began to see how we might actually benefit from our misfortune. Now, with the postseason on the horizon, I want the kids to maintain the same confidence and rhythm, to be in what I like to call "ready-to-play." That is no guarantee that I'll use them, but if I do, I need to trust they'll do the job. Too often, if a player believes he has little chance of receiving any minutes, his concentration will lapse, and he will not be ready if an emergency—injuries, fouls, whatever—forces me to call his number. On this team, finding enough time for four guards is extremely challenging, eased slightly by moving Kobe to small forward for eight or ten minutes a game.

March 29
Los Angeles

We took a step forward in recent days, recording double-digit victories at home over Sacramento and Minnesota, two of the teams we're chasing to secure the best overall record in the Western Conference. The guys moved the ball well and displayed the type of aggressive defense that wins championships. Credit should also go to Shaquille, who has suddenly become a force again on the boards, pulling down thirty-four in the two games. For the longest time, the staff stressed how vital it was for him to rebound. Only recently, after someone on our team pointed out his recent inconsistency—in February, against the Wizards, he finished with only two rebounds in thirty-four minutes!—has Shaq shown a renewed commitment. Rebounding, much like defense, requires tremendous will, especially on the offensive end, when players must bang through a wall of bodies. I've been around some great rebounders over the years, such as Jerry Lucas, but none were greater than Dennis Rodman. The Bulls would never have won their last three rings without Dennis. With his leaping ability and uncanny sense of knowing where the ball would bounce off the rim, he snatched rebounds from taller, bulkier opponents. Rebounding is the most overlooked aspect of the game. To his credit, Jerry Krause always understood its value, searching, year after year, for the best rebounders coming out of college. He drafted Horace Grant and Charles Oakley.

Against Sacramento, Kobe was brilliant, scoring thirty-six points only hours after returning from another pretrial hearing in Colorado. People wonder how he is able to focus on basketball after such an emotional and physically draining experience. I don't wonder. Kobe views these games in particular as opportunities to vindicate himself, to say, in effect, "You've seen my face in the courtroom. Now I'm going to show you the court where I dominate." He has been dominant since the All-Star game, limited only by the shoulder injury he suffered against Seattle. During our streak, he has averaged more than thirty points, and has recorded at least six assists in eleven of the last twenty games. His performance reminds me of the run he went on in February 2003, when he scored more than forty points in each of nine straight games.

"Kobe, Shaq isn't running the floor well," I told him then. "We need to get more scoring. We're too methodical, too predictable. I want you to be the push man and explore the offense, and if we don't have anything, get us into it." In a game against Washington in late March, he attempted 13 three-pointers, making nine of them. He was, I felt, sending me a message, "I'm going to take full advantage of the license you gave me, and stick it right to your best guy's face," referring to MJ. I wasn't offended. If this was the mindset Kobe needed to perform at his rarefied level, so be it.

I told the press yesterday that Kobe has reclaimed his role as the "top player in the game." He is not the only one who sends messages. My message was twofold, to reward Kobe for his play, and to balance the ledger for the comments I made in the *Daily News* piece, in which I called Shaquille "the focal point." Looking back, I don't regret for a moment my comments about Shaq. I have always considered it very important to let him know that he's our primary threat on offense. I'm convinced it motivates him to compete with a sense of invincibility, to be, as he likes to call himself, the MDE (Most Dominant Ever).

I was feeling good about Shaq, Kobe, the team . . . until last night. Suddenly, I saw signs again of the disharmony that forever threatens to define this season. I shouldn't be too surprised. The signs have been there all along, even during our recent success. Two weeks ago, we had trouble taking our group picture—*our group picture!* The guys couldn't stay in the right chairs or put their hands in the right place or wear the right uniforms. In the film session afterward, I couldn't resist. "It's the male ego that doesn't want to be told what to do that you guys are fighting against all the time," I said. "You couldn't even conform to a team picture." The inability to conform, I explained, was also reflected in poor ball movement. "Five guys have to go through a concentrated effort of organizing themselves on the floor," I said. "It only takes a small amount of effort to get it done in a correct way, but if you don't want to do it, if you resist, it won't work." Kobe was back to his selfish ways, in another battle for his manhood, this one against Utah's Raja Bell. Kobe scored thirty-four points, but he needed twenty-three field-goal attempts and twenty-one free throws. In the second half, he took fifteen shots, nobody else taking more than five.

"They're making you get in your attack mode," I told him when he came off the floor during a timeout late in the game. "You're going to have to pass the ball. They're not calling the fouls for you."

He was in no mood to back down. "I'm going to fucking crush them," he said. "I just haven't found my shooting yet."

Today at practice, we spent the entire session reviewing our mistakes. There were probably twenty offensive possessions in which players drove through pressure, threw poor passes, lined up on the wrong spots on the floor, or ran improper routes. In last night's game, we finished with a season-low twelve assists, on twenty-seven field goals.

"If we played a game like that in the eighties," Kurt Rambis said, "Riley would have had us on the court in a knock-down, drag-out practice."

"I am not Riley," I reminded Kurt. "I don't believe in that," I said. "I know they were horrible out there, but I'm not going to break them down physically. These guys are too valuable to waste on the practice floor."

Besides, extra practice is not the answer. The answer is a different mind-set. Too frequently, our players defer to Kobe or Shaq, worried that "if I don't get the ball to Kobe, he's not going to pass

the ball to me and he's going to have the ball a lot more than I am."
I try to discourage this attitude, insisting that "you have to be able
to turn them down. If you go to them every time they ask for the
ball, you're going to screw up our offense. You have to show enough
personal strength and fortitude to be able to do that." Offensive execution isn't my only concern as the season heads toward its final
two weeks. The other is our longtime nemesis, the screen roll. We
did an excellent job of defending it in the Sacramento game, not allowing Bibby to get behind the screens, but we must become more
consistent. The Kings will find a way to adjust, and the Spurs,
whom we will probably meet in the playoffs, will run it with Parker
and Duncan on almost every possession. We couldn't stop them
last year, which is why we signed Gary. The staff is ready to pass
on suggestions but as usual, would prefer the guys to come up with
their own solutions. "You've been here for eight years and you still
haven't figured it out," I told Shaq and Fish today. "Are you capable of talking about it? That is your job."

On the subject of jobs, my future remains up in the air, which
is fine with me. Of course, I always keep in mind that whatever decision I make, or the Lakers make for me, will have a direct bearing on the future of my assistants and their families. "We're going
to have to look out for ourselves," Jim Cleamons's wife, Cheryl,
said to me recently. "We're in a vulnerable position. We want to stay
in Los Angeles." Jeanie and I find the subject almost impossible to
avoid. "What cues did I ever miss that your dad sent me?" I asked
her. "He said in Hawaii, 'I want to keep everything going the way
it's been going for the next couple of years.' That doesn't mean anything about salary, does it? All it means is that he wanted me to be
a part of the coaching staff for two more years." I have every right

to determine my exact worth. "Six million dollars five years ago," I said, "isn't six million dollars today." I could probably receive more money if I signed with another franchise, she said. "Are you telling me that you haven't increased the ticket prices?" I asked. "And if that's the case, why wouldn't the coach's salary be increased five years later?" To me, it's a matter of respect more than the money. Did I do the job or not? And if I did, don't I deserve a raise? The answers may come sooner than I think. Dr. Buss wants to meet.

APRIL 9
Los Angeles

Our meeting turned into dinner at his house, which I could tell right away was not going to produce any answers. There were other guests, including two teenage girls, his two teenage sons, and a few characters I did not recognize. Familiar with Jerry's lifestyle, this was not totally unexpected. I'm very comfortable around him, able to converse on a wide assortment of topics, such as travel and literature. He has been astute enough to maintain his distance from the locker room, the team's sanctuary, and has dealt in a professional manner with a potentially very awkward situation: his daughter dating his coach. I have never heard him utter a single remark that could be construed as demeaning or disrespectful toward me. He loves to tell the story about our first meeting in 1999. "All I want to do is win another championship," he told me. "I think we can get three or four championships out of this squad," I responded. Yet despite the success of our professional relationship, I have no real clue as to how Jerry ticks, especially his penchant for hanging out with young girls and dancing till three in the morning. I'm sure Jerry is just as puzzled in his attempts to understand me and my Zen Buddhist ways.

I'm puzzled about something else, my team. Tonight, for the third game in a row, we got into a deep hole, down by nineteen in the second quarter to the Grizzlies, who were playing without Pau Gasol, their leading scorer and rebounder, and Bonzi Wells, their third-leading scorer. We rallied in this game, but we hadn't been able to recover in the prior two, losing at home to San Antonio and Portland, our first back-to-back defeats at Staples in more than a year. The loss to the Spurs, which halted our eleven-game winning streak, was not a huge shock. For one thing, we were due, and for another, the game tipped off at twelve-thirty P.M. When I arrived in LA, I was told that Shaquille wasn't the same player in the afternoon. "Shaq, you've got to go to bed before two in the morning," I warned him. "If you're up till three or four, you'll be tired by the time the game starts." He grumbled a bit, but seemed to get my point. Against the Spurs, he finished with an ordinary seventeen points and nine rebounds. Regardless, I viewed it as a minor setback, a game that will be long forgotten in the weeks ahead. The Portland loss did upset me. They embarrassed us with a 25–2 run on our floor. Desperate as they may be—the Blazers are battling Utah and Denver for the final playoff spot—that should never happen.

So why the poor starts? Tex blames it on the wrong personnel. "You're not putting your best players on the floor to start the game," he tells me. He would prefer that I start Fish, who, he insists, is a much better fit for our equal-opportunity offense. "Sometimes," I counter, "you don't always put your best players on the floor." Fish, off the bench, provides a spark that energizes the entire team, which, I'm quite certain, Gary would not be able to bring. I wonder, too, if our players take seriously enough the idea of gaining home-court advantage. They tend to become cocky, assuming that once they turn up the intensity for the playoffs, it will not matter where we play. What they fail to grasp are the many unanticipated variables—fouls, injuries, quirky plays, etc.—that can unfold in any game at any moment.

APRIL 13
Los Angeles

With the playoffs less than a week away, we need to be coming together. Instead, we're coming apart. At the center of the latest turmoil is—who else?—Kobe. This time, in a strange twist, he's being crucified for taking too *few* shots: only one, unbelievably enough, in the first half of Sunday's game in Sacramento, which we lost by seventeen points, ruining, in all likelihood, any chance to win our division. He finished with eight points, his lowest total ever in a game in which he played at least forty minutes. The theory being tossed around is that Kobe, stung by criticism for his shot selection in recent games, decided to show the Lakers how stagnant the offense can become when he doesn't assert himself. "I don't know how we can forgive him," one anonymous teammate was quoted as saying in today's *Times*.

I don't buy into that theory. I watched the tape and witnessed nothing unusual that would make me suspicious of Kobe's intentions. Early in the game, he tried to be a playmaker, the role we want him to assume, and then in the second half he became more active, taking twelve shots. If he were less energized than usual, a more logical explanation was that he might have been distracted by his off-the-court situation. Because of how magnificently he's performed this year, people tend to forget that this is a man who may lose his career, his freedom. What goes on in his mind, from day to day, is impossible to imagine. John Black, one of Kobe's allies, told me a story that could mean everything, or nothing. When Kobe made a surprise appearance at a recent team function in Santa Monica, Black thanked him on behalf of the organization. "Don't have long to be in the gold armor," Kobe said.

Today at practice, Kobe went from player to player, shoving the article with the anonymous quote in their faces. I have rarely seen him that incensed. "Did you say this?" he demanded of each player. Later, during a team gathering, he pursued the interrogation. "Right here and right now," he said, raising his voice, "I want to know who said this shit."

Nobody said a word, until Karl finally broke the silence. "Obviously, Kobe, no one said it or no one wants to admit they said it," Karl said. "You've just got to let it go now." Karl and Kobe, who have become buddies, launched into a shouting match that I had to stop.

"We have to get over these types of things," I told the guys. "You can't be playing as a team if you're going to be harboring sentiments that aren't good toward each other." Desperate measures, I'm beginning to think, might be in order. Maybe we'll return to meditation, something, anything, to improve our karma.

"Are you feeling like you're going to come back next year?" Jeanie asked me.

"Well, not if Kobe Bryant is on this team next year," I told her. "He's too complex a person. I don't need this."

At least Shaquille and I seem to be rounding into playoff form.

"Are you just going to sit there or get in the fucking face of those officials?" he shouted after he was called for an offensive foul against Vlade.

"What for?" I fired back. "For what you just did? You screwed up. I didn't screw up. You screwed up. I'm supposed to bail you out after you did something like that? You've played here thirty times. You know you can't stick a shoulder into Vlade, because if he falls down, the crowd will yell, and the officials will be human, and they'll react to it. That's who they are."

APRIL 15
Open skies

The ball left Kobe's hands, headed for the basket, a game, a division on the line. When it dropped through the net from behind the arc, when he and his teammates celebrated a remarkable double-overtime victory at the Rose Garden in Portland a few hours ago, it made no sense, and then again, total sense. Despite everything— the feuds, the injuries, the hearings, the futures in limbo—we are the Pacific Division champions, the number-two seed in the playoffs, ready to chase our fourth title in five years. Two Kobe three-pointers, one to tie the game in regulation, the other to win it, capped a typically chaotic two days.

The night before, at home against Golden State, we fell behind again, by ten at the half. I remained confident. "Keep plugging away," I told the troops. "They've had a great half. This is a team that thrives on playing in front of their bench. But they have to come and play in front of our bench in the second half. All those shots that are going in are not going to happen for them in the sec-

ond half. You've just got to find a way to play through it." Sparked
by Kobe's forty-five points, a season high, we rallied for a five-point
triumph. "I hope you didn't tire them out too much," I said afterward. For us to win the division, we needed to beat Portland and
receive help from Golden State, who would be hosting the Kings.
Our trip to Portland did not start with a good omen. Shortly after
midnight, the landing gear on our charter was unable to retract,
forcing the pilot to fly back to Los Angeles. Once we realized we
might be stuck on the ground for some time, I sent the players
home, opting instead for a late-morning flight. Missing our usual
shootaround would be better than missing our usual sleep. Besides,
we could watch video on the plane, or at least that was the plan. The
videotape machine didn't work. What will happen next? Actually
I wasn't too concerned. Only one week since we last faced the Blazers, I was confident we knew what to expect.

Knowing it was one thing, solving it another. For a team eliminated from the playoffs for the first time in twenty-two years, Portland played as if their whole season were on the line, leading by
seven heading into the fourth. We were still trailing when word
came that Golden State had beaten the Kings, information I wrote
on the board during the next timeout to provide a little extra motivation. "You've got to push through this thing," I urged them.
They did, especially Kobe. I suppose I should marvel at the two
shots he made. I don't. I've seen too much, from him, from Michael.
I am gratified. As the number-two seed, if we advance past Houston, we'll almost certainly face the Spurs in the second round. Some
suggested that this wasn't the sequence I had in mind, that I would
rather have secured the number-four seed, setting up a potential
second-round matchup against Minnesota, an easier opponent, pre-
sumably, than San Antonio. Utter nonsense, I assured the team,

which brought up the same suspicions to me at practice a few days ago. I believe the goal is to win every game, developing momentum and confidence, and then see what scenarios play out.

We're headed toward Los Angeles. Toward what else in the days, perhaps weeks, ahead, I cannot begin to predict. Will this team unify, will it demonstrate the sacrifice, the selflessness, that all championship squads display? Will it fulfill the expectations that started in July? Or will it fall short, the fissures, never far below the surface, proving too deep to overcome? Will it go down as the grand experiment that failed, remembered more for its trials than triumphs? The plane is about to land, the next part of the journey about to begin.

EIGHT

ROUND ONE: HOUSTON

APRIL 16
Los Angeles

I asked the team to meditate with me this morning. The session did not last long—fifteen, maybe twenty, minutes, but it was long enough to remind the players that they must rely on each other more than ever in the coming weeks if they hope to complete their mission. A great game from Kobe or a great game from Shaq, or great games from both, will not be enough. We need to develop a oneness of thought and action, to find the space where together we can become more receptive to the spiritual growth that is required this time of year. The challenge will be extremely difficult. These men strive to be individuals, separate, unique, naturally opposed to joining forces. We held a few sessions earlier in the year, but I stopped because I felt the room was tainted by the acrimony that began to emerge last season. There were emotional statements made that I wouldn't want to repeat, the cruelty more malicious than I could imagine. I've decided it is time to try again, to ask for a deeper, more sustained, commitment. Meditation has worked in the past for this group, most notably on the morning of Game 7 of the 2002 Western Conference Finals in Sacramento. Normally, when we assemble for a session prior to our pregame buffet, the players arrive a few minutes late, but on that occasion, they were early, eager to attain total focus. At that moment, before we went over strategy, I knew they would be ready for the challenge. We knocked off the Kings in overtime in a very hostile environment, Arco Arena, headed toward our third straight title.

To eliminate the negative karma, I made changes in the meditation room, putting up photographs from our championship seasons to replace several Native American pictures. I wanted the players to feel more of their own presence. I also smudged the area with sage and sweetgrass, much like spreading incense, only a heavier smoke. At first, I asked everyone to breathe, to center themselves, to shut their minds down, and allow any external sounds—a door slamming, a voice in the hallway, a phone ringing—to pass without identifying them. The brain will demand attention, but, like throwing a pebble into the water, its waves will soon start to recede, followed by a period of wonderful tranquillity. For about ten minutes there was total silence. Did the players achieve peace, a oneness of thought? Were they able to let go, to open their consciousness to a new level of trust? Probably not.

In Chicago sometimes we meditated three times a week. There were eight or nine guys who benefited from the sessions. Here on this squad, Fox and Fish are the only two, I suspect, who will profit. The rest will walk out and never approach this space again. What I am trying to instill in them is simply too far removed from their more practical, more materialistic, commonsense world. They think we're wasting our time, at best tolerating the intrusion. If that's the case, why do I bother? Because, at least for this short period, we become part of what I call a conspiracy, literally "breathing together," learning how to be centered when everything around us moves too fast.

Also, I need to go into this space for myself as much as for anyone else, to put me in touch again with the spiritual aspect of the game, which, by its very nature, is impossible to define. It is not logical or illogical, emotional or nonemotional; it is, rather, the unseen, players tuning in to one another, becoming aware of each other's presence. I often felt this connection when I played for the Knicks in the late 1960s and early 1970s. I recall one game in which Tom McMillan, Bill Bradley, and myself did everything right—screen roll, drop pass, give and go, etc.—for five straight minutes. I never felt more engaged. Basketball, unlike football with its prescribed routes, is an improvisational game, similar to jazz. If someone drops a note, someone else must step into the vacuum and drive the beat that sustains the team. One slight drop-off, one guy in the wrong spot at the wrong time, and the whole unit will fail. The conventional approach is to run designated plays. But I choose, and this is the essence of the triangle, to play into an opponent's energy. If they apply pressure in one spot, step into the opening. Many players strive to embrace the energy for themselves, to be, as they say, *in the zone.* But that is not the kind of basketball I'm talking about. You can find that in the playground. I want to see a group of players in the zone.

I followed meditation with a lecture, and with everything at stake, this was no occasion to hold anything back. Needing to grind in the last few days against Golden State and Portland, we're drained, physically and mentally. On the other hand, the accomplishments of the past week have helped us believe in ourselves, which is absolutely essential. To succeed against the best teams in the league, we will need to improve with each quarter, each game, each series. "Since October in training camp," I told them, "we have lied to one other about how dedicated we were going to be toward this season." I didn't single out a specific player. Only by making the guys realize this was a matter of collective, not individual, guilt could they respond together, as a team. At the same time, adhering to the Positive Coaching Alliance principles once again, I searched for the right words to make them feel better. "We're so individually tied to our own needs and wants that we end up lying in our *good intentions*," I continued, "but that's really okay. We know that you had good intentions, and that's what we are looking for. We went through the thing a few days ago with Kobe, and now we have to think about being as tight as we can be, if we can have this dream happen, of winning a championship."

First things first. The Rockets will be no pushover. The teams split four games in the regular season, the Lakers losing by twelve on Christmas Day in Los Angeles, and again by double digits in Houston seven weeks later. We played without Karl both times, and in the second contest, a rusty Kobe was thoroughly outplayed by Cuttino Mobley. The guys, healthy at last, took the next two, rallying from fifteen back in Houston, and then, only two weeks ago, prevailing at Staples, 93–95. In the last game, I was most encouraged by how aggressive Shaq was in defending Yao Ming, which will be the key matchup of the series. He limited Yao's touches, which is the way to contain him. With most opponents, Shaq freelances in the paint, opting not to play defense on his own man until he catches the ball, making him a reactor instead of an actor. But against the seven-foot-five-inch Yao, who can hit the midrange jumper and runs the floor well, Shaq can't afford to be passive. The performance—Yao was only three of fifteen from the field—gave Shaquille the confidence that he can stop this guy. In their prior two duels, Yao outscored Shaq 62 to 52, leading many "experts" to conclude, prematurely, that the gap between the two big men has significantly narrowed. These were only two games, two *regular season* games.

Yao will be an important force in the league for years to come, but he will never be as good, as athletic, as dominating, as Shaquille O'Neal. Nobody will. The gap will widen in the playoffs when Shaq takes his game to the next level. During the regular season, Shaq is unable to watch video for more than five or six minutes at a stretch. But once he's matched up against the same opponent for two or three games, he develops a feel for his tendencies, exploiting his weaknesses. Dennis Rodman was the same way. He might watch video on his own while riding the bike, but in a group setting, he would sit with a towel over his face, in his own world. We will need Shaquille to rotate, preventing their smalls from open looks in screen rolls. Both Mobley and their other starting guard, Stevie Francis, can penetrate and score from long range. Yao will have a lot of opportunities with the ball, but Van Gundy doesn't fully trust him yet. He is going to try to beat us with his guards.

They will also look for production from starting forward Jim Jackson, who is their most dependable veteran, and backup Maurice Taylor. I don't anticipate the Rockets will try to break us down off the run. Van Gundy prefers to control the tempo, calling signals, looking for a final score in the eighties.

Van Gundy, I'm quite certain, will also try to manipulate the refs, through the press. As a Knicks assistant coach in the '90s, he learned from one of the game's provocateurs, Pat Riley. During the 1992 Chicago–New York series, Riley complained how the Knicks wouldn't stand a chance if the officials put Michael on the line every time he drove to the hoop, a transparent ploy to give his thugs, excuse me, defenders, the license to stop MJ. I wasn't about to let Riley have the stage to himself, pointing out that Patrick Ewing took steps every time he made his move in the lane. In one postgame press conference, I said it was clear the NBA and Madison Avenue must be rejoicing because the series had "seven-game officiating" attached to it. I was hammered by the league for that accusation with a fine and by the media with a *New York Post* cartoon showing a character looking like me under the word *whiner.* Van Gundy started this year's lobbying campaign weeks ago. In a magazine article, he criticized the refs for how they officiate Yao. With Van Gundy, there is also a personal element in the dynamic. He remains convinced that in 1999, during my one-year hiatus from the sport, I was plotting behind the scenes to steal his job, which was never the case. I met with his former boss, Dave Checketts, but only as a courtesy—Checketts was close to Red Holzman, who died in November 1998—and never inquired about the coaching position. I told Checketts it was very possible the Knicks could advance deep into the playoffs since they were built to beat the

"Touching all the lines"—October training camp,
University of Hawaii.

Kobe and his legal angels heading into the
courtroom in Eagle, Colorado.

Gary and Karl joining in the run for the ring.

The Lakers coaching staff (*left to right*): Kurt Rambis,
Jim Cleamons, me, Frank Hamblin, and Tex.

Mitch Kupchak being collared by Shaq
after celebrating Shaq's 20G points.

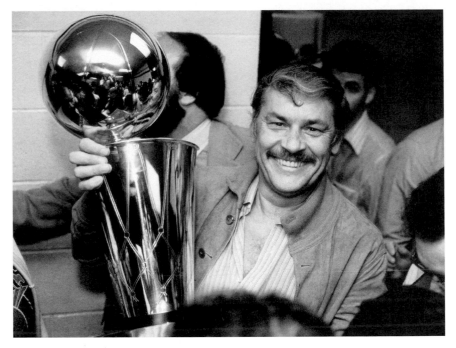

Dr. Buss and one of the trophies he proudly loves.

Jeanie and me making a public appearance—
one for the club.

A medley of role players (*clockwise from center bottom*): Rick Fox, Kareem Rush, Luke Walton, Bryon Russell, Devean George, Derek Fisher, Brian Cook, and Slava Medvedenko.

Los Angeles Times
SPORTS

'I definitely don't need advice on how to play my game. I know how to play my guard spot. He can worry about the low post. I'll worry about mine.'
Kobe Bryant

'As we start this new season, [stuff's] got to be done right. If you don't like it, then you can opt out next year. If it's going to be my team, I'll voice my opinion.'
Shaquille O'Neal

It's the Return of Star Wars

Two days before Lakers open season, Bryant and O'Neal are at odds again

By Tim Brown
Times Staff Writer

J.A. ADANDE

Kobe, Shaq Need to Put Team First

MARK HEISLER
ON THE NBA

There Might Not Be Any Turning Back

ON THE DEFENSIVE: *Smarting to retaliate, Kobe Bryant says he won't change his game.*

SENDING A MESSAGE: *Shaquille O'Neal made it clear that he is taking control of the Lakers.*

LA Times headline.

Fisher's glorious shot—the Lakers redeemed.

Shaq puttin' the clamps on young Yao.

Shaq at the line can make one squirm.

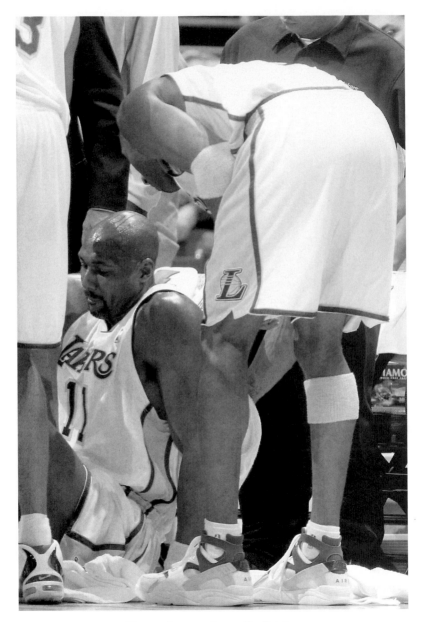

The way fortunes change. Karl's injury
against Phoenix, December 21, 2003.

Take these words...and go away...the press.

Making sure Tom sees the game the "right way."

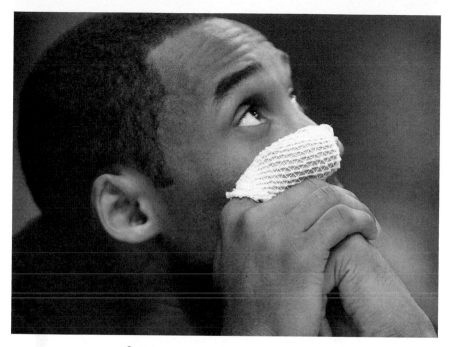

One more difficulty in a season of hardships.

Kobe's buzzer beater to win the Pacific Division.

The last postgame press conference. My greatest boosters (*left to right*): Charley, Ben, Brooke, and Chelsea with the visible stress of a playoff loss on their faces.

Miami Heat, which they did on a last-second Allan Houston shot that received the friendliest of bounces. The Knicks lost in five games to the Spurs in the NBA Finals.

How far we advance will depend, to a large extent, on one variable we can't control: injuries. After a regular season defined by their frequency—Karl's knee, Shaq's calf, Kobe's shoulder—we're banged up again. Kareem is nursing the ankle he hurt in February, while Horace, who tore cartilage in his right hip, will miss the entire playoffs. The loss is substantial. Horace, at age thirty-eight, did exactly what we wanted, backing up Karl and Shaq. If anything happens to either of them, the only bigs available will be Slava and Brian Cook, both inexperienced on this pressurized stage. I'm also not sure what we can expect from Fox, who dislocated his right thumb in the first quarter of the Memphis game in the last week of the season. Fox is a valuable player, someone who can hold our concepts on offense and make key stops on defense, so critical in the playoffs when every possession is magnified.

With the roster set, I've made an important decision. For the first time in my coaching career, I have assigned one player the responsibility for calling the signals on the floor. Normally, the triangle, by its very nature, does not require set plays, its actions determined by the movement of the defense. Too often, when offenses run plays A, B, or C, defenses catch up, implementing strategies specifically designed to stop plays A, B, or C. By the time the playoffs start, they know every set in the other team's playbook. What do you do then? This Lakers team, which has sputtered from day one in the triangle, needs to have plays called, at least five to ten a game. Trying to signal them from the bench would afford the Houston defense an extra opportunity to read them. Someone on the floor needs to take on this job. Ideally it would go to the point guard, in this case Payton, but I've had trouble getting Gary's attention on the court. He's always chatting with the refs or one of his teammates. I don't know how George Karl, his longtime coach in Seattle, put up with it. I've never seen any player so perpetually distracted. Instead I'm giving the opportunity to Kobe, who knows the offense as well as I do. Also, as always, I'm trying a little psychology. By trusting Kobe, I'm hoping he will show more maturity, more selflessness than ever.

My chief concern at this point is that the guys don't seem to be taking the other squad seriously enough. We've been trying to tell them they can't turn the ball over and must be attentive to Houston's three-point shooters. "You can't get sucked in," we explained. "You have to rebound better, offensively and defensively." But the message does not seem to be getting through. Our veterans assume that Francis will be out of control, that Mobley will be inconsistent, and that Yao will be worn down by Shaquille. They assume the Rockets, a young team that hasn't been in the playoffs, will fold under the pressure. They assume a lot.

APRIL 18
Los Angeles

Too much, it turned out. Last night, beginning our quest for a title, and a place in history—no team since the '60s has won four titles in five years—our execution was abysmal at both ends. Houston controlled the tempo throughout, a typically slow, methodical Van Gundy tempo. They walked the ball up, treating every possession like it was a football game, while we went through our offense without any real purpose. We did not know how we wanted to attack Houston, where the double-teams were coming from, or when they were coming. Throwing the ball into Shaq, and having him kick it out to the perimeter, was not the problem. The problem was operating anything efficiently out of the triangle, of finding a way to move their defense.

I was not consoled by the final result, a 72–71 victory, knowing this level of play will send us home early again. So much went wrong, starting when Kobe was assessed his second foul six minutes into the game, with us leading 10–6. "That gives Houston a chance to stay in this," one of my assistants said. They stayed in it, all right, going on a 10–4 run to end the quarter, and trailed by only six at the half, despite committing fifteen turnovers. Karl was missing jumpers, going one for nine, and Shaq was missing free throws—two for seven. "You don't have to shoot those shots," I told Karl during the break. "If you feel like your legs aren't up to it, move the ball out and get the rest of the team involved." I warned them about Houston's tendency to play well in the first few minutes of a quarter. "You can't let them get the lead," I said. Third quarters have been a problem for the Lakers since I took over here, mostly because Shaquille refuses to use the time allotted to warm up, preferring to save his energy for the game. Shaq scores 60 to 70 percent of his points in the first half. When I was with the Bulls, I can remember games in which Shaq would score twenty or thirty points in the first half, and less than ten in the second. "I know you don't like to warm up," I've told him a million times, "but it would really help us if you would." We don't expect him to work up a sweat, or even take any shots, just walk to the end of the court and loosen up long enough to get his heart rate going. "I can't play forty-two minutes if I do that," he insists. Sure enough, the Rockets won the quarter, 17–9, to go up by two. We were four of twenty-one from the field.

In the fourth, the bench came through, Kareem hitting two threes, Fish one. But after Karl missed another jumper with about a minute to go, Houston took possession leading 71–70. A basket here would put us in real jeopardy, but Taylor missed, and Karl snatched the rebound. Most coaches would call a timeout at this point. I let them play, figuring we would wind up with a better look if we didn't allow the Rockets an opportunity to set up their defense. At least that was the plan. As the ball moved from player to player, nobody was willing to take the big shot.

We needed a timeout to reorganize, but because our bench was at the opposite end of the court, it was up to the players to arrive at this conclusion. The position of the bench is an often overlooked factor in the game. Generally I prefer the team to play defense in front of our staff in the fourth quarter. We can relay which side the picks are coming from, and encourage them to be more aggressive. Besides, they need to know I completely trust them to execute properly on offense without my help. Only in this situation, the seconds ticking away, my help was essential. Finally, with the twenty-four-second clock winding down, Kobe forced a long jumper, a horrible shot in the game's most critical possession. The ball did not reach the rim but fortunately it did reach the hands of Shaquille, who bailed us out with a dunk, fouling out Yao in the process. Shaq missed the free throw, and our lead was only one with seventeen seconds to go. During the Houston timeout, I told them to be ready for Francis to penetrate, a strategy that worked extremely well for the Rockets throughout the second half. I considered putting Fox in, but he had been on the bench for a long time. Ultimately, Francis did just what we anticipated, driving by Fish, forcing Kobe to rotate over. When Francis reached the baseline, he kicked it out to Jackson in the corner, one of his favorite spots. His jumper to win the game hit the rim. We were very fortunate. Overall we shot 32.9 percent. If it weren't for Houston's twenty-two turnovers, the outcome would certainly have been different.

Also disconcerting was the overly physical nature of the proceedings, which in my postgame press conference I likened to mud wrestling. I was entirely confident we would prevail in that style of play. My objection stemmed more from the fact that I didn't believe it was aesthetically pleasing. The television ratings have declined in recent years, and games like the one last night are not likely to attract a new legion of fans. Part of the problem has been the absence of continuous play, of what is referred to as end to end action. When I coached in Puerto Rico, a very enjoyable experience, we often went a full twenty-minute half with maybe one stoppage. A dead ball went immediately from out of bounds into play. It was like soccer. Now, in a business dominated by the almighty dollar, by interrupting the game for commercials every three minutes, there is no continuity, no flow. The quality has definitely been affected. I worry that it may destroy the game. Everyone says we owe television for our great fortunes, but will the twelve-year-old at home be patient enough to sit through commercial after commercial?

Equally disturbing was the fact that only a few days ago, the league sent a tape to both teams, detailing the types of infractions—illegal screens, palming the ball, three seconds, etc.—the officials would not overlook in the playoffs. We showed the tapes to the players. So what happens in the first game? They overlook them, of course. Why bother sending a tape, which must have taken them a lot of time, if there's no follow-up from the refs? What the NBA doesn't understand, and this happens year after year, is that officials are determined to keep the star players in the contest. They haven't called illegal screens in three months! All I ask for is consistency. If players are allowed to get away with three steps, with moving picks, we need to know in order to manage the game accordingly.

APRIL 19
Los Angeles

I approached Kobe before Game 2 tonight, telling him his effort in the opener was probably his worst playoff performance in five years. He was four of nineteen, only one of eleven in the fourth quarter. "I hope you have something for them tonight," I said. "I hope you made an adjustment to where you're bringing the ball from because he (Mobley) was on top of you every time you turned." I wouldn't be so bold with every player, especially only hours before a playoff game, worried about damaging their confidence. With many I would give them an ego boost, searching for the words that would allow them to play at their potential.

But Kobe is one who definitely does not need an ego boost. "I got something for them," he promised.

"What are you going to do?" I asked.

"I'm going to post him up."

I asked if perhaps the assignment of calling signals might have been too much for him.

"No," he assured me. "My teammates just forgot about me out there," Kobe said. I urged him to stay involved, told him that even though he was calling plays for the others, he needed to assert himself. He certainly did, finding the seams in the double-team to score from inside and outside, finishing with a game-high thirty-six points. Kobe played with a lot of energy, and so did the rest of the guys. Karl, again left open by the Rockets, hit his shots this time, chipping in with seventeen points.

Even so, the score was 51–51 when, three minutes into the third quarter, Shaq was signaled for his fourth foul. The conventional move in this situation would have been to take him out, saving him for the fourth, especially when Shaq isn't very good at adapting his game to avoid more fouls. Duncan is a master at staying out of the fray, as was Willis Reed, my former teammate, and the Celtics' Dave Cowens. The Celtics used to leave Cowens in with four fouls in the *first half*. If anything, Shaq makes *more* mistakes when he lands in foul trouble, reaching in when drivers come down the lane. "You wouldn't commit a foul like this if you didn't have the fouls on you," I've told him. "So why would you do it now?" The key to playing well in foul trouble is to move your feet and keep your hands away from the offensive player. I took the gamble tonight because I could move Shaq over to cover Kelvin Cato, a limited offensive player, while Karl, at least for a short stretch, could take Yao. "If Cato drives at you," I told Shaq, "stay out of his way." I did not want the Rockets to gain the slightest momentum. The gamble paid off, Karl bodying up Yao, causing turnovers and missed shots. In the meantime Kobe found his rhythm, highlighted by an acrobatic layup with his back to the basket. Finally, four minutes later and leading by five, I took Shaq out, moved Karl to center and inserted Luke Walton as the power forward. I was very pleased with the adjustments we made defensively, getting on the top of screens. Despite Shaq's foul difficulties, Yao had only four rebounds. We prevailed 98–84.

APRIL 22
Los Angeles

We're leading 2–0, so why am I not feeling very comfortable? Two reasons, actually. One has to do with Gary Payton, frustrated yet again over his lack of playing time. I kept him out of the entire fourth quarter in Game 2 because we were up by double digits and Fish was playing with tremendous energy. Gary had left the floor in the second quarter with back spasms, though he went back into the game. In the fourth, there seemed to be no need to take any chances. Fish throws his body around in a unique, endearing way, taking charges, fighting through multiple screens, creating opportunities for us that ignite the crowd. Fish is also an excellent spot shooter. His numbers were way down this year, about 35 percent from the field, but that was mainly because surrounded by second-unit players unfamiliar with the triangle, he didn't receive the same open looks. Yet he handled his reduced role in a very professional manner, never griping, never going to the press. Now, with Kobe and Shaq demanding double-teams, Fish can find his spot and wait for the pass out of traffic. Benching Gary is no reflection of his abilities. In a need situation, where the game is very tight, he's the perfect player to put in to get some things accomplished defensively. But if the game has entered what I call a lull situation, and Game 2 was a prime example, I prefer a shooter who is staying warm.

Of course, my rationale will not do anything to appease Gary, a star in his former NBA life. Throughout the season, when this issue came up, I claimed I was saving him for the playoffs. Well, what was I saving him for *now*? On Monday night, during my postgame address in the locker room, I heard an angry voice in the background. When I finished I went to check out this voice. It turned out to be Gary. He was behind a closed door in Gary Vitti's office. "I tried to talk him down," Vitti explained, "but he's really emotional." He sure was. Gary was on the phone to his agent, shouting. "I'm fucking disrespected," he said.

I didn't get to Gary until practice a couple of days later because we gave the players a day off. "I know I yelled at you on the floor the other night and you were unhappy about it," I said, referring to an out-of-bounds play in which it seemed he failed to switch quickly enough, resulting in a dunk. When I reviewed the tape the next day, I realized he was not responsible for the breakdown. "I'm going to make a mistake once in a while as a coach," I told him. I've always believed a coach should be willing to admit fault. Players must feel they're being treated fairly. Once my admission settled in for a moment or two, I got after him a bit. I rarely come down hard on anyone, but this is the playoffs. They must be willing to take direction. Like they say in the military, in the time it takes to question an order, you might be dead. "You can't bring the mood of the team down simply for your own personal reasons," I told him. "You're not a coach and you don't think like a coach. I have to do what's best for the psychological nature of this team. So in that regard, you're going to have to do your best job to have an attitude that's correct about it."

"No problem," he said. "I'm done with my anger," he went on. "I'm sorry about what happened. I know there are some things about this situation that don't fit me, but I want to do my best. I will be competitive." I appreciated his response, but I know the matter is far from resolved.

My other concern revolves around a familiar problem, Shaquille and his errant free throws. In the first two games, he was only five of seventeen, including the miss following his dunk late in Game 1, which could have cost us the victory. He knows Van Gundy will not hesitate to call for the Hack-a-Shaq, which absolutely scares him to death. He's searching desperately for a solution. The latest has him hoisting shots about a foot behind the line, which makes no sense. I broached the topic with him in practice. "What are you doing standing behind the line?" I asked. "Now you're shooting them a foot *long*. What is that all about?" When I realized he wasn't going to be receptive, I gave up. I am simply not going to deal with him when he's in that kind of mood. I'll revisit this issue another day.

APRIL 23
Houston

Since the Lakers seized control of this series four days ago, my thoughts have drifted on occasion toward the Spurs, who also captured the first two games of their opening-round matchup against the Grizzlies. Last night when the coaching staff, Mitch, and I went to dinner downtown, we were set up in a private room with a television to watch Game 3 of the San Antonio–Memphis series. We know the Spurs very well, but there are always more nuances to pick up, tendencies to later break down on film. The Spurs won a close one to take a 3–0 lead. Parker was the star for the first three quarters, Duncan the closer, with Turkoglu providing a huge lift with eighteen points. Nonetheless, defense remains their forte, a challenge we'll have to deal with soon enough.

Perhaps not as soon as we think. Tonight the team that should be occupying my undivided attention, the Rockets, sparked by an acrobatic Francis, held serve on their floor, 102–91, to make it a series. We succumbed to the same breakdowns, mental and physical, that have plagued us the entire year—poor coverage on pick-and-rolls, failure to follow the basic principles of the sound offense, etc. etc. etc. The guys couldn't stop the Rockets' penetration and when they rotated over, Francis or Mobley, who combined for forty-eight points, easily found the open man. The Rockets converted nine of sixteen from behind the arc. Francis nearly finished with a triple-double, adding nine rebounds and seven assists. Taylor hit some key jumpers down the stretch. "Don't lay behind the pick," we kept telling Shaq. "You can't sit behind your screener because the guard is going to turn the corner and come at you. You have to get out and show your [chest] numbers at the player." I'm concerned about this problem for this series and beyond. "If they don't solve screen and roll," I told the coaching staff, "they're just setting themselves up for failure against San Antonio. That's all Parker does, is screen rolls."

Shaquille, meanwhile, was five for fourteen from the line. If he had made his free throws, we might have had a chance to win the game. The problem is driving him crazy, and I can't worry about his mood any longer. "If you don't make your free throws," I told him, "we're not going to win. You can't put us or yourself under that kind of strain." I know he's capable. My first year here I stayed on him, and he went on to make nine out of nine in Game 4 of the

Western Conference Finals against Portland. In practice Shaq shoots free throws with more confidence, but under the pressure of a ball game, his hand tightens up, flattening the ball's trajectory. He looks like he's chucking it toward the basket. Many of his attempts don't come close, offering him little opportunity to receive the bounce that on occasion bails out the pure shooters. His knees hurt, so he can't properly use his legs, and his wrist is broken, which results in the awkward release. I've mentioned to him numerous times that he needs to practice visualization. "Tell yourself 'I can make them,' " I said. "You need to see yourself making them. You can't go back to your fearful state, which becomes, 'I want to make sure I hit the rim. I don't want to airball it. What if I airball it and everybody laughs?'" Another idea I've put forward is shooting them underhanded, reminiscent of one of my contemporaries, Rick Barry. "It may be the easiest way," I said. "Oh, no, I'd be embarrassed," he said. The most frustrating aspect is his tendency to experiment with a new method every week or two. "Just find something you believe in," I told him. "If you keep changing, it will always be a wreck."

During the 2000–2001 season, the Lakers hired Ed Palubinskas, who played for LSU in the 1970s. A shooting fanatic, Ed taught Shaq how to put the ball high on his fingertips and release it with a leaning, instead of a bending, technique. Shaq developed a true, consistent arc. But when Ed asked for a yearly salary and a championship ring, we let him go. Without Ed, Shaq was unable to sustain this technique. The press made a big deal out of his dedication, showing up at the arena today about three hours before tip-off to work on his free throws. To me it was not a big deal. That was exactly what Shaq, as a professional, should be doing.

Another important factor has been our inability to hold productive practices, reflected in a lack of execution. Too often, with players nursing one ailment or another, we haven't been able to develop the rhythm we'll need night after night to advance. Players can take numerous shots, go through a series of drills, and participate in two-on-two games, but there is no substitute for racing up and down the court for ten, maybe fifteen, minutes with very few stops to work on ball movement. In past seasons players who weren't on the playoff roster were able to take part, replacing those with aches and pains, allowing everyone else to get in the necessary work. We taught them how to run the opponent's offense. They didn't learn the whole system, but enough plays to simulate the challenges the starters and main reserves would be facing. In Chicago, there was one player, Dicky Simpkins, who was unstoppable in practice, and helped us prepare for Karl Malone. Normally I put the guys through rigorous practices but I haven't been quite as hard on them this time. If they couldn't absorb our concepts in the first two hundred practices since training camp, it doesn't seem very likely that a breakthrough will come now.

There is a bright side to this loss, which was not totally unexpected. The Rockets were 27–14 at home, holding opponents to very low shooting percentages. The bright side is that finally perhaps our guys will recognize that they can't put forth the minimum effort and expect to prevail against a quality team. I thought our performance in Game 1 would be the wake-up call, but, cocky as ever, they brushed it off, figuring the Rockets were lucky. With Jackson's miss from the corner, a shot he often converts, *we* were the lucky ones. Then, after coasting in the second half of Game 2 to win by double digits, the assumption was that we would stroll into Houston and finish the series. That assumption is gone.

APRIL 26
Los Angeles

Should I discuss Gary's complaints in front of the whole squad? Or should I leave it alone? I went back and forth on the matter until finally, in a team meeting Saturday, I opened the door without referring to him directly. If the players did indeed have a problem with his behavior, or how I dealt with him, then it should be out in the open now, not simmering under the surface, a source of division. "Is there anything you guys want to address?" I asked. "Everybody cool? Everybody know their role?" There was only silence. Obviously it was not a problem for them. This is not a group to hold anything back. If they felt Gary was acting like a jerk, they would say something. They clearly understand his tendency to go off on rants. "Then I expect you all to give me the best of what you've got, and Gary, regardless of how many minutes you've played or want to play, if I have to put you in with three minutes to go in the game, I want to feel you'll work hard during that time."

Yesterday, when I came into the locker room, I made it a priority to reinforce the point. "Are you ready to play a fourth quarter if we need you?" I asked.

"Yes," he said. "I'm okay now," he said. "My anger got the best of me."

During the team meeting, I also addressed our recent inability to properly finish quarters. In Game 3, we were up by five midway through the opening stanza, but were outscored 17–6. In the second, Houston ended the quarter on a 10–4 run. "Are you tired?" I asked them. "Do you need more direction on the floor?" They didn't answer, again. "I think you guys are tired," I continued, "and don't want to admit it. You know what you have to do. You have to have a better choice of shots." Kobe appears the most fatigued. He wants to play the whole game but for obvious reasons doesn't possess the same energy he's demonstrated in the past. I limit his practice time and try to squeeze in the maximum amount of rest for the minimum amount of missed game minutes. I wonder how much of his desire to remain on the floor stems from the fear that once the playoffs end, the only court left in his immediate future is the one in Colorado, which he cannot control. Yesterday during halftime of Game 4, he stood in the hallway, talking on his cell, Mitch told me later. That was a first in my coaching career. He was on with his wife, Vanessa, I presume. Perhaps he was telling her that after experiencing stomach problems earlier in the day, he was feeling much better. Perhaps he just wanted to hear her voice. He is in a place I cannot pretend to know.

Yesterday's game belonged to Karl, who will not let this chance for a championship, maybe his last, slip away, not against this team. The Rockets have left him open since Game 1, choosing to double-team Kobe and Shaq. Karl made them pay for it, scoring thirty points, his high as a Laker, including twenty in the first half. I'm amazed at what he can do at the age of forty. I was also impressed with Gary, who finished with thirteen points, seven assists, and six rebounds. I played him in the fourth quarter this time. In many cases when the spotlight shines on a player, even a negative spotlight, he focuses more intensely than ever, determined to prove himself. Yet leading by fourteen late in the third, we failed to close out another quarter, letting the Rockets cut the deficit to ten heading into the fourth. More ominously, we gave them and their fans a reason to believe. Usually if a team can maintain a double-digit advantage heading into the last seven or eight minutes of a playoff game, the team trailing will lose that belief, falling out of character.

Houston didn't waste the momentum, clawing back into the game. We made the task easier; our players consistently moved to the wrong spots, even after I made the offense as basic as possible. "All I'm going to do," I told them, "is have the guard dribble the ball into the wing. You're going to go down in the corner and we'll throw the ball to the top. If you're open, we'll hit you. If not, we'll go back into Shaq." It was a nightmare. If they couldn't operate this simple stuff, I wondered, how could I ever expect them to go far in the playoffs? With thirty-nine seconds left, Francis tied the game with a jumper.

After both teams missed, we got possession with three seconds left. I called a play for Shaquille in front of the basket. Shaquille? Wouldn't he be the *last* option? Won't they foul him immediately? Exactly. He would only have to hit one of two free throws, the scenario with the best possible odds. Despite his recent ineptitude, Shaquille is a career 53 percent shooter, while last-second shots, historically, have been successful only 25 percent of the time. However, Kobe, the first option, broke it off. Instead of coming off the baseline to set a pick for Shaq, he went to the top, in effect destroying the second and third options, Fish and Karl. With no more timeouts, Gary inbounded the ball to Kobe, who missed an off-balance jumper. "This is the first time I've ever seen a game where you had no timeouts at the end," Fish said. There was one other occasion, I reminded him—Game 4 of the 2002 Western Conference Finals against Sacramento, when Robert Horry hit the jumper at the buzzer.

In overtime I observed a lull in our energy, which had been at a high level throughout the game. Mobley made two layups off screen rolls, the second putting us four down with 2:24 to go in the period. The guys were despondent about losing the lead and anxious about the shots Kobe missed down the stretch. I began to wonder if he was going to shoot every time he touched the ball. Jeanie has a term for it, "rich people shoplifting," the tendency to initiate behavior which is detrimental simply because the perpetrator knows he or she can get away with it. During a timeout, I got on the guys, which is not my normal style. "We're not going to lose this," I told them. "Don't give this game up. You've got to suck it up and play with all the competitive spirit you've got." We were still trailing by four when Karl made the biggest play of the game, hitting a runner and drawing the sixth foul on Yao. On the ensuing possession, Kobe stole the ball from Jackson, made a driving layup, and was fouled. We closed with a 9–1 run to win 92–88.

I was extremely proud of how the guys overcame their despondency. During the rest of this playoff run, however long it lasts, there are bound to be other moments of similar despair, when a game, perhaps a season, will suddenly appear lost. If we can summon the same fortitude and resiliency we showed today, especially on the road, there shouldn't be any obstacles we can't overcome. I've never coached a championship team that at one time or another in the postseason didn't reach a crisis point. In the first year with the Lakers, it came in Game 7 of the Western Conference Finals against Portland, down fifteen early in the fourth quarter. In 2002 it came in Game 7 against Sacramento, down nine in the third. But with this current group there is one thing that worries me. I still sense a lack of the cohesiveness, the oneness every team requires to win a title. There are always signs—anticipating when a teammate will be beat on defense, trusting someone will be in the designated spot, displaying an unwillingness to lose. So far, I haven't seen any of these, and time is running out. Achieving oneness does not guarantee success, but it greatly enhances a team's chances. Except in the rare blowout, no matter how poorly you may perform, there comes a point late in every NBA game when the margin is not substantial, maybe six or eight points. The team closest to that oneness is usually triumphant.

APRIL 28
Los Angeles

Tonight was Kobe's night, which seems to always be the case when he plays in the hours after attending a hearing in Colorado. He is out to prove his greatness to anyone who still doubts him. This week has been an even tougher ordeal for him, flying back and forth for three straight days. Arriving on the court only about fifteen minutes before the tip, he needed a little time to get his focus. But after I gave Kobe an early rest, the focus was back. He scored fourteen points in the second quarter. Nonetheless, in a close-out game, we trailed, 48–47, at the half. The fans were restless. Going back to Houston for a Game 6 was not a scenario anyone was willing to contemplate. "We can't play any worse than this," I told them in the locker room. "We'll get it together." We did, outscoring the Rockets 25–9 in the third. Suddenly the third quarter, a problem forever, has become a strength. Shaquille, although he still won't warm up, hits the court ready to play. Tonight Devean scored seven points in the quarter, with two steals, both from Jackson. When he plays under control, utilizing his raw skills—on our team, only Kobe is a better all-around athlete—he becomes a huge weapon for us. I won't let myself get too excited. From one game to the next, I never know what to expect from him.

The final was 97–78. One series down, three, we hope, to go. We won't enjoy this triumph for long, not with the long-awaited rematch against the Spurs only a few days away. Some wonder whether we might have been better off facing them in the Western Conference Finals, not the second round, that we'd be better prepared after playing perhaps Minnesota or Sacramento. No matter. We've been preparing for this team, in one way or another, for a full year, since they ended our bid for four straight championships. I recall the day in August when Tex and I finally watched the video of Game 6, noting our inadequacies, vowing to do better the next time. I recall the moment when, before heading for Montana, I learned we were likely to sign Karl and Gary, the power forward and defensive stopper we didn't have against Duncan and Parker. For the longest time, I couldn't envision a way to beat the Spurs. Now I can. But what I believe isn't what matters. My players must believe, starting right now.

NINE

ROUND TWO: SAN ANTONIO

APRIL 29
Los Angeles

I was awake at six, in the office by eight, the video room by nine. In contrast to last year's playoffs, when I underwent the angioplasty, I'm prepared to devote my full energy and attention to the task at hand: dethroning the San Antonio Spurs. Jeanie was convinced that it was my lack of drive, of willfulness, that limited us more than any other factor in 2003. I experienced chest pains and shortness of breath. Walking up stairs was an ordeal. I don't know how I made it through the day. At first I assumed the fatigue was related to the normal playoff cycle—late games, late flights, the endless practices and video sessions. The angioplasty, which I had between Games 3 and 4, had a lasting impact on my children. For thirteen long seasons, they had witnessed the anxiety I go through as a coach in the National Basketball Association, heightened during the playoffs. Thirteen seasons was enough, they believed. I told them last spring that I would honor the last year of my contract with the Lakers. I know they'll be on me to quit this time.

Many experts proclaim that the winner of this series will be the overwhelming favorite to be crowned NBA champion, discounting the remaining contenders—Sacramento, Minnesota, Dallas, and the Eastern Conference playoff teams. I won't go that far, but I will concede that nobody is playing at a higher level than the Spurs, who won eleven in a row to close out the regular season, and swept the much-improved Memphis Grizzlies in the first round. Jerry West and Hubie Brown have done a marvelous job with the Memphis club, and its future is bright, but Memphis was taken apart by the Spurs. I see a definite similarity between the Spurs and the 2000–2001 Lakers, who went 15–1 in the playoffs. Of the nine NBA championship squads I've coached, that unit put together the most impressive postseason run, destroying opponents in the fourth quarter.

This San Antonio team is not the same one that defeated us last year. Gone are David Robinson, Speedy Claxton, Steve Kerr, Stephen Jackson, and Danny Ferry. The newcomers include Horry, Rasho Nesterovic, and Hedo Turkoglu. Nonetheless, on balance, anchored by Duncan, their two-time MVP, they appear just as potent. Parker, still only twenty-one years old, has shown remarkable growth this season. What impresses me the most about this kid is his ability to play equally well at two or three different speeds—a solid pace, a quick step, and a chase step, in which he challenges the middle of the defense. He can go to his left almost as well as to his right. People have wondered how Parker could possibly still be on the board when San Antonio selected him with the twenty-eighth pick in the 2001 draft. He was nineteen, for goodness' sake, and playing in Europe, where it is very difficult to assess the level of competition. For every Parker or Dirk Nowitzki or Toni Kukoc, there are twice as many projects who will never pan out. Europe has yet to produce a true franchise player in the NBA. If Parker had displayed the same skills in the NCAA Tournament, he would have been a lottery pick. He can nail the three-pointer, which makes him even more dangerous. Bruce Bowen, their small forward, plays exceptional defense on Kobe, chasing him from one end of the court to the other. Kobe will have to grind for every bucket. On offense Bowen can hit the three-point shot from the baseline. Turkoglu is another accomplished shooter, who has been playing extremely well.

Their bench is very productive, led by the Argentinean, Manu Ginobili, who can pass, penetrate, come off screen rolls, shoot threes, and play aggressive defense. Early in the season, with both Duncan and Parker sidelined, Ginobili scored a career-high thirty-three points in double overtime against us. Horry, who saw less playing time this season, has geared up for his stage, the playoffs, hitting some big three-pointers against Memphis. Since I started coaching in 1989, I can't think of a player, except for Michael Jordan and maybe Reggie Miller, who has nailed more clutch shots. I wonder if the guys will be ferocious enough against Rob, a friend and former Laker, who played such a vital role in our success. Gene Shue, who coached the Baltimore Bullets in the late 1960s and early 1970s, once told his team before a playoff matchup against the Knicks: "I know a lot of you guys really like the Knickerbockers.

They're good guys, but you've got to develop a hatred for them if you're going to beat them." Hatred seems a bit extreme. I prefer to see them develop a warrior mentality, in which they honor their opponent. Too many players today degrade their opponent. "He's garbage," they'll say. He is not garbage. Your opponent is who makes you a better warrior.

On the negative side for the Spurs, the loss of David Robinson may prove critical. Although he was limited in the last season of a superb career, David was able to guard Shaq for twenty, maybe twenty-five minutes, sparing Duncan from working too hard on the defensive end. Nesterovic, a free agent who was with Minnesota last year, is a decent player who can hit the medium-range jumper and block shots, but Shaq dominated him in the playoffs last year, averaging twenty-nine points. The Spurs will also miss David's leadership. Duncan has inherited that role but he's a quiet, less forceful leader than David, who inspired the team and the crowd. Even so, many people are picking the Spurs. During the regular season the Lakers took three of four games, but in the last meeting on April 4, they ended our eleven-game winning streak, 95–89, at Staples. Parker finished with twenty-nine points and nine assists. "I don't know how we're going to beat this team," Tex said today. Tex is usually pretty upbeat.

For starters we will need to solve our longtime nemesis, the screen roll. They killed us with it last year, which led to the acquisitions of Karl and Gary. I'm confident these two will make the difference. After some initial difficulty containing Stevie Francis, they both stepped up, curtailing Houston's options. Gary was able to go over the picks, while Karl came out to trap. Parker will be much tougher to handle. Unlike Francis, he does not lust to score, preferring to set up Duncan or one of their three-point shooters. He is also, despite his inexperience, more decisive and reliable than Francis. Gregg Popovich, their coach, is prone to run screen rolls for the first three quarters, and then ride Duncan as much as possible the last ten minutes of the game. Our challenge will be to force the Spurs to rely on Duncan earlier in hopes of tiring him out. When the offense revolves around Tim, the supporting players become tentative, standing around, taken out of their normal game. We will also need to get Shaquille more involved. In the Houston series against Yao, he wasn't the force he usually is. But against Nesterovic and San Antonio's other bigs he will possess a distinct size advantage. Popovich will try to counter by persuading the refs to keep track of possible three-second violations. He works the officials almost as persistently as Van Gundy. Shaq must be wary of committing offensive fouls, which would restrict his aggressiveness on defense. Malik Rose, only six-foot-seven, is excellent at drawing offensive fouls.

I don't get the sense that our players truly understand how effectively the Spurs have been competing, although not even a month has passed since they beat us in our building. I compare this case of temporary amnesia to a trip to the dentist. You know the drill is going to be unpleasant but you don't remember exactly how unpleasant until it's administered. Suddenly the memory of the past experiences rushes to the surface. While the team may be impressed by Duncan's production in the post, it doesn't automatically grasp the high level of execution required to feed him properly from a variety of entry angles. Teams attempt to disrupt the passer or double-team Duncan, but the Spurs, with their spacing, intelligence, and patience, usually find a way to counter any scheme.

Finally, we must find a way to force the Spurs, who haven't lost since March 23, to doubt themselves. The best way is through our own high level of execution: make it tough for them to pass. When they receive the ball, make sure they're not in their familiar, comfortable spots. Put a body on them, a hand in their faces, making them shoot off-balance. Encourage them to wonder how in the world they will get any decent scoring opportunities. Gradually the frustrations will mount, creating confusion, creating . . . doubt. Once those doubts creep in, they tend to fester, gaining power with every errant pass, every missed assignment, every call that should have gone the other way. They know they beat us last year, but they also know we beat them the year before, and the year before that. In those days, they were a team that often fell apart in the fourth quarter. Parker may be especially vulnerable. Two years ago he was thoroughly outplayed by Fish. He was so out of control that Popovich limited his minutes. "You have to make sure," I reminded the guys, "that he doesn't remember last year's playoffs as much as he remembers the playoffs two years ago."

May 3
Los Angeles

We didn't create much doubt yesterday in Game 1, except maybe in our fans. The guys, down eight at the half, began to discover their rhythm in the third quarter, but in the fourth there was one mistake after another—poor passes, ill-advised shots, missed assignments. I called timeouts, changed personnel, but nothing got us clicking. I did not anticipate that the Spurs would be so successful at fronting Shaquille, a strategy that because of his jumping ability, has failed over the course of his career. The Celtics tried it for a couple of seasons, and so did the Pacers, but most teams realized its futility. Our offense, with its ability to feed the ball into the post from a variety of different positions, was built for that kind of defense. Even so, throwing the ball over the top is no easy feat. A lanky, agile defender like Nesterovic, with help from Duncan, was able to cause turnovers. The Spurs fronted Shaq even when he was in the midpost. In the fourth, we forced the ball into Shaq time after time when the angle simply wasn't there. Earlier in the game he drew two three-second violations in three possessions. He was thinking, "I got my three-second call, so now I'll park my ass in there," but he should have known that Dick Bavetta, a veteran ref, wouldn't go for that kind of defiance. Bavetta's first call was, "I'm going to give you a warning." The second was a "f---you" call. Shaq finished with nineteen points and thirteen boards, but converted only three of thirteen free throws.

The kids, Kareem Rush and Luke Walton, looked overwhelmed by the moment. Kareem was pressured into traps. Luke threw a poor pass. "I don't know if these young players will be able to give us anything in the playoffs," Frank said. I'm not ready to concede that point, not yet. I believe in the kids. They showed me a great deal in December, January, and February. I'm confident they can show me more in May. The Spurs, who went on a 19–2 run, prevailed 88–78. "You weren't ready for this game," I told the team at practice today. "This is exactly the kind of pressure we were talking about. You can't make these types of turnovers without a loss." Especially frustrating was that this was clearly a game we could have stolen, planting immediate doubts. Nonetheless, the players weren't fazed. For the fans and the media, every playoff setback is monumental, a symbol of deep fissures, but players realize the other team has to beat them four times.

Our challenge remains the same, to contain Parker and Duncan. Parker (twenty points, nine assists) was too much for Gary and for Kobe, who covered him briefly in the first quarter. He proceeded to drive by Kobe for a layup, then hit an open three on the next possession. I had seen enough. The kid simply has too much foot speed. Gary, more frustrated than ever, has pleaded for an opportunity to go right back at Parker, to exploit his height advantage to post him in the lane. His impulse is common among today's players, who are generally more dedicated to repairing their wounded pride than to following the overall team concept. Common or not, I rarely sign off on this impulse, certain it would disrupt our normal offensive flow. Besides, if Gary properly carries out his assignment in the offense, his chances to score on Parker will be there. "He needs your support," I told the players today. I bumped into Kobe in the bathroom before practice. "Is Gary okay?" I asked. "Is he going to implode? Do you feel any of the tension he seems to be creating around himself?" Of course he feels the tension. The whole team feels it. The whole city feels it. I'm trying to be empathetic, but there is a limit to my tolerance. This isn't Atlanta in early March. This is the playoffs. "If you don't solve your problems, I'll get someone else in there," I told Gary. "We'll just do it a different way." He called to say he would be late for practice today, due to "personal problems." I didn't ask what they were, and he didn't offer. I never try to pry into players' lives. Was this Gary's idea of a protest statement? I'd go crazy if I were to speculate about that kind of stuff.

Stopping Duncan will be equally difficult. In Game 1, he showed tremendous leadership. In addition to his production—

thirty points, including twelve in the fourth—he argued vehemently on behalf of his teammates on numerous calls. Finally, when he complained about one on himself, an obvious pushoff of Shaquille, I stepped in. "Tim, why don't you just play basketball and quit bitching all the time," I said. "If you want to be a referee, get a fucking whistle and come out and be a referee." He stared at me, perplexed. "You know what the hell I'm talking about," I said. I'm sure his response wasn't too flattering, but with the noise in the arena, I couldn't hear it. To be honest, I admire Tim for defending his teammates, for working the officials from the opening tip. Such loyalty impresses the refs, who will be subtly persuaded to give Tim's team a break later in the game. One break could mean the ball game. Unfortunately, on our squad, nobody will assume the spokesman role. Kobe and Shaq will argue, all right, but only about calls that affect *them,* which is not the same thing. Karl and Gary have reputations that hinder their effectiveness. On prior Lakers squads Robert Horry and Ron Harper would speak out for the group. In Chicago it was Michael and Scottie.

There were certainly enough poor calls. The most frequent violation was San Antonio's attempt to get away with questionable screens. Duncan or Nesterovic constantly pushed off with their hands, which is clearly against the rules. Once, Duncan was kicked out of a game against Golden State, but that was only because he screened the wrong guy, referee Jack Nies. The coaching staff and I couldn't help but laugh when Nies picked himself off the floor and tossed Duncan. If this trend persists I might have to pull one of the beat guys aside and say, "Look, you've got to write something about their screen roll. Their big guy is knocking off the defender, and they're doing it illegally." I've never tried this with a writer before but I may have no choice.

At least we're licking our wounds at home and not in enemy territory. After yesterday's afternoon game we flew back to Los Angeles, arriving at about seven P.M. It wasn't even dark yet. I've always believed that if players can sleep in their own bed, and practice on their own court, they will be better prepared. They can go for a whirlpool or a steam bath, lift weights, or arrive at the facility in El Segundo before practice to work on their shooting. If we had stayed in San Antonio for another two nights, our time at the arena would have been scheduled and restricted. Plus the players, with plenty of time to kill, would have been subjected to excited fans and accounts of their Game 1 failure on local television. Our hotel in San Antonio is located in the heart of the noisy downtown area. One night there was enough.

MAY 8
Los Angeles

If I thought the overtime in Game 4 against Houston was a crisis point for this team, that was nothing compared to the crisis we face right now, down two games to zero to a San Antonio squad which hasn't lost in six weeks. In Game 2 on Wednesday, the Spurs seized a 33–17 advantage in the first quarter, Parker leading the way with sixteen points. The lead remained sixteen at the half. Our guys were plagued again by turnovers. The Spurs, believing they escaped with an average performance in the opener, were determined to elevate their play. I began to feel I was watching a video of last year's dismantling. Could it be, I wondered, that after the moves we made, and the 18–3 start, we were doomed to the same fate against the same team? There was too much dribbling and too little ball movement, and the transition defense was abysmal. We made a run in the second half, narrowing the deficit to two. By moving Shaq around in the lane and changing the angles of the entry passes from different sides of the floor, it became tougher for Nesterovic to front him. Our lob passes were more precise, coming off the dribble before the defender was able to pressure the ball handler. Shaq finished with thirty-two points and fifteen rebounds. But Parker, held to only six points in the second and third quarters, went off in the fourth, resulting in a second consecutive ten-point triumph. He finished with thirty, his career high in the playoffs. The guys simply ran out of gas, shooting only six of sixteen in the fourth. Almost six minutes passed without a field goal. Two offensive rebounds off missed free throws also killed us.

Kobe scored only fifteen points, neutralized by Bowen, who was given what I call a license to hunt by the refs. He was jarring Kobe, pushing him, using his arms and hands to keep him from good looks or penetration. Kobe was seventeen for forty-three in the two games, and many shots were forced. In Game 2, he shot only two free throws, which should be impossible. A lot of times the license to hunt is granted when the officials perceive that the player's teammates have demonstrated great defensive intensity. I discovered this during my career with the Knicks. In the early '70s, I came off the bench and was very physical, but the refs let me play. But in 1975, after DeBusschere, Lucas, Meminger, and Reed left, I led the league in fouls and I wasn't playing any differently. The players around me were different. The Lakers rarely profit from this license because Shaquille doesn't guard his man very tightly. We try to maintain a certain physical presence, but aren't allowed to get into guys' faces.

Upon our return here, the city was bracing for the worst.

The fans weighed in on talk radio: *Bench Gary Payton, he's no Hall of Famer. . . . You're a bunch of dysfunctional individuals, not a team. . . . Knock Tony Parker on his ass. . . . Kobe's taking too many tough shots. . . . The bench isn't stepping up. . . .* On and on it went, or so I heard. One writer even had the nerve to ask me, "If San Antonio were to win this, would they be considered a dynasty?" A dynasty? They haven't won *this* yet. I took note of the somber mood but did not become discouraged. The Spurs merely held serve, and our players are still in good position to even the series and create some doubt in their minds. I also believe there is another level defensively we are capable of attaining. Some coaches, scanning the papers for bulletin-board fodder, may try to inspire their team with quotes from the naysayers, but I don't operate that way. The lone exception was during my first year in Los Angeles, when, after we posted a 67–15 record in the regular season, one publication printed ten ways teams could knock us off in the playoffs. I read the list, and frankly, some of the ways—Shaq's free-throw ineptitude, poor transition defense, the inability to stop screen roll—made pretty good sense then, as they do now. I pasted them on the board in the locker room. But now on this occasion, I must make sure the players haven't lost any faith. The coaching staff may devise a dozen different tactics to contain San Antonio's screen roll, to penetrate its tight defense, to get Gary more involved, to feed Shaq in deeper positions, and to free Kobe, etc. etc., but unless the guys *believe* we can prevail, those tactics won't mean a thing.

Today during a team meeting I asked each player to speak in front of the whole group and affirm his commitment to winning Game 3, an idea Jeanie suggested. I started with Shaquille. "Bring it on," he said. "Just bring me the ball, and we're going to win.

Trust me." One by one, everyone piped in. "This is what I always dreamed about," Luke said. "This is what every kid wants to do." Karl was the most enthusiastic, reminding me of the first meeting, back in training camp. Slava, with his thick Ukrainian accent, was wonderful. "I'm here to play," he said. "I'm going to give it everything I've got." Even Kobe was passionate. He can be hot or cold in these situations, either anxious to be part of the group or anxious to be isolated from the group. Kobe has remained committed throughout the playoffs. On the plane to San Antonio before Game 1, he watched video of the Spurs. I was impressed. Typically, guys watch movies, listen to music, or play cards. They don't check out screen roll.

These affirmations represented a move in the proper direction but they weren't sufficient. The players needed to develop a deeper sense of urgency, a mind-set that could guide them through perhaps the most challenging week of their basketball careers. I went around the room, reminding each one where he stood in his contract situation and mentioned the unlikelihood that many of them would ever play for the Lakers again. If the theme for the 1997–98 Chicago Bulls was "The Last Dance," then for this Lakers contingent it might well be "The Last Chance." Kobe, Karl, Gary, Fish, Slava, Horace, and Bryon Russell can become free agents in July. There is only right now, I told them, no tomorrow. They needed to approach every game as if it were the last. I included myself in the speech. "This is it for me," I said. I found out afterward from Chip Schaefer that they took my comments to mean I was retiring. I'll have to correct that misconception. That is not exactly what I said, and besides, the last thing I want to be is a distraction at this most precarious time.

With a renewed sense of commitment, the players proceeded to go through one of our most rigorous practices in a long time. Normally by this point of the season, guys are nursing fifteen to twenty minor ailments. They require twenty minutes of warm-up exercises and stretching before they can go on the court. But today was different. They stepped right into it with no hesitation. We worked on simplifying the offense, adopting a modified version of the triangle. The pure version is too difficult for this group, especially Karl and Gary. This was my concern seven months ago in Hawaii and it remains my concern. Karl is uncomfortable on the wing and Gary seems incapable of properly reading and reacting to the defense. A large part of the system the Lakers teach is moving without the ball, but Gary needs to have it in his hands to feel fully engaged. Therefore we practiced screen rolls with him, using dribble penetration to initiate our normal actions. A more involved Gary would force Parker to play defense. We also worked on our rotations against Duncan in the post, and on vacating a space to throw the ball over the top to Shaquille.

May 9
Los Angeles

No more speeches. No more team meetings. No more tweaking the triangle. This afternoon at Staples we went out to prove something to our fans and to ourselves. Consider the point proven. In our most proficient game of the playoffs, we overwhelmed the Spurs, 105–81. Shaq was dominant, with twenty-eight points, fifteen rebounds, and eight blocked shots, the type of playoff performance he turned in routinely during his twenties. Kobe, freed to operate by harder picks from Karl and Shaq, added twenty-two points, along with six assists. If the officials were going to ignore our complaints about San Antonio's illegal screens, we figured that if we can't fight 'em, join 'em. The effort from our two stars wasn't reflected only in the stat sheet. During a scramble for a loose ball in the first quarter, both ended up on the floor. I never like to see Shaq pick up a foul away from the basket, but in this situation, it was worth it. He fired up the team and the crowd.

For the first time we reminded Parker, held to only eight points, of the playoffs two years ago. In recent days it seemed like the whole city of Los Angeles was calling for the Lakers to knock Parker down to make him think twice about entering the lane the next time. I never endorsed this idea. In the '60s, '70s, and '80s, it was the standard approach to deter aggressive penetrators—I can't recall how many times Mark Price, the former Cleveland guard, was knocked down by the Pistons—but it won't work in today's NBA. The risk of a flagrant foul—an automatic two shots and possession—or worse yet, a suspension, is too severe. Furthermore I didn't want us to be perceived as the bullies in the series. The refs would then be more likely to call the game tighter against us, figuring we were the physical club while the Spurs played the right way. At the same time, whenever Parker drove toward the hoop, we were determined to force him into dead ends, to erect a wall of defenders to block his path. "In the playoffs," the saying goes, "there are no layups."

In devising a strategy to contain the screen roll, I came to a sobering conclusion: Gary and Karl were not going to be the solution. Stopping Francis was one thing, stopping Parker another. Gary couldn't get over the top of San Antonio's picks. Typically guards lose some of their athleticism and explosiveness at the age of thirty-three or thirty-four. This was why I asked Gary back in July if perhaps he had lost a step. No way, he said. Well, what was he going to say? Yes, coach, I'm a step slower? It was also why, against his wishes, I limited his minutes during the season. In today's Game I chose instead to plug the screen roll with a player from the nearest wing. The new wrinkle confused Parker, who lost the ball on several occasions. Shaquille's blocked shots were another key factor; they led to us outscoring the Spurs 18–10 in fast-break points. We're usually content to play our opponents even in that department. There is also a psychological effect. "Don't worry about a blocked shot," I tell players. "Shoot your shot. If it gets blocked, it gets blocked." Nonetheless players will begin to hesitate if they fear their shots will be rejected.

Yesterday Gary went on one of his classic rants. "Blame me," he said to the press, who have done just that since the series started. "Go ahead. Put it on me. It's Gary Payton against San Antonio. I'm down, 2–0." Today, just as Gary did in Game 4 in the Houston series, he answered the criticism with a solid performance, fifteen points and seven assists. The criticism has been too harsh. I know he's been tough to handle, but in December, January, and February, when this team seemed to suffer another injury every day, Gary was a warrior, guiding the kids to much-needed victories. He has missed very few games in his fourteen-year career. Karl chipped in with thirteen points, six rebounds, and five assists, and helped limit Duncan to only ten. We were concerned about keeping their three-point shooters in check. If Duncan and Parker scored twenty-five apiece, the Spurs would still probably need an additional thirty or thirty-five points to win. "What's going to beat us," I told the players, "is if Tony gets his points *and* he gets ten assists. Your job, as an individual, is to make sure your guy doesn't get his average. Don't allow any career nights." In Game 3, there were no career nights.

MAY 11
Los Angeles

The passion we brought to the floor in Game 3 was not evident in the first half of tonight's Game 4. Neither was the precision. The Spurs, hitting from long range this time, were leading by ten. They made the proper adjustments, especially on screen roll, and now it was our turn, before it became too late. I was at a loss, just like the fans who constantly complain that they can never be sure which Lakers team will show up. If they're frustrated, imagine how I feel. Players often explain a loss by saying, "we didn't match their intensity." The phrase is overused but accurate. Less talented teams with greater intensity defeat more talented teams all the time. Matching intensity does not mean initiating aggressive, frenetic action. That often causes players to go out of control, out of character. Matching intensity means competing with full alertness, with a commitment to sound principles and execution. Little things—good footwork, proper spacing, a hand in a shooter's face—make a big difference. "You guys are going to have to be more decisive," I said in the locker room. "You need to support each other."

In the second half, the passion and precision returned. Sparked by Shaquille, with fourteen points, including four of five from the line and seven rebounds, the Lakers outscored the Spurs by fifteen in the quarter to go up by five. In the first four games we have outscored the Spurs in the third quarter by a combined forty-four points. At halftime, we ran through about five minutes of video with ten to fifteen sequences from the first half, the coaching staff very precise about the adjustments that had to be made. The Spurs hung around in the fourth, but Kobe was unstoppable, scoring fifteen of his game-high forty-two. The press tried to make a big deal about whether Kobe, attending another hearing in Eagle County, would make it back in time. I wasn't concerned. Kobe told me there was a good chance the court would recess in the early afternoon, which it did. He arrived at Staples nearly three hours before tip-off. The final was 98–90.

Outdueling the Spurs twice in Los Angeles was only the first step in puncturing their sense of invincibility. The Spurs still have every right to feel good about themselves, keeping in mind that they haven't lost on their home floor since March 1, to the Grizzlies, a span of seventeen games. In last year's playoffs, San Antonio allowed a 2–0 lead to slip away, secured Game 5 at home, barely, and clinched the series in LA. The key for any team is to find something, anything, to believe in to ward off the demons of self-doubt. Nonetheless, fighting for our survival, we've held serve. The critics on talk radio will shut up for now. I'm proud of the guys. They affirmed their commitment, the willingness to sacrifice that we first talked about in Hawaii. They are not lying to each other any longer. The road ahead will only be tougher, but I think they're ready.

MAY 14

Open skies

The Fisher shot. Everybody wants to reflect on the Fisher shot. So do I, but there were other developments earlier in the day that set the stage for the magical moment. In the late morning, we went through our normal video session—well, normal for us. I showed the guys clips from the animated movie *Shrek*. For years I've spliced in clips from films or television shows to break up the monotony. Players will lose focus watching themselves race up and down the court for ten straight minutes. I often resort to comedies, really stupid stuff like *The Three Stooges*. In Chicago, I put the package together myself, which took hours but provided me with a great feel for the opponent. But the technology has moved beyond me. Now I have a video expert who puts it together.

Of course I'm not just trying to lighten the mood. Each clip comes with a message that registers, I hope. A clip of Mo hitting Curly with the frying pan might be shown after a clip of a player throwing an errant pass. The idea is to instruct without bruising egos. The player laughs, and no offense is taken at being cited for a mistake in front of the group, but the message gets through. Yesterday, by showing *Shrek*, I was trying to compare the story of an ogre winning the heart of a princess to the challenge we face in the playoffs. Can this team, by embracing the basketball gods, turn an ugly season into a championship? Did the players pick up on this message? I doubt it, just like I doubt they learned much from our meditation session prior to the Houston series. Yet I feel an obligation to put the possibility out there. I went back and forth between *Shrek* and clips of positive actions from Game 4. The players felt good about themselves, geared up for the shootaround.

I can usually tell a lot from a shootaround. If the players appear ragged, disinterested, going through the motions, it is extremely unlikely they will be inspired for the game seven or eight hours later. There was no such concern this time. The execution was ideal. They worked on defending the screen roll, putting Gary into more of a playmaking role, and applying pressure on Parker. "We have to win here," I told them, "and this game will be easier than the pressure of a Game 7." In Game 7s, the nerves take over. Players must possess refined motor muscle movements that will react smoothly. They can't afford to snap, pull, or short arm their shots. The players have a term for the latter—"alligator arms." In Game 7 of the 2002 Western Conference Finals, the Kings, a tremendous shooting team, suddenly couldn't make their free throws, the easiest shot in the game. If they had prevailed, they probably would have captured their first NBA championship. The visiting team is always the underdog in Game 7, losing 75 to 80 percent of the time. I'm not suggesting there isn't substantial pressure in a Game 5. There is, but at least players operate with some margin of error. In the Sacramento series, we lost Game 5 on a Mike Bibby shot with eight seconds left. The loss was devastating, but we regrouped to win Game 6 in Los Angeles. Tonight, I told them, is what I call an "opportunity" game.

Early on we seemed primed to capitalize on it. Our lead was seven at the half, despite very little production from Shaq, who was plagued with three fouls. The offense was moving the ball. The defense was forcing turnovers. The team was unified, committed. For the first time in the series, the Spurs looked uneasy at home, frightened, most notably Parker, who was only two of ten from the floor. The best players in the world are not immune to insecurity. Several years ago, in a game against the Clippers, their coach, Alvin Gentry, kept instructing his players to foul one of our guards, Lindsey Hunter, on purpose. The staff was dumbfounded, until Hunter missed six straight free throws. He was scared to death.

In the third quarter, we extended the lead to sixteen, due primarily to eleven points from Devean George, who hit three shots from long range. The kid has endured a tough season, and I haven't made things easier, benching him after his ill-advised post-up move down the stretch in Atlanta. He has persevered. But tonight so did the Spurs, led by their own unlikely hero, local product Devin Brown. A three from Brown cut the lead to nine entering the fourth, reminiscent of the Rockets' late spurt in the third quarter of Game 4. The Rockets built on that momentum and almost stole the game. Teams possess a tremendous psychological advantage if they can enter the fourth quarter with a double-digit lead. Even if the opponent hits three straight three-pointers, the lead will not completely evaporate.

Even so this was no time to panic. I rested Shaq to start the fourth. Normally I wouldn't hestitate to rest both Shaq and Kobe at the same time, but in a game this critical, with scoring at such a premium, I couldn't take that chance. We were fading, the Spurs surging. It was going to be a struggle for either team to score eighty points. With about ten minutes left, I gave Kobe a blow. He didn't seem to be thinking very clearly and his shot was flat, which is what happens with fatigue. His condition reminded me of Michael's in Game 5 of the 1997 Finals against Utah, when he played despite the flu and scored thirty-eight points. Kobe sat out barely more than a minute. Gary didn't sit long, either. "Get Gary back in there," Shaq pleaded. "Don't go with the kids now. We've got to have the veterans in there."

Fatigue was setting in for both teams, and shots, good ones, were missing by a mile. With eleven seconds to go, Kobe made a twenty-one-foot jumper to put us on top, 72–71. He focused, used his legs, somehow finding just enough energy to get that thing to go down. The Spurs called time. I alerted the guys to look for Duncan to take the last shot, either using a screen roll or dribble weave. In a similar situation against us earlier this season, Duncan took the shot from the top of the key. He missed but he had a good look. We could not give him a good look again. "Be prepared," I told Shaquille. He was, getting right in Duncan's face, but it didn't make a difference. Duncan, falling to the ground, hit an eighteen-footer with .04 seconds left. The crowd went wild. Their Spurs, it seemed, would win with a miracle. "What an incredible shot that was," I said to my coaches. I would need to say something else to my players. Their faces were blank when they came off the floor.

"Keep your heads up," I told them. "There's a way to win this game, and we're going to find it." From my vantage point, Duncan's shot actually dropped through the net with .09 seconds, an argument that went nowhere with the refs. But at least there was .04 seconds left. A tenth of a second less and according to the rules a lob near the basket would have been our only option. I grabbed the chalk and diagrammed a high screen that could free Kobe for a jumper, and a back pick that could set up Shaq for a lob. Payton was to throw the inbounds pass. "Rob knows this play," I said, referring to Horry, "so we might have to change this. Gary, remember, we still have a twenty-second timeout." I'm an eternal optimist but I do live in this world. When the guys broke the huddle, it was obvious we would need our own miracle shot.

The Spurs called time to check out how we planned to line up on the floor. Naturally during the next huddle I changed the plan. I moved the back picks to different areas of the court. But the Spurs knew what was coming. Neither Shaq nor Kobe was open. Gary signaled for our final timeout. I changed the line once again, telling Kobe to pop out from the middle of the pack and Karl to set a pick for Fish. Shaq would head toward the hoop from a different angle. Normally, if I were coaching the defense, I would have someone guard the inbounds passer, who is often the most dangerous player in this scenario. But in this case there was no time for a return pass. Popovich would be criticized later for leaving Payton open, but I would have done the exact same thing.

And then it happened. Gary hit Fish, who hit the winning bucket. A game was won, a hero born, a season saved. I could not have been more pleased, for our team and for Fish, who has made as big a sacrifice as any Laker this season. In the last year of his contract, he's lost valuable playing time and perhaps a chance to earn more money on the open market. On occasion he forced the action and once snapped at me for taking him out of a game in Oakland. I don't mind when a player gripes at being removed. He is showing pride, competitiveness. Fish has always kept the ultimate goal in mind, a championship. He made some key shots down the stretch this season and missed others, but I often told my coaches, "Derek really believes in himself. He wants to hit a last-second shot."

The scene in the locker room was chaotic, to say the least. "You little m-----," Kobe said to Fish. "Way to kick their ass." I hugged Fish. There was no need to say a word. The players, one after another, were high-fiving him. After a minute or two, I brought the group together in a circle. "Congratulations," I told them, "way to step into that spotlight. This has given us the opportunity, and we have to go out in two nights and finish this off." I went to meet with the press. While I was away Kobe hyperventilated, then collapsed, and was put on a table in the training room, two IVs attached to his arm. His eyes started to roll up in his head. With some fluids in him, he would be okay. The kid is remarkable. He didn't have one of his greatest nights, but he hung in there, and made a big shot that was overshadowed by the two that came afterward. Everyone hung in there. Perhaps this team can be compared to the story of *Shrek*. Perhaps this ugly season can end in a championship.

MAY 15
Los Angeles

Closing a team out, especially the defending champions, is no easy task. In the first half tonight, we proved my case, and the score was tied at halftime at 39. The Spurs outrebounded us 25–15. The third quarter was equally ragged, and our lead was only four. But I wasn't too concerned. I saw doubt in the faces of the San Antonio players. Losing the two games in LA didn't do it. Losing Game 5 at home did. For the quarter, they went three for twenty-three. In the fourth Kobe went off, scoring sixteen of his twenty-six. He was running the screen roll to near perfection. Gary was solid again, with fifteen points and seven assists. Popovich went to Hack-a-Shaq late in the game, but it didn't work. Shaq made five of his last eight free throws. We won, 88–76, becoming only the eighth team in NBA history to rally from an 0–2 deficit in a best of seven series. Popovich greeted me at half-court. "I hope you get your tenth," he said, referring to a tenth title.

I'm not thinking about a tenth title. All I'm thinking about is the effort this team, on the brink, displayed over the last week. I've been around some great teams and some great players, but this truly was one of the most courageous efforts I've ever seen. To lose to the Spurs for the second straight year, with all the changes, all the hype, would have generated an immediate purge. The Last

Chance would have been the lost chance. Instead we could celebrate tonight, for a few hours at least. "I can't believe we beat this team four times in a row," Tex said. I can't believe it, either.

After every playoff game, I address the team. I don't pretend to offer anything especially profound or revealing. I talk about the schedule for the days ahead. Perhaps the most important thing I do is take a piece of chalk and write on the blackboard how many more victories it will take to earn a ring. Tonight I wrote eight, which usually seems like a large number. But tonight, by beating the defending champions, eight doesn't seem very large at all.

TEN

ROUND THREE: MINNESOTA

May 20
Minneapolis

I have nothing against the good people of Minnesota but I was hoping to avoid a trip to the Twin Cities. I wanted to start the Western Conference Finals in our building, putting doubt in the opposition right away. Our postseason record at Staples over the years has been outstanding. I also wasn't too crazy about another series of long plane rides. Going back and forth to Sacramento, about an hour north of Los Angeles, would have been infinitely more bearable. Unfortunately the Kings didn't cooperate with my desires or their own, losing a tight Game 7 to the Timberwolves.

For most of the regular season, Sacramento appeared the team to beat, even without Chris Webber in the lineup. Peja Stojakovic was an early MVP candidate. But once again the Kings found a way to falter, first squandering the Pacific Division title and the number-one seed, and now bowing to the Wolves after seizing home court advantage in Game 1. They were up ten with four minutes to go in Game 2, lost, and were never on top in the series again. They looked old, suddenly, Webber struggling to get up and down the court. Bibby and Stojakovic were a combined seven for twenty-five in Game 7. The Kings also lost their poise, especially Anthony Peeler, who was forced to sit out Game 7 for elbowing Kevin Garnett, a former teammate, in Game 6. The Kings were already short-handed without backup guard Bobby Jackson.

On the other hand, opening on the road offers a special opportunity, especially against a team unfamiliar with this rung of the playoffs, and one which will have trouble regrouping, mentally and physically, only forty-eight hours after the biggest night in the history of the franchise. They celebrated, and so did their fans, as if they had captured the NBA Finals. All they had done was emerge from the second round, only halfway to a championship. The Timberwolves must now prepare for an entirely different challenge from an entirely different team. The Kings settled for jumpers. The Lakers will pound them inside with Shaq. Bibby penetrated and dished to three-point shooters. Kobe will penetrate and finish. The task facing Minnesota is unfair. In the first round of the playoffs, teams sometimes received two or three days between games but now, suddenly, on the verge of their biggest test yet, the Wolves have only one full day to prepare. Television rules again. I understand basketball is a business, but one has to wonder: what kind of product does the league want to show?

Nonetheless, Minnesota will be a formidable opponent. The two major acquisitions they made in the off-season, Latrell Sprewell and Sam Cassell, have transformed the Wolves from a solid club to a legitimate championship contender. The franchise has made an amazing comeback from a devastating setback. In 2000, Commissioner David Stern fined the organization $3.5 million and took away five future first-round picks for breaking the spirit of the salary cap rules in re-signing Joe Smith, the former number-one selection in the entire draft. Most observers assumed Minnesota would be stuck for the rest of the decade with a nucleus of Kevin Garnett and interchangeable role players. But Kevin McHale, the vice president of basketball operations, found a way to reload. The Wolves, eliminated in the first round in seven straight years, finally cleared that barrier by defeating the Denver Nuggets in five games. Conventional wisdom holds that by making it past Sacramento, Minnesota will believe it has already accomplished enough this time around. Teams in this situation often let down. But Garnett possesses too much competitive zeal to allow this team to let down. Cassell, who earned two rings for the Rockets in 1994 and 1995, wants his third. Sprewell, who took the Knicks to the Finals in 1999, wants his first.

Containing Garnett, the league's MVP, will be our chief priority. I don't imagine we'll resort to double-teaming him, except perhaps late in the game. Putting another man on him earlier would allow his teammates to set rear picks, freeing their three-point shooters. This is an outstanding jump-shooting team. I do anticipate trying to surprise him with a defender from the blind side when he goes for his familiar spin move. He takes a single hop to his left and then goes right, pointing his right shoulder at the basket. Otherwise we are simply going to have to live with the things

Garnett can do. He hits mid-range turnaround jumpers with consistency and penetrates. I'm confident Karl will neutralize him to some extent at least. Karl missed the first two regular season games against the Wolves, but on March 12, in his first action in nearly three months, he was able to frustrate Garnett, stripping the ball, bodying him up. Garnett is wiry, looking almost like a corpse.

One factor in our favor is that Garnett is exhausted, physically and emotionally. I first noticed the signs late in the regular season. "We've got to push him hard," I told the coaching staff, "so that in fourth quarters, he's forced to struggle." Minnesota, trying to claim the number-one seed, rode him hard in the final weeks. I've tried over the years to rest my starters as much as possible heading into the playoffs, though on one occasion the strategy resulted in a confrontation with Phil Harrison, Shaq's stepfather, who sat on the bench the whole fourth quarter. I was walking off the court in San Antonio after a loss in the final game of my first season with the Lakers. The game meant nothing, the number-one seed long secured.

I was blindsided by Harrison. "You blew the game," he said.

"Look," I told him, "I want to rest my players for the playoffs."

Sprewell will also be a focal point of our defense. On the open floor he is one of the most dangerous players in the game, slashing to the hoop or pulling up for a mid-range jumper. He also possesses three-point range. Sprewell has gone to great lengths to repair his reputation since the infamous choking episode in 1997 with P. J. Carlesimo, his coach at Golden State. Sprewell was suspended for the rest of the season. The incident came as a surprise to many in the league who never perceived him as a true malcontent. Now at the age of thirty-three, he is a respected team leader who competes with tremendous spirit. Normally keeping Cassell in check would be another important component. He shoots with unreserved confidence from the perimeter, and goes coast to coast. But Cassell, an All-Star for the first time this season, has been hobbled by an injured hip and back, and it seems obvious he won't be near 100 percent for this series. He might score his usual twenty points but he will not be healthy enough to play the full-court pressure defense that teams like to deploy against us. If Flip Saunders, the Minnesota coach, leaves him in for his offense, we must make him pay at the other end.

If Cassell is sidelined, what will Flip do? Will he put in Darrick Martin, the journeyman? Or will he resort to a small lineup, with Garnett at the point? Either way they will miss Troy Hudson, the lead guard who averaged 23.5 points against us in last year's playoffs. Hudson played in only twenty-nine games this season. Still, their bench is more than adequate. Backup guard Fred Hoiberg is a player we've coveted for years, an ideal fit for the triangle. He can move without the ball, catch it, and then shoot without putting it on the floor. Mark Madsen, a backup center, played the three prior seasons in LA before signing with Minnesota as a free agent. I felt bad we couldn't keep Mark, but the choice was between him and Slava, who possesses more all-around skills. Mark is a high energy guy, a rugged rebounder, who can change the complexion of a game without scoring a single point. Wally Szczerbiak, a swingman, has been injured for much of the year but is a dangerous scorer when he's on. I would vote for McHale as executive of the year, except for the questionable acquisition of former Clipper center Michael Olowokandi, the first pick overall in the 1998 NBA Draft. A lot of pundits were high on Olowokandi, including Jerry Krause. "He'll be as good, if not better than Duncan," he told his coaches. Jerry can fall so deeply in love with certain players that he loses any connection with reality. Then again, Jerry could say anything he wanted about Olowokandi. He wasn't the one making the pick.

I feel very good about our chances. Minnesota captured the first three games during the regular season, but in two of them we were missing key players. In late March, with Karl approaching top form, the Lakers returned the favor, 90–73, at Staples. Kobe scored thirty-five points. Shaq added twenty-two, and pulled down eighteen boards. The defense was magnificent, holding Minnesota to 31 percent from the field. There seems to be no reason we can't produce the same type of inspired effort in this series. The players, feeding off their comeback triumph over the Spurs, appear to sense the same opportunity, especially Kobe. Kobe has not been a very good practice player since maybe my second or third season here. There have been times when his practice habits have been more destructive than instructive: Kobe seemed interested mainly in finding another player to challenge him. The sessions turned into one-on-one battles over manhood instead of exercises in polishing team concepts. But this week he has displayed a whole new level of commitment. He's been relentless about making sure his teammates pay attention to the coaching staff. Maybe he realizes that ultimately, after the incident in Colorado, the feud with Shaq, and the conflicts with me, there will be another happy ending in Hollywood after all.

May 21
Minneapolis

The crowd was going nuts. With three minutes left in the third quarter, their dear Wolves were even at sixty-seven with the dreaded Lakers. Maybe the victory over Sacramento was just the start. Maybe there would be many more nights to celebrate in the days and weeks ahead. I was concerned. This was a game we could not allow to slip away. The Wolves would only start to gain even more confidence, their energy fully restored. "We've just got to go out there with a strong run," I told the guys. "This team has still got to be tired from the other night. Stay strong, and we'll get them." It is generally assumed that a team mounting a rally is in better position to win the game, but the opposite is often the case. The team that has been trailing for most of the way has to expend a tremendous amount of energy to catch up. Yet climbing the mountain is only the first step. It means nothing if the same effort can't be sustained.

The strong run came. Fish nailed a three, then another three, and then Kareem hit one. Just like that, the lead was nine. Minnesota cut it to only two with about four minutes left, but Fish hit another bomb, his fourth in five attempts, to put the game away. Fish finished with fourteen. Our ball movement was excellent, resulting in twenty-nine assists on thirty-seven field goals. I usually feel pretty good when we finish with about twenty-five to thirty assists in a game. Shaq was overpowering, with twenty-seven points, eighteen rebounds, and four blocks. Minnesota kept sending in a different big—Madsen, Olowokandi, Ervin Johnson, even Oliver Miller—but nobody could stop Shaquille. Fouling him wasn't effective, either. He converted nine of eleven free throws, reminiscent of the Portland playoff game four years ago. What happened this time? Well, a man named Dennis Hans e-mailed Mitch, pointing out that Shaq needed to revert back to the method he learned from his former shooting instructor, Ed Palubinskas. During the Houston series Shaq had worked with University of Houston coach Tom

Penders. "Whoever has been tinkering with Shaq's shot," Hans wrote, "has made a mistake because now he's combining orthodox things with the unorthodoxy he previously learned." Mitch handed the e-mail to me, and I gave it to Shaq, who apparently read it on the plane. At long last has this problem finally been solved? Of course not. I've seen Shaq experiment with many theories. I have my own theory. It's called luck.

MAY 23
Open skies

I warned them.

"You guys have been in this situation before," I said during practice. "You remember what happened a few years ago in Phoenix."

"Phoenix was entirely different," Kobe interjected. "We were up 3–0."

That was not the point. The point was that this team let down in a playoff game, and that was inexcusable. I was determined it would not happen again. In Game 4 of the 2000 Western Conference Semifinals, the Suns coasted 117–98. At halftime, they led 71–48. "I don't care how much you guys *think* you remember," I continued. "This Minnesota team has got a lot of pride. They're an emotional team. We can't let them get any momentum."

I warned them, and yet it didn't make the least bit of difference. The Wolves came out with tremendous energy in Game 2 tonight, squaring the series, 89–71, matching the Lakers' all-time playoff low. To me, it seemed like our players underestimated the Wolves, perceiving Garnett, MVP or not, as a mere adolescent, not the mature, composed man he's become in this, his ninth season. I am frustrated. This was another opportunity that slipped away. "When you get that second game on the road," I told the guys in the locker room afterward, "you can really squelch a team. Now we're going to be in a series."

Cassell, who sat out the fourth quarter in Game 1, played only the first forty-three seconds, but Minnesota compensated adequately with Martin, who came through with a career night—fifteen points, six assists, and zero turnovers in thirty-six minutes. "Wasn't this the kid, about ten years ago," I asked my coaches, "who wanted to make a name for himself in Vancouver by guarding Michael at the end of the game?" The same kid, they said. Michael made him pay. Tonight we didn't. Martin, who spent part of the year with the Sioux Falls franchise in the CBA, will never be a star, but I've always contended that everybody at this level is capable of bringing something to the court. Otherwise they wouldn't be here. When a team loses a top-notch player who would typically attempt about fifteen to twenty shots per game, all that means is that someone else will take those shots, and in many cases he's going to score. It may not be at the same level of proficiency, but the difference will not be severe. Unless there is a complete breakdown, which is rare in playoff basketball, every game will be winnable in the last five or six minutes. The substitute may bring a physical presence, an infusion of energy, something the star could not. In this case, with Martin in the lineup, the Wolves applied full-court pressure, taking valuable seconds off the twenty-four-second clock before we were able to initiate our offense.

Minnesota was also very successful at setting hard back picks on our forwards and centers, which freed their three-point shooters. Karl tried to run through one pick, set by Martin, and was tossed from the game. The officials lost control, issuing seven technicals in the last quarter. No matter. I am confident the Wolves will not profit in the long run from trying to turn this series into a physical affair. The aggressiveness may have worked in Game 2, but our guys know how to play this brand of basketball. Shaquille is almost impervious to contact: he is pounded and punished more than any player in the game today, maybe ever. Karl, an unbelievable specimen, is a master at throwing his body around, while Gary and Kobe can bang pretty well for guards. The only true bruiser on the Minnesota squad is Madsen, but he's not going to score. To endure long stretches in a physical contest, teams need players on the floor who can also put up points.

Shaquille was ineffective, scoring only fourteen. I wasn't quite sure what was wrong with him. Perhaps it was the short break since Game 1 on Friday. I've always believed that one of the reasons the Lakers raised their level of play in the postseason was Shaq's ability to rest between games. In the regular season, we might play four games in five nights, a grueling stretch that exacts a heavy toll on his body. There is no perfect solution. I suppose I could limit his minutes in the winter months, but his presence is invaluable, and if a player doesn't see at least thirty-five minutes of action, he becomes rusty. The game has certainly changed. In my day the centers stayed on the floor until maybe the last few minutes of the half, running, essentially, a straight line from one basket to the other. This saved a tremendous amount of wear and tear. In one season, Wilt averaged—*averaged*—forty-eight minutes a game. That will never happen again. I shouldn't put the entire blame on Shaq. Minnesota closed the entry angles extremely well, making it very difficult for us to feed Shaq in his favorite spots.

On offense our strategy since I took over this team has been to establish Shaquille first and switch the emphasis to Kobe in the second half. If defenses try to guard Shaq straight up, he will dominate. I don't care who the defender is—Ewing, Robinson, Olajuwon, Mutombo, anybody. If defenses pack the lane, it will open up great looks for our three-point shooters. In the second half, when Shaq may tire a bit, Kobe will break down the defense through penetration. Today, however, the early emphasis was Kobe, who scored nineteen in the first half. This was not the plan, which greatly concerned me. "This is the absolute wrong way to attack a team," I told the guys during a timeout. What's wrong with Kobe going off early? A lot, actually. It becomes tougher to get Shaq involved, to develop his rhythm. Also, if Kobe assumes the brunt of the scoring in the first half, how do we attack the defense in the second? With Shaquille? I don't think so. The opposition will put him on the line. Tonight he was six for fourteen. In this series Minnesota will rotate three or four defenders, able to waste six fouls apiece. Keep going to Kobe? That isn't so easy. Eventually the opponent will plug the lanes, like the Wolves did tonight. Kobe scored only eight points in the second half.

May 25
Los Angeles

In Game 2, we tried to force the ball into Shaquille without the corner being properly filled. As a result the Wolves packed the high side, forcing Shaq out of position, too deep behind the backboard. Yesterday in practice we worked on executing the triangle on the weak side, allowing Shaq to move across the lane. The key is patience, waiting for him to find the spot where he can best attack. Another priority was finding more opportunities for Gary, who scored only eight points on Sunday. Gary will never be a focal point in this offense—he left that role back in Seattle—but he can't be a complete bystander, either. Some players need early involvement to maintain their focus for the whole game. Gary is one of those players, and because he is not a spot-up shooter, he has to dribble, to play with the ball a little to make something happen for himself. If it does, if he scores, say, eight, ten early points, he will settle in, and the pressure will be off for the rest of the night. He doesn't have to think, "where am I going to get *mine?*"

Tonight he got his, scoring fourteen of our first eighteen points, leading us to a 24–17 advantage after one quarter. I was happy for Gary. He knew this season would be about sacrifice, but it turned out to be much tougher for him than he expected, than *we* expected, and his problems only accelerated in the playoffs. He sat out a couple of fourth quarters in the Houston series, and went on that famous rant after Parker torched him in the first two games in San Antonio. Now at least, this was a moment for him, perhaps to mollify the cynics who have been on his case for months. Meanwhile Kobe was scoreless in the first half, attempting only two shots, but this was more like the way we wanted to operate. He proceeded to score eleven points in each of the third and fourth periods, including back-to-back three-pointers, to give us an insurmountable seventeen-point lead. Minnesota went to Hack-a-Shaq in the fourth, but the strategy backfired. Shaq made six of his last nine foul shots, after going two for his first thirteen. We prevailed, 100–89, to take a 2–1 series lead.

Darrick Martin, the unlikely star of Game 2, did not score in eighteen minutes and recorded only one assist, prompting Flip to use Garnett at the point. Martin simply was not prepared for the intensity of a road playoff game. The challenge is entirely different than playing in front of familiar, friendly faces. To me it seemed like he was fouled on a few occasions but didn't get the call. That's usually the case with subs. The key is to score even when fouled, which will establish credibility. The next time they might get the benefit of the doubt. Subs will also have to absorb more contact, the defender figuring he can get away with more aggressive play.

MAY 27
Los Angeles

This afternoon before heading to Staples for Game 4, I returned a call from an old friend. Did this friend have a secret to containing Garnett? Garnett had twenty-two points, eleven rebounds and seven assists in Game 3. Or would this friend offer advice about how to set better screens? Or did he want tickets? None of the above. This old friend knows very little about basketball, everything about life. His name is Roshi Kwong. The roshi and I met in the mid-1990s after he heard about my book *Sacred Hoops*, which touched on the relationship between basketball and Buddhism. He has taught throughout the United States and travels every summer to Iceland and Poland to lead retreats, in which, for ten, twelve hours a day, he sits and meditates. The subject soon turned to meditation and the breath. He suggested a breathing technique. "Remember," he said, "the breath controls the mind as the mind controls the body."

Shouldn't I be entirely occupied with basketball in the hours leading up to such a pivotal contest? Lose this one, and the series would be even again, forcing us to win another game in their building. Without denigrating its importance, to me at least, everything doesn't revolve around the game tonight or the game after that. I see myself as fairly well balanced, though that wasn't always the case. Perhaps winning nine championships has removed some of the extra pressures other coaches experience. Perhaps winning nine championships has helped me realize that the Larry O'Brien Trophy is not the key to finding real peace. I am not interested in Roshi Kwong giving me a tip for Game 4. I am interested in him giving me a tip to lead a happier, more fulfilled, existence. I thanked him, wished him well on his journey ahead, and continued my own.

The proper plan of attack worked again tonight. Kobe, returning from another court hearing in Colorado, acted as a playmaker in the first half, a scorer in the second. His seven points in a row helped us close the third quarter with a 19–6 run. This team has done a marvelous job this series of ending quarters, one of the keys to victory in playoff basketball. We finished the first quarter with a 7–2 spurt, the second, 15–5. One way to close well is to force the opponent into the penalty phase as quickly as possible and then determine the most effective method of capitalizing. For us that usually means giving Kobe the room to operate. He will more often than not get the calls and the nearly automatic two points. Another reason for our late-quarter success has been a change in the substitution patterns. During the regular season, I put the second unit in the game with a minute or two left in the opening stanza, allowing the subs to develop a rhythm heading into the second. I applied the same strategy at the end of the third quarter. In the playoffs, however, I leave at least four of my starters on the floor for the entire first and third quarters, inserting the reserves at the start of the second and fourth quarters. After a long rest the first unit returns to finish the second and fourth quarters. The opening three minutes of the third quarter will often determine the outcome. If a team falls behind in the first half, there is always a chance to watch video, to make the proper adjustments. In the second half that same opportunity is not available. Adjustments can be discussed only during timeouts.

Shaq was relentless on the boards again. His scoring during the playoffs is always a vital factor, but his rebounding and intimidating presence in the lane are even more significant. He finished with nineteen rebounds tonight, his fifth game in a row with at least 16. He puts his full attention to the task in critical games. Also coming up big was Karl, who nearly recorded a triple-double—twelve points, eleven rebounds, and eight assists. We're not expecting huge numbers from him, but if Karl can make Garnett play defense, and force him to work hard on the offensive end, it will be a real plus. Garnett scored twenty-eight points, but Cassell was able to play for only five minutes. I feel bad for Flip. Martin might have another game or even two, but he won't consistently give the Wolves what Sam provided the whole season, scoring and on-court leadership. The final score was 92–85. Three down, one to go.

Midway through the third quarter, I was assessed a technical, and all I did was ask Jack Nies, the lead official, a very innocent question: "Would you take a look, Jack, at how Garnett travels the next time he makes that move?" What's so horrible with that? I was cited, perhaps only because I had the nerve to . . . stand up. The officials let other coaches routinely roam the sidelines without any repercussions. But when it comes to me, who normally sits stoically, standing up was perceived as a threatening gesture. There was a time in pro basketball when coaches were not expected to leave their seats during play. If they did, the refs glared at them, and they would sit down again. In the '70s coaches—Tommy Heinsohn of the Celtics comes to mind—started to influence the game with their imposing presence, walking from the baseline to half-court to protest a call or shout instructions to their players. These days they're confined to a designated area, the coaches' box, but many ignore the restriction, a violation the refs rarely enforce. In the Houston series, Van Gundy left the box constantly.

May 29
Minneapolis

We returned to the Twin Cities for the last time in this series, I hoped. Although after our performance in Game 5 tonight, I'm not so sure. I thought we gave a pitiful effort in Game 2, but looking back, that was our "A" game compared to this showing. There were signs earlier in the day. When I left the coaches' room to bring tickets to the box office, I noticed there was an unusual amount of horseplay going on in the locker room. Boys will be boys, I told myself, continuing with my business. But when I returned a few minutes later, the players were still goofing off. Some coaches would come down pretty hard on this kind of behavior. That has never been my way. I believe players have every right to be in a jovial mood before a game, even a playoff game. But this display seemed to be crossing the line. So I went inside. "Guys," I said, "we've got to start getting ready. We better get our minds in the right spot."

Their minds were in the right spot, or so it appeared. Late in the first quarter, our lead was ten, the Wolves obviously feeling the pressure of elimination. The longer they trailed, the more desperate they would become, the more out of character. But we didn't hold on long enough to force that desperation. Minnesota proved that it, too, can close quarters, ending the second with a 13–0 run to assume a 46–40 lead. Spearheaded by eleven straight points from Sprewell, the Wolves seized a sixteen-point advantage with six minutes left in the game. There was another run, from us this time, which sliced the lead to six. Kobe was heating up just in time, and our defensive pressure was forcing them into poor scoring opportunities.

The game was suddenly winnable . . . if only the refs would have given us a chance to win it. Down 86–80 with just under three minutes to go, Kobe penetrated and kicked the ball to Gary, who passed it to Fish at the top of the key. While Fish was loading up for the shot, Shaq was signaled for a three-second violation. "Let the game happen," we told the official. I have no direct evidence, but I bet Flip was yelling "three seconds" in the ref's ear. Hoiberg converted a three-point play on the next possession, and our momentum was gone. The Wolves hung on, 98–96, forcing a Game 6 in Los Angeles.

Too often the three-second call in professional basketball is wrongly applied. The rule was originally adopted in the 1930s to stop Adolph Rupp's University of Kentucky bigs from setting rough picks in the lane. The problem is that back then the lane was six feet wide. The lane is sixteen feet wide now. To account for this extended space, players should be allowed to reside in the paint for up to five seconds. In spirit the rule is designed to stop players from parking in the lane or making a series of moves without delivering the basketball. But in reality Shaq is frequently cited when he's simply sliding from one position to another, which can take as long as three seconds. In this particular incident, Shaq was most definitely not violating the rule's spirit.

Nonetheless, we did not lose this game because of one call that didn't go our way. We lost this game for numerous reasons. One reason was our tendency to do far too much dribbling, a common error in today's pro game. The dribble, in fact, has replaced the pass as the primary means to move the ball toward the basket, to generate shots. Sadly the beautiful, rhythmic, around-the-horn ball movement practiced by championship teams in the '60s, '70s, and '80s is increasingly rare. For years it has been true that once the offense executes the fourth pass in any given possession, the defense will be on its heels, out of position. But the kids in the playgrounds today focus almost exclusively on the dribble, not the pass. There is a whole treatise about the small man being able to do so many things off the dribble that it's almost supplanted the dunk as the single most spectacular moment in basketball, Allen Iverson being the player who, perhaps more than anyone, has helped foster this movement.

Following the Game I went to the press room. I hate this ritual, especially after a loss. There is so little of any real substance that can be discussed at this moment. I usually can't wait for those magic words, "one last question." Tonight the last question came from a familiar voice in the back of the room. "How do you think the team will respond?" the person asked. It was Kobe, who would be next in the line of fire. "They'll win," I said. "They'll win." Even so, I wonder, what will be the cost? That is why I badly wanted to win this one. I've become concerned about how many minutes Karl is putting on his forty-year-old body. His knee is far from 100 percent. I don't think you can ever afford to play any extra games in the playoffs. Over the years this Lakers squad has been keyed for almost every playoff contest, winning twelve close-out games in a row since dropping Game 5 of the 2000 Finals at Indiana. I don't care about the streak. I care that we have to play a game we should have avoided.

MAY 31
Los Angeles

There wasn't much giddiness in the locker room before tonight's game. The boys were not being boys. The boys were being determined young men, total professionals, anxious to end this series. Perhaps the most determined was Shaquille, who had complained he didn't receive enough touches in Game 5. Shaq, who took only eleven shots in the game, has gone public with this same issue on numerous occasions throughout the years. This time, when Kurt relayed Shaq's comments to the coaching staff, Tex responded, "Let's count them." I don't recall counting before. The tally showed that, in fact, there were at least seven or eight instances in which Shaq did not punch in the lane and ask for the ball. If a player posting up wants the basketball, he doesn't receive it automatically. He must make a move to secure position in front of his defender and present a target. Shaq didn't do that. He came out of the lane or gave up on the sequence. There's a passive-aggressiveness to Shaq's behavior. He says, "you've got to bring me the ball." Yet in reality, he should be securing the offensive rebound, or be more active. "Show everybody how aggressive you are by demanding the ball," I've told him many times. "Be aggressive in the lane so that it's obvious to your teammates that you want the basketball. They'll give you the ball."

Tonight from the tip-off, it was obvious: Shaq wanted the ball and he was going to get it. He was also active defensively—too active, actually. With about two minutes left in the second quarter, the Lakers ahead 45–40, Shaq was signaled for his third foul. Everyone in the building assumed I would yank him. But without any real offensive force to guard, I gambled that he could restrain his game sufficiently to stay on the floor for two lousy minutes and still be relatively effective. Minnesota is not the kind of team to keep pushing the action into the middle of the lane. Furthermore two of the calls against Shaq were highly questionable. I felt the referees owed him one, which is generally how it works in this league. Maybe so, but not this time. A minute later, bumping Sprewell near the corner, he was cited for his fourth. It was another bogus call in one of the worst officiated quarters I could remember. There were twenty-three fouls, fourteen against us. Kobe, with three, was also in foul trouble. A game this physical takes on a whole new identity. Players start recklessly throwing their bodies around to draw yet another foul. My main problem with the second quarter was that it was being officiated much more tightly than the first. In this game for some inexplicable reason, the referees altered their philosophy between periods. I don't think Ed F. Rush, one of the officials, should be permitted to work this far into the playoffs. He has a leg injury, and he can barely run down the court. As we headed toward the locker room, I had never heard LA fans so angry with the officiating.

In the locker room the guys were upset. "Forget about the officials," I told them. "You have to rise above it." They did exactly that. Yet early in the fourth, the game was deadlocked at sixty-eight. With each passing moment, the Wolves, even without Cassell again, gained more confidence. A return trip to Minnesota seemed possible, too possible. But then Kareem Rush took over. Bill Bertka, the former assistant coach here, had a phrase for whenever an unheralded player rose to the occasion. He called it *paying the rent*. In the fourth quarter of the biggest game of his life, Kareem paid the rent.

His first three-pointer put us ahead 71–68. His second extended the lead to eight. His third blew the game open. I am very proud of Kareem. In training camp we challenged him to become serious about basketball. He accepted the challenge. In practices he went all out during intense three-on-three battles when he was teamed with Luke Walton and Brian Cook against Slava, Fox, and Bryon Russell. Throughout the season, I played him extensive minutes in the fourth quarter to prepare for precisely this moment. There were still other unresolved issues: Would he step into big shots? Would his teammates respect him enough to get him the ball at the right time? Would he attain the credibility with the refs to get calls? He looked overwhelmed against the Spurs but tonight he hit six of seven from behind the arc. Slava, meanwhile, hit four of four from the field. Because of them, there will be no Game 7.

After the game there was a ceremony on the floor to honor the Lakers, the new 2003–4 Western Conference champions. A few of the players stayed to receive the hardware, but I went to the locker room. This was not the particular piece of hardware we set out to claim for ourselves back in October. Some teams may revel in such an accomplishment, but for this franchise, this year especially, it's either a banner or bust. I probably should stop for a few moments and take it all in but I'm too concerned. This team hasn't played well since Game 4, a trend that must be reversed immediately. We stunk in Game 5, survived in Game 6. There are six days between now and Game 1 of the Finals. I hope that's enough time.

ELEVEN

THE FINAL ROUND: DETROIT

JUNE 5
Los Angeles

We made it to June, to the only destination that matters, the NBA Finals. Eleven months ago this moment was inevitable, with two Hall of Famers in pursuit of their fourth title, and two others their first. But one month ago, down two games to none to the league's defending champions, this moment was inconceivable; we were a team without a soul or, in the opinion of many observers, a chance. But here we are, four games away from the sport's ultimate achievement. The final four will be the most difficult four. Our opponent, we learned this week, will be the Detroit Pistons, who outdueled the Indiana Pacers in a low-scoring, hard-fought six-game series. For me the irony of facing the Pistons is inescapable. In 1989 and 1990, the Pistons beat the Bulls in the Eastern Conference Finals. They did what no other team could do—stopped Michael Jordan. Finally in 1991, when we circumvented the "Jordan Rules," fully adopting the concept of team play, the Bulls swept the Pistons in four games. In Game 4, the Bad Boys were more ill-behaved than ever, walking off the court before the buzzer sounded. To this day that display remains the epitome of poor sportsmanship. Chuck Daly, their coach, was very upset with his team's conduct. Now, thirteen years later, I will be taking another playoff team to Detroit, in all likelihood my last.

Long gone are Bill Laimbeer, Rick Mahorn, Isiah Thomas, and the rest of the group that won back-to-back championships, but one of its leaders, the former guard Joe Dumars, now head of basketball operations, has done an excellent job in putting the current squad together. Dumars has not been timid. Within days of bowing to the New Jersey Nets in the 2003 Eastern Conference Finals, he fired Rick Carlisle, replacing him with Larry Brown. Carlisle had led the team to back-to-back fifty-win campaigns. In February Dumars pulled off the season's most important trade, acquiring power forward Rasheed Wallace in a three-team deal. The Pistons, 34–22 at the time, closed at 20–6, and then beat the Bucks (five games) and Nets (seven) before they took on Indiana. Against the Nets, they showed tremendous resiliency, winning Game 6 on the road after a heartbreaking triple-overtime defeat in Detroit. This Detroit unit resembles the one from years ago, particularly on the defensive end. In March the Pistons held their opponents under seventy points in an NBA-record five straight games, the streak broken when the Nets' Aaron Williams tipped one in with one second to go during an 89–71 loss. During the year teams averaged only 84.3 points against them, on 41.3 percent shooting.

Even so our players do not appear to be affording them the respect they deserve, not yet anyway. Neither do the writers, who act as if the Lakers have already won the title. The only debate is whether we will sweep the Pistons or require five games to make it official. This kind of overconfidence is unsettling, especially when I believe it is totally misguided. Sure the Eastern Conference has been outmatched in the Finals since the Bulls' reign ended in 1998, winning only six of twenty-six games. Not a single series has gone the distance. Sure, the battle between the Pistons and Pacers was difficult to watch. But the Pistons are very athletic and well coached. They play together the right way.

The biggest difficulty we may encounter with the Pistons is our lack of familiarity. We knew the Rockets, the Spurs, and the Wolves extremely well, facing each team in the last three weeks of the regular season. There were no surprises. We haven't faced the Pistons since way back in November, when we split the two contests, and that was before they acquired Rasheed Wallace. Our players need to grasp a team viscerally to really get their minds wrapped around the challenge. I don't mean their opponents' cosmetic games: Does he prefer going to his left? Does he panic when double-teamed? Does he easily lose confidence in his shot if he misses two or three in a row? I mean their *internal* games. What can we do to get inside their heads, to irritate them, to push them away from their comfort zone? The answers do not come from dissecting video or poring over scouting reports. The answers come on the hardwood, in a guy's face, seeing how he reacts or doesn't react.

The pressure of attempting to visualize this opponent is disturbing my sleep. Who is the key to their club? In every prior playoff series, the key was obvious: Yao/Duncan or Parker/Garnett. But in this series there is no clear-cut star. Is the key Chauncey Billups, the point guard who torched us in both regular season games this year? If it is, do I consider putting Kobe on him instead of on their talented shooting guard, Richard Hamilton? I didn't like the way Gary guarded Billups. Early in his career Billups, the third overall pick in the 1997 draft by the Celtics after only two years at University of Colorado, displayed wonderful athleticism but was too selfish for a point guard. Rick Pitino dumped him and he wasn't the last coach to be fed up with this kid. Billups shuttled from team to team, five in only six years. He appears settled at last, but is still prone to too much individual play. "This isn't a Larry Brown prototype point guard," I told the team. "Brown likes Mark Jackson, Eric Snow, guys who aren't thinking about scoring. They may score but they think about running the offense and feeding their teammates first. Billups is thinking about scoring first. So we have to make him do things that take him away from the team game." I'm not convinced that Billups is the key. In Game 1 of the Indiana series, he scored seventeen points in the first half, yet the Pistons trailed, 48–41.

Or is Hamilton the key? Tex believes he might be, although I regard him as essentially a perimeter shooter. Hamilton, who helped Connecticut win a national championship, is very similar to Reggie Miller, a high-energy guy who runs around the court looking for screens. The knock on Hamilton has been his toughness. A few years ago, when he played with the Wizards, he scored about fifteen against us in the first half but wasn't very productive in the second after Kobe started to body him up. "I just don't think this kid is physical enough," Michael told me afterward. In 2002, the

Wizards traded Hamilton to Detroit in a package that landed Jerry Stackhouse. I asked Kobe today about Hamilton. The two played high school ball against each other in Pennsylvania. "I've been kicking his ass for ten years," he said.

Or do we need to focus on the Wallaces, Rasheed and Ben? They are not related, except in degrees of intensity. Other teams have been able to neutralize him, but Rasheed, the longtime Blazer, has always been a very effective post-up player against the Lakers. In the 2000 Western Conference Finals, he was probably Portland's most dangerous threat. Two years ago we put Shaq on him late in the game, which we might have to do again if Karl struggles. Rasheed has real anger-management problems, which have been well documented, but he has behaved himself in Detroit so far. Ben, meanwhile, has shown great progress. When he first entered the league with Washington, I figured he was another Bo Outlaw— wonderful physique, woeful touch. He turned out to possess more all-around skills than Outlaw, becoming a stalwart on the all-defensive team, one of the league's premier rebounders and shot-blockers. Yet at six-foot-nine and 240 pounds, Wallace is too small to contain Shaquille. What will Brown do? Will Wallace play behind Shaq? He's not that type of defender. Maybe Brown will put Rasheed in front of Shaq, and have Ben come over from the back side, similar to San Antonio's approach. Brown and Popovich, his former assistant, are good friends. Will Brown call him for tips? Brown is opposed to the double-team and will try instead to draw offensive fouls on Shaq, a strategy that worked well in their victory over us in November. Shaq picked up three quick fouls in the first quarter, and played only thirty-one minutes. Wallace has always rebounded well against Shaq. In the November game playing thirty-three minutes, he outrebounded Shaq, fifteen to ten. Because Wallace doesn't have a big body and is very athletic, he can maneuver around him.

The other Detroit starter is small forward Tayshaun Prince, the former University of Kentucky star. The Lakers brought Prince in for workouts twice during draft week in 2002, but wound up with Kareem Rush when he surprisingly slipped down the list. Prince has a strange shooting motion but he's so lanky that small defenders have trouble handling him. He plays like a guard and is quick enough to cover Kobe.

Their bench is also very accomplished. At six-foot-seven and 245 pounds, Corliss Williamson, a.k.a. the Big Nasty, creates a lot of space in the post and finishes well. Mehmet Okur, their seven-foot backup from Turkey, is a solid outside shooter. Another seven-footer, Elden Campbell, the former Laker, can also contribute. Last summer we thought about signing Elden to back up Shaq, but went after Horace instead. Elden has been in the league for fourteen years, but is still only thirty-five.

Perhaps the key is Brown. In his first year or two with a new team, he is able to motivate his players to elevate their games far beyond prior levels, a sign of an excellent coach. Eventually, however, Brown wears his team down with his persistence in playing the game "the right way." He is never satisfied. After a certain period, the players stop listening to him. Doug Moe, his close friend and the former coach of the Denver Nuggets, told me a story that captures the essence of Larry Brown. "It was the start of the season," Moe recalled. "I was in Boston one night after a game, and Larry called me after his game. We talked for about a half hour. He wanted to trade this guy, he wanted to trade that guy, and I ended up talking him down, mollifying him. I hung up the phone and thought to myself, 'What the hell am I doing? My team is 2–4. His team is 6–1!' " I look forward to going against a Larry Brown team. He stresses sharing the ball, setting picks, boxing out, applying pressure on the ball and passers, and contesting shots. Our guys will have to execute better than ever.

Or ultimately, perhaps the key isn't any one player or even their esteemed future Hall of Fame coach. Perhaps the key to the Detroit team has been right in front of me all along, its defense. None of their players, it seems, believe they have to score twenty points for the team to prevail. Everyone seems comfortable with the game flowing naturally, dictated by their collective tempo, by their aggressive, intense defense. One night the leading scorer might be Billups, another Hamilton, another Rasheed Wallace. But on every night, their athleticism will result in turnovers, runouts, and more often than not, victories. The two Wallaces are as quick as any big men who have ever played the game. Why is it so important to identify the key, the soul, of the opposing team? It's important because if you can manage to disrupt their key and create a negative mood, the featured player and the team in general may quickly lose confidence. Suddenly, the other players might become desperate about getting the star on track, and he may force shots, taking the team out of its regular offensive flow. Guys may start to bitch at one another, and then you've got an opponent on the ropes. Professional players maintain their composure better than high school or college squads but are still susceptible to breakdowns.

Heading into Game 1, my most serious concern is Karl. In Game 6 of the Minnesota series, he collided with Fish, injuring his right knee, the same one he hurt in December. This was precisely why I was so disturbed about giving away Game 5. There could have been no Game 6, no collision. At first there didn't seem to be cause for too much concern, but Karl's knee ballooned on him overnight. If that weren't disconcerting enough, Karl, who believes our medical staff misdiagnosed the earlier injury, went to see his own doctor. The guy aspirated thirty-five cubic centimenters of fluid from Karl's right knee. Vitti was bothered. Draining the knee should be the last resort, he said. Karl's knee became sore and impossible to bend. Suddenly the absence of Horace Grant looms larger than ever. Horace could have played an important role against the Wallaces, but without Karl, Slava will be the only big to assist Shaquille. Brian Cook isn't seasoned enough for this level of intensity. Karl isn't the only one ailing. Fish underwent therapy for a tear of the medial collateral cartilage in his right knee, which he suffered in Game 5, while Devean has a sore left knee and a troubling ankle. From Tuesday through Friday, there were only nine healthy bodies available for practice. I'm also concerned because the last time the Lakers went against a Larry Brown–coached team in Game 1 of the Finals, we lost to the Sixers in overtime 107–101. Brown is excellent at coming up with a game plan.

JUNE 7
Los Angeles

No wonder I was concerned. From the Rasheed Wallace three-pointer that opened the game to the lock-down defense that closed it, the Pistons were in control for most of the way in Game 1 last night, prevailing 87–75. I watched Karl very carefully, and it was clear he couldn't slide laterally to defend the screen roll, which was such a big part of our comeback against San Antonio, and he was also ineffective going to the basket. He was at least able to irritate Rasheed, who committed two fouls in the first quarter and played only twenty-nine minutes. The real factor was Chauncey Billups, who completely outplayed Gary, scoring twenty-two points, eight in the first quarter. Detroit also benefited from a big game by Prince at both ends. Prince hit a couple of incredible shots, including a three in front of our bench, finishing with eleven, but more important, kept Kobe from going off. Kobe scored twenty-five, but needed twenty-seven field-goal attempts. Instead of trying to drive to the hoop, Kobe settled for difficult shots with Prince in his face. He simply did not know how to attack this kid. More than a few times it looked like Prince hit his arm, but there was no call. Our only other player in double figures was Shaquille, with thirty-four, on thirteen of sixteen. We probably should have kept pounding it into Shaq because Brown was going to keep playing him straight up. Shaq could have scored forty, maybe forty-five. The other starters—Karl, Devean, and Gary—*combined* for twelve points. The Pistons dictated the tempo, dragging out almost every possession to the last possible moment. Their bench outscored us 19–4, led by Williamson with seven in only eleven minutes. Fish was one for nine, Kareem zero for three. "This is going to be a long series," I told the coaching staff.

The players don't seem to feel the same sense of urgency. They just lost Game 1 of the NBA Finals, yet they're still not giving the Pistons enough respect. They lost Game 1 in 2001 and came right back to win four straight, three in Philadelphia. Why, they figure, shouldn't they be able to do that again? The way they see it, Kobe won't have another poor shooting game, and Prince won't bank in another off-balanced jumper to beat the shot clock. I realized I needed to shake them up. Going through the video of Game 1 this morning, I found a way. There was a scene of Brown, with a camera in the huddle, telling his players that the Lakers weren't guarding anyone. I decided to show this clip to the guys today, running it back four or five times. Brown was absolutely correct. We weren't getting to their shooters. "If you don't get your feet underneath you, we're not coming back here," I told them. What worries me most is that the Pistons defeated us by twelve in our building even though one of their prime threats, Hamilton, scored only twelve, on five of sixteen, and committed six turnovers. What worries Tex most is our offense. "It's about us getting out there and scoring," he said. "I don't know if this team can score enough points."

JUNE 9
Open skies

I've seen it all again in the last twenty-four hours, a microcosm of a season I will never forget, on or off the court. Gazing down from the clouds, trying to retrace the events of last night and this morning with some sense of clarity, I find the exercise too familiar, too painful. I wonder: does this happen in other cities, to other franchises? Do teams come through with a miracle finish and then the very next morning destroy the good vibrations with unnecessary venom? No, of course not. This only happens with the Lakers.

Last night was incredible, Kobe hitting a three-pointer from four feet beyond the arc with 2.1 seconds left to force overtime in Game 2. I called for "what the fuck," the play I learned from Red, who could never remember its name. There are options for everyone on the floor, though Kobe would certainly be the main target. The ball went from Shaq to Luke to Kobe, freeing him to attack against Hamilton, caught on a switch. This was a break. Kobe would have had a tougher look against Prince. Larry Brown was unfairly criticized for failing to foul Shaquille. I would not have fouled Shaq, either. What if he made the first free throw, missed the second, and we secured the rebound, then nailed a three-pointer? Do the math. That would have been a four-point play, and the Pistons might have lost the game right there. In that scenario I would foul only if there were one or two seconds left on the clock. In the overtime we played our best stretch of the first two games. The first basket in overtime is always crucial, even more than the one that breaks a tie heading into the last five minutes of regulation, although the time remaining would be roughly the same. It's purely psychological, as if an entirely new ball game has started, one with even greater tension, the advantage going to the team that strikes first. We struck first with a Shaq dunk fourteen seconds after the tip. For the period we outscored Detroit 10–2, for a 99–91 triumph. The series is magically, mercifully, tied 1–1. Besides Kobe, Luke Walton—seven points, five rebounds, eight assists—came through with a magnificent effort. In the second quarter, he changed the whole complexion of the game.

This morning was incredible as well—incredibly sad. The coaches met first to look at the video, to see how we managed to squander an eleven-point third-quarter lead, almost allowing the Pistons to go up 2–0, a perhaps insurmountable advantage with the next three games in Detroit. Billups had gone off again, for twenty-seven points, including thirteen of fourteen from the line, and Hamilton added twenty-six. The Pistons kept up the pressure while we grew tired. In addition Karl aggravated his injury. To watch him struggle to run up and down the court was difficult. He worked so hard to rebound from the injury in December, and now on the verge of finally achieving his dream of winning an NBA Championship, his body won't permit him to give anything close to his normal 100 percent. The basketball gods can sometimes be most cruel.

Yet even a severely limited Karl Malone has been able to keep Rasheed Wallace from hurting us in the first two games. At one point Vitti told him to go into the locker room to get his knee checked out, but Karl refused. Karl is a true warrior.

The conversation with the coaches in the video session turned to the issue of Shaquille and his defense on screen roll, which was largely ineffective again. "When I'm all done," Tex blurted out, "I'm going to expose this guy as overrated."

"Tex," I immediately shot back, "how can you say those kinds of things? The reason I came here to coach this team was because of Shaq." Tex started to line up his usual litany of anti-Shaqisms—he has terrible footwork, he's not coachable, he can't make free throws, and so on. I continued to defend the big fella, pointing out his outstanding field-goal percentage over the years.

"Yeah," Tex countered, "but those are all dunks."

Finally I added with caution, "you know what I've always said, that Shaq can sense your mood." Sure enough, about forty-five minutes later, with the players now in the room to watch clips of Game 2, I was showing a sequence of Billups hitting a three-pointer off a screen roll late in the third quarter when the incident happened, the one that has darkened the mood of the whole team, and certainly mine.

"I think this is the time you want to step out on Billups," I said to Shaquille. "I think he wants to score at the end of quarters."

I started to show the next sequence when Tex, sitting in the row behind Shaq, interjected: "Phil, hold on a second. I think Shaq wants to say something about that play."

Shaq did not have a comment, except a nasty one directed at Tex. "Why don't you just mind your own business, old man?"

I asked for an explanation.

"Shaq shrugged his shoulders and threw up his hands when you said something," Tex said.

Shaq insulted him again. "I told you to shut the fuck up," he said. "We don't need to hear from you about this shit. Just mind your own business."

Tex said, "This *is* my business."

This was not the first time Shaq and Tex had exchanged words. The poor dynamic between them is almost inevitable. Tex feels Shaq doesn't work hard enough. Shaq feels Tex is too negative. Tex believes in the sound principles of the offense. Shaq believes in the sound principles of *his* offense. But this was by far the worst exchange I could remember, especially given the timing, only hours before heading to Detroit to play the next three games of the NBA Finals.

I sent the players to the practice court, while Tex bolted from the room and went upstairs to his office. "I'm not going on this trip," he said. "I can't do any good." I then tracked down Shaq, who had gone to the locker room, and asked him to apologize to Tex.

"You're not doing the right thing," I told him.

"I know I'm not doing the right thing," he admitted, "but I don't give a fuck. I'm sick of the guy's comments." Soon it was too late to repair the damage, at least here in Los Angeles. We had a plane to catch. Sitting here now, unable to focus on Xs and Os or stopping Chauncey Billups, I wonder if there is anything I could have done or said to defuse the situation. Tex made the trip after all—the other coaches kidded him that he couldn't bear to part with the per diem money—but I keep asking myself if I had failed him, this wonderful eighty-two-year-old man who has meant so much to me, by not defending him more aggressively in front of the whole group.

Why did this happen? Why now? Why after our stirring victory in Game 2? Defending screen rolls is paramount to our success in this series, just as it was against Houston, and especially against San Antonio. If we can't find a comfort zone, in which honest differences of opinion are openly exchanged without hostility, how can we possibly hope to solve our dilemma? Against difficult odds, caused by injuries and implosions, this team has come together in recent months. The only goal we care about is still in range. We can't afford to implode again.

JUNE 11
Detroit

Shaq apologized, finally, at yesterday's afternoon shootaround. He went over to Tex and gave him a big hug. Tex accepted the apology. I hoped this was the end of it; other basketball-related concerns needed to take center stage: How do we free Kobe? How do we stop Billups? How do we get to that magical eighty-five- or ninety-point mark that should spell victory? At the shootaround, I was eager for the guys to take tons of shots. The rims at the Palace differ from the rims at Staples. If the ball skips off the backboard with too much force, it won't drop through the net. I also was closely monitoring the players' activity level. The first game after changing time zones is always the most challenging. On Monday night we arrived at our hotel in suburban Birmingham at about nine-thirty P.M. local time. An hour or so later, there must have been about five hundred people on the roof of the garage across the street, shouting "Let's go Pistons!" Their exuberance is understandable; these fans have had little to cheer about in more than a decade. The kids are sick of hearing the same Bill Laimbeer or Isiah Thomas stories over and over. They want to be able to tell stories of their own, eventually, to their kids.

They will have wonderful stories to tell about Game 3. They will tell how their heroes broke out to an 8–0 lead and never trailed. Their Pistons, if one believes the press, were supposed to be "devastated" by the manner in which they lost Game 2. That is why one has to be very wary of automatically believing the press. If anything it was the Lakers who lost an opportunity in Game 2. Leading by eleven in the third, if we could have coasted to a convincing double-digit victory, we might have been able to put some doubt in the minds of the Detroit players. They would have left town with a split, but also with a reminder that their defense is not impenetrable. But instead they left thinking they should have won both games.

Our critics say this team has a tendency to not always be focused, but there are too many other factors—poor shooting, injuries, the quality of the opposition—that can affect the outcome. Last night, there may have been no lack of effort, yet there certainly was a lack of execution. There was confusion, miscommunication, an inability to read the defense and follow through on basic concepts. Kobe was being forced into crowds, taking off-balance shots. It was embarrassing. Yet as poorly as we competed, we trailed by only seven points at the half. The game was still very winnable. In the fourth, the difference in athleticism between the two teams became glaring and perhaps ominous. The Pistons extended the lead to 20 with an immediate 9–1 run. Every attempt we made to play pressure defense to match their intensity backfired. It got to the point where I told the guys: "Don't even pressure their guards on the perimeter. Get back in a sink defense. We can't afford to get any more fouls called. Play them soft except for the guy on the ball." The change in defense made no difference, only feeding into the perception of the Pistons as the more aggressive team versus the soft Lakers. Detroit was in the penalty phase early in the quarter again and capitalized. The final was 88–68, the lowest point total in Lakers' playoff history. For me this was new and uncomfortable territory. Throughout my coaching career, when my team was 1–1 in the finals, we were always keyed up for the critical Game 3.

Looking at the stat sheet in the locker room, one stat got my attention: the discrepancy in free throw attempts, 30–13 in favor of the Pistons. *Thirty to thirteen!* How does that happen in an NBA Finals game? Were the Pistons that much better than us on defense? Or are they merely profiting from their reputation? Teams recognized for their defensive intensity will often get the benefit of the doubt. There were certainly plenty of questionable no calls, such as when Prince ran under Kobe while he was shooting a jumper and twisted him around. The discrepancy deserves a comment, but what, exactly? If I choose to harp on the refs, I risk sounding like a whiner—perhaps the *New York Post* can dig up that old cartoon from the Bulls-Knicks series—or worse yet, incurring their wrath. Then we might receive even fewer calls. I'm also concerned the players would use the issue as a crutch, picking up technical fouls, which we did far too frequently in the Minnesota series. In my package of notes to the team before the Finals, I wrote: "We have had five consecutive games in which we've been T'd up . . . this has to stop. Regardless of how bad they are, they are not picking on you or us . . . IT'S NOT ABOUT YOU."

Teams establish a tone. If they actively defend, if they work hard, if they force the action, the referees take notice and lend credibility to their effort. In basketball the second foul, the reaction to the initial contact, is the one most often called. Yet at the same time, I have to let the refs know I'm not pleased with this disparity. In yesterday's game the Pistons plugged the lane. As a result we settled for jumpers, including twenty-seven shots from three-point range—more than a third of our total field-goal attempts (74). A jump shot does not force the action.

Wearing a brace, Karl gave another courageous effort tonight, but once again was severely limited—five points and four rebounds in eighteen minutes. I took him out for good halfway through the third quarter. I played Luke a bit at the 4, but he committed three fouls in less than six minutes in the first half, finishing with only four points, two assists, and three rebounds. The Pistons were ready for him this time, and the 4 is not his real position. Kobe, meanwhile, was only four for thirteen for eleven points, the worst game I've ever seen him have in the playoffs. He was so frustrated at one point, I had to sit him down. Instead of having him dribble or use a screen roll, we tried to get him in a quick isolation so he could face up and attack. It worked on a few occasions, but we couldn't get the ball to him on a steady diet. Shaq only scored fourteen. The most remarkable stat of all: Kobe and Shaq took a combined five free throws.

JUNE 12
Detroit

For the first time in ten trips to the NBA Finals, the team that I've coached is trailing in the series 2–1. Yesterday the guys watched the tape until the fourth quarter, when I shut it off. "We can't play this way," I told them. With no change in Karl's condition and no clue about how to halt this sudden Detroit juggernaut, I looked elsewhere for guidance. "This is a must game for us," I said. We have to throw everything we can at this ball game. You've had a chance to look at the last game, to reflect. So I would be very interested in anybody's impressions or input that they would like to leave with me." Nobody said a word. Apparently if there was to be a clue forthcoming, it would have to be up to the coaching staff. Just then Shaq put his arm on my shoulder, leading me over to the corner. "Let's go in the bathroom," he said. "We'll talk."

Shaq did most of the talking. He asked me to play Bryon Russell, the veteran small forward who has seen very little playing time since the fall. The idea is ridiculous. Of the twelve players on the playoff roster, Russell is the one *least* prepared to play. "Shaq, Russ doesn't know the offense," I told him. "We've got to have guys who know the offense." The Lakers signed him only as a stopgap measure until Fox recovered from his foot surgery. In fact I've been wondering lately whether we made a mistake by cutting Jannero Pargo in February instead of Russell. Pargo possesses the kind of foot speed to stay with Billups up and down the court, the way Tyrone Lue did against Allen Iverson in the 2001 Finals.

There were other causes for concern on defense as well. "We need to rebound and get after the ball," I told Shaq. "We need size to compete with the Wallaces. Slava and even Brian Cook will have a chance." Moments later, the rest of the cavalry came in— Kobe, Fox, Fish, and Devean. This wasn't a meeting. It was a convention. Fox took charge, suggesting the unit that won the three titles, now all present and accounted for in the men's room at the Palace of Auburn Hills, should start Game 4. Karl, he said, wasn't healthy enough, or Gary effective enough. "Coach, we just need a chance to be on the floor," Fox pleaded. "We know how to take this team apart. The Pistons are doing the same thing we faced in Philadelphia."

I repeated to Fox my concerns about rebounding. "Who is going to take on the role that Karl has played, and what if Shaq isn't having one of his active days?" I asked.

"I'll box out," Fox insisted. "If I can't do the job on Rasheed Wallace, then take me out of the game. I'll take him. We need a shot. It would be great if we got a shot early because we need to get a lead."

"I can't guarantee you that," I said. "I want Karl to go out there. I want him to do the things he's done against Rasheed, even though he might not be able to sustain the effort."

Fish was next. "It just takes ball movement and player movement," he said. "We know how to do this with the offense you have taught us for the last four or five years."

Finally it was Kobe's turn. "You know how much I hate this fucking offense," Kobe said, "but I'll settle in and we'll just execute the triangle and get the ball into Shaq and beat them up on the inside."

I got the point. "I'll let you guys have a chance out there, as a group of five, at some point," I said. "If you can show me something, great, but I have to coach what I think this team has to have. I feel very strongly about that. I'll make those decisions."

The meeting was over. It lasted five minutes, seven tops. I thanked them for their input and I meant it. I always encourage players to show initiative and to have faith in their ability to do the job. On many occasions team members have approached me one-on-one with suggestions, but this was the first time I could ever recall a small group gathering to offer a specific plan. For a team that could easily be down 3–0, the confidence level is pretty high. Game 4 on Sunday night is an opportunity to, pardon the cliché, seize the day.

I went back to the hotel, and thought about whether this plan might actually work. The problem is Karl. I know that if he is going to help us at all, the best chance would be in the first eight to ten minutes of the game, before his knee stiffens up again. "Don't worry that you're not one hundred percent," I told him today. "We'll take whatever you can give us. You give our club a sense of resiliency, and that's what we need. Get us through the first quarter and then we'll find a way to do it after that with other people."

JUNE 14
Detroit

The number on the blackboard in our locker room remains three, still where it was almost a week ago—three wins to a championship. But there is another number I would not dare to write down, though it is in everyone's mind—one loss to elimination.

Since 1985 when the league switched to the 2–3–2 format for the Finals, no home team has swept the three middle games. Even the Chicago squad in '98 lost once to Utah during that stretch. In 1993 we captured the first two games in Phoenix and then dropped two of three on our court. To beat the higher-seeded team three times in a row is an enormous task. Yet the Pistons, after withstanding a more sustained effort from us in Game 4 last night, are on the verge of doing just that.

We played the game the right way this time, feeding Shaq early and often. I started Karl again, believing he afforded us the best opportunity to contain Rasheed Wallace, who was due to have a breakout game. Midway through the second we led 32–29. To be on top in this game, we felt, was critical. The Pistons were never behind in Game 3. The challenge grows increasingly difficult for the team trailing in a playoff game. Teams tend to lean on their marquee players to rescue them in a hurry. Except Detroit doesn't really have a marquee player. When they need a bucket, do they go to a screen roll with Billups? To Hamilton coming off a screen? To Rasheed in the post? If there was a true big-time scorer, they wouldn't hesitate to go to him four or five times in succession. In a deficit situation every shot attempt becomes more urgent. Is it a good shot? Or is it a force? Is it taken in the context of the offense?

The Pistons went through a dry spell in the second period, but were bailed out by entering the penalty period with more than eight minutes left. Pointing out the foul discrepancy obviously had done no good. For the half the Pistons attempted twenty-three free throws to only eight for the Lakers. I can't overemphasize how much that hindered our cause. Good looks are more infrequent in playoff basketball, so when one team takes a lot more free throws than the other, the advantage is substantial. Free throws are the easiest shots in the game. There is no defender in your face, no contact. On offense I was disappointed we didn't ride Shaquille more. Clearly on his way to another monster game in the Finals, he did not attempt a single shot in the last six minutes. Kobe tried to assert himself, attempting fourteen shots in the half. I didn't think too much of it, until one of my coaches showed me the stat sheet in the locker room. Why, I wondered, did Kobe keep firing it up when Shaq was securing such deep position in the paint? What happened to Kobe's pledge in the bathroom meeting to run the triangle? He seemed too intent on making up for his miserable performance in Game 3. Still, we were down by only two points.

In the third, Karl couldn't run anymore. I put Slava in, which allowed Rasheed to operate more freely. He scored seven points in the quarter. Yet entering the fourth, the game was tied at fifty-six. One strong quarter, one lousy strong quarter, and we would be assured of at least one more game at Staples. This was the moment for our defense to lock down the Pistons to a total ideally in the teens. So much for the ideal. Detroit scored thirty-two, an explosion in a low-scoring contest. Hamilton went off for eleven, establishing the tone with the first two hoops of the quarter. I called time immediately. "Don't screw it up," I said. "Give yourselves a chance." The chance was still there with about eight minutes left, the Pistons up by only two. A Ben Wallace free throw made it 63–60. But when Ben missed the second, he collected his own rebound, and layed it in. Nobody bothered to box him out from outside the lane, an unpardonable sin at such a critical stage. Wallace is a worse free-throw shooter than Shaq! Rasheed, meanwhile, scored another ten in the quarter, finishing with twenty-six, the breakout game we expected. The final was 88–80. The guys played as well as we could play, committing only ten turnovers, but there were a number of reasons we came up short.

No reliable backup for Karl. "Slava is in over his head in this series," Tex said. If only Horace were healthy. Rasheed Wallace might have enjoyed some moments against him but he wouldn't have had the confidence that he could go to the baseline and dominate.

No outside shooting. We were only three for sixteen from behind the arc, Fish zero for three. It is impossible to know how much the knee injury may be causing his sudden struggles, but Fish was on fire against San Antonio and Minnesota. In four games against the Pistons, he's only eight of thirty. That is not like Derek Fisher, not in the playoffs.

No contribution from Gary. Against my better judgment, I played him forty-three minutes in Game 4. Initially I felt we needed some three-point shooting to spread a defense that collapses around penetration, but Shaq encouraged me to leave Gary in there. Gary managed only eight points and five assists, while Billups notched another twenty-three. I put Kobe on him late in the game.

Finally, no consistency from Kobe again, who converted only eight of twenty-five attempts.

In the locker room afterward, he was steamed. "How can they let this guy get to my arm on every shot?" he asked, referring to Prince. Kobe was astute enough not to make an issue out of it with the press, which would make him appear a sore loser. But the play of Prince can't fully explain Kobe's poor production. After the game at a banquet set up for the team at the hotel, Dr. Buss came over to my table. He had the explanation. "I think our young man has hit the wall," he suggested. "The whole weight of the whole season has finally caught up to him. He just looked so tired out there tonight that he didn't have the energy to finish this game off the way he's done it in the past."

I nodded. "Maybe you're right," I said.

Even so, I remain optimistic. Kobe, tired or not, is due to have a big night in Detroit, and if we can utilize Shaq in the same manner we did in Game 4—he finished with thirty-six points and twenty rebounds—the guys can send this series back to Los Angeles. All this team has to do is a hit a couple of threes, get to the line, and we will put together that eighty-five- to ninety-point total that should be enough.

JUNE 15
Detroit

Tonight, in a couple of hours, I might very well be coaching my last game, for the Lakers or anyone. There are countless memories, from Chicago, from Los Angeles, and from so many other arenas across America. I started in the fall of 1989 and except for a one-year hiatus, it has been my calling ever since. I've worked with great players, great coaches, great . . . oh, enough reminiscing for now. I do not plan on tonight being my last game. I plan on two more games after this one, culminating with a celebration at Staples next Sunday night.

First there is a Game 5 before we can contemplate a Game 6, or a Game 7. "Our goal is to just get this series back to LA," I told the guys. Our cause would certainly be enhanced if the refs would give us a fair shake. In Game 4, the Pistons shot forty-one free throws to our twenty-two. "I hate to say this, Jerry," I told Dr. Buss at the buffet afterward, "but I think we wuz robbed." Going over the tape yesterday, Kurt Rambis discovered twenty-five separate sequences which illustrated the inconsistency of the calls. Mitch phoned the league offices in New York to complain, but got nowhere, which was to be expected.

Today during the walk-through I went over the matchups for the game.

"Let me take Billups," Kobe volunteered. "Let me see if I can slow him down."

"I don't know," I responded.

Shortly afterward when I entered the locker room, Kobe brought the subject up again.

"I'd rather you take Hamilton," I said, "and then perhaps make the adjustment."

Kobe mentioned his real motive. "I just said that to see if Gary would say, 'No, let me have him. He's mine.'" Gary didn't say a word. "I think he's scared," Kobe said. "He doesn't care if I take Billups or not."

So here we are, not exactly in the appropriate mind-set, I suppose, heading into an elimination game in the NBA Finals. In a few minutes, four of my five children will stop by to wish me luck and coordinate postgame plans. Last night, seven of us went to dinner two blocks away. The street was filled with fans, split down the middle in their loyalties. They shook my hand and cheered until we turned the corner and then yelled, "Pistons suck" or "Lakers suck." My kids laughed. Having them in Detroit has been wonderful, especially if tonight is indeed the end.

JUNE 16
Detroit

So many emotions, so little time, the alarm clock next to my bed approaching two A.M. The morning routine will be the same as always: bags at nine, bus at ten, plane at eleven. Only we're not headed to another game. We're headed to summer instead, a loser in the NBA Finals, the number on the blackboard staying at three forever. Outside the Detroit fans are still cheering, the new generation of youngsters able finally to tell their own stories of glory for years to come. The journey started in October, on the beaches in Hawaii, a team built for a championship. Now in mid-June, the journey ends, in Detroit, Michigan, without a championship, with a future more uncertain than ever.

I never thought it would end this way. Even tonight, moments before game time, I was confident, and so were the players. We went over the Xs and Os, of feeding Shaq on the move in the lane, of how to defend the screen roll, of avoiding unnecessary fouls. "I don't want you to bitch at calls," I said during my five-minute pregame address. "You must remain determined and strong. The referees will measure your mental ability to accept adversity. We don't want to be in the penalty situation in the first four minutes of a quarter and have to be passive defensively." Then for positive reinforcement, I showed a short clip of highlights from Game 4, interspersed with a scene from *Miracle,* the movie chronicling the inspiring story of the 1980 U.S. Olympic hockey team that defeated the Russians. In the scene an injured American player courageously joins his teammates on the ice. When the clip ended, our players stood in a circle, put their hands in the middle, and offered the usual words of support. Everyone was focused on the task ahead.

Or so I thought. Moments later a cell phone went off, a clear violation of team policy. Jamal Sampson, our injured young reserve center, looked at his phone, but it wasn't ringing. The phone that was ringing belonged to Kobe. I couldn't believe it. Worse yet I couldn't believe that he answered it and started talking in a hushed voice. We were about to go on the court for the most important game of the year, and Kobe was allowing himself to be distracted by a phone call. I didn't ask who he was talking to and I didn't care. He shouldn't have been talking to anyone.

Finally the game was under way, and for the first few minutes, our side was in good shape. Slava, subbing for Karl, who didn't even suit up tonight, hit four jumpers, staking us to a 14–7 advantage. "When Rasheed Wallace keeps beating me up and down the floor," Karl told me, "I know I can't go." The Pistons appeared a bit tentative, yielding perhaps to the inherent tensions of a close-out game. There was enormous pressure on us to keep the series alive, but there was also significant pressure on them to end it. Lose this game, with the champagne on ice and the fans itching to celebrate the city's first NBA title in fourteen years, and the entire complexion of the series would change. The Pistons would have to fly back across the country and try to close us out on our court, against a veteran team with three rings in four years. These thoughts had to be going through their minds.

But with eight minutes to go in the quarter, Shaq had been cited for a loose ball foul, his second. The call was unbelievable. Ben Wallace jumped forward and did one of those acting jobs, the ref buying it completely. There was no discernible push from Shaq, no arm movement whatsoever. I started to get the feeling the refs wanted the series to end. Otherwise why call a phantom foul in this situation? They knew we were already down one big, and wouldn't survive long without Shaq. Usually a second foul is called in a game of this magnitude only if the perpetrator is overly aggressive or there's a collision, but the contact must be obvious, and this was not obvious at all. Either way I had no choice. I put Brian Cook in for Shaq. If the refs were going to call a foul like that at this particular point in the game, what would they be willing to call for his third foul? Of course, with the middle open, the Pistons proceeded to score eight straight points in less than two minutes, removing our lead and, apparently, their jitters.

At least we weren't settling for jump shots, and consequently, the calls weren't one-sided anymore. Early in the second, we regained the lead. "We want to finish strong, " I told the guys. "They're going to try to make a run to end the quarter." The run came, all right, lifting the Pistons to a 55–45 lead at intermission. Yet even then not all hope was lost. If we could somehow keep the margin within six or eight points heading into the fourth, anything could happen. "This team can't score fifty-five points in a half, and you've just given them these points," I said. By now it was too late for words. The trend continued: the Pistons beat us to every loose ball. Ben Wallace played the game of his life.

The outcome long decided, I took in the last few minutes. It didn't feel right. I am spoiled, taking nine prior teams to the Finals and departing with the trophy every time. No series even went to seven games. When the buzzer sounded I congratulated Larry Brown and signaled to my kids in the stands to meet me outside the locker room. Inside I consoled my players. "This is a fitting ending," I said. "Fifteen years ago, when I started coaching, I got beat in the Eastern Conference Finals by Detroit worse than you guys got beat. There was a lot of anger in the locker room about losing, about not getting to the Finals. This time there is just disappointment that all the effort we gave in the course of the year and all this talk about sacrificing didn't give us the finish we wanted. We have to give it to Detroit. They earned the championship, and you guys have nothing to feel bad about."

The speech, my last probably, was over. I then hugged the players one by one, starting with Shaquille, who hesitated for a moment but finally wrapped his arms around me. I hugged Kobe, telling him how much I admired the effort he gave in this series. I hugged Brian Cook. "Sorry I couldn't give you what you needed," he said. "Don't worry about it," I told him. "Everybody has to be a rookie." I hugged everyone, except Karl, who was in street clothes. At one point I became so sweaty I went into the bathroom to wash up. Fox was in there, sobbing. Another hug. I feel bad for him. He worked incredibly hard to recover from his foot injury, only, like Karl, to be injured again.

Finally I headed to the media room, escorted by my sons, Charley and Ben, and daughters Chelsea and Brooke. My other daughter, Elizabeth, left town after Game 4 to return to her job in DC. "This is the only time you'll have a chance to go on with me," I told them. For years I've kept my kids out of the spotlight, respecting their privacy. But now with the spotlight on their dad about to fade, maybe for good, I wanted them by my side. The reporters asked about my plans, hoping to hear the "R" word, but I wasn't about to announce my retirement just yet. I said the chances of coming back were very slim. When I walked off the podium, I saw Larry Brown on the other side of the curtain. "Your kids played really well," I said.

On the way to the hotel I spoke to Jeanie, who congratulated me for a great season. "It was hard to watch Detroit celebrate," she said. I thanked her for her perseverance. At the hotel there was yet another buffet. I was sitting with the kids when Jeanie's father approached me. "I suppose we better have our luncheon this week before I head off to Europe," Dr. Buss said. I knew he wasn't too pleased, but he was most supportive. "I never anticipated this team would go this far," he said. "It's a miracle what you did. I can't believe the success we've had the last five years. It feels like it's gone by so quickly." I know what he means.

So what happened, anyway? How did we fail in our quest? Sifting through some preliminary thoughts in a Detroit hotel room, before the appropriate distance offers a chance for deeper reflection, the injury to Karl Malone was certainly one factor. By the end of the Minnesota series, Karl was clearly our most valuable player. He guarded one younger, more heralded performer after another— Yao, Duncan, Garnett—holding his own each time. Even on one leg, he was able to frustrate Rasheed Wallace. If Karl could have given us one more game, one more *half,* say, the second half in Game 4, things might have been different.

I wonder, too, about Kobe. Maybe Dr. Buss is right. Maybe the whole weight of this most troubled season finally caught up to the young man. Entering the series there didn't seem to be anyone on the Pistons who would be able to stop him, but Prince did. Or maybe the Pistons were simply the superior team. Somewhere along the way, I finally realized the key was Chauncey Billups. I started Kobe on him in Game 5 and then switched back to Gary. Billups made only three field goals, but went to the line eight times. We never stopped him.

Or finally, maybe I'm the one to blame. Maybe I was incapable of communicating the selfless concepts required to produce success. I needed to take them to that place where I took them before, fostering a collective consciousiness, a collective soul. Only in achieving that degree of oneness can a group of men truly make the necessary sacrifice to win a championship. Maybe I should have made a bigger deal about our victory over the Timberwolves. Maybe that would have lifted everyone's spirits. Well, enough maybes, for now. I feel like I let the city and the owner down. Winning a championship can bring a city, even one as diverse as Los Angeles, together. I'm sure my thoughts will become clearer in the days and weeks ahead. The clock by my bed has turned to three. Bags at nine, bus at ten, plane at eleven.

TWELVE

A NEW JOURNEY

JUNE 16
Los Angeles

Nothing about this season was normal, so why should the first few hours *after* this season be any different? On the bus this morning, we discovered that Kobe, Karl, and Fish would not be making the trip to Los Angeles with everyone else. The scuttlebutt was that Kobe and Karl hung around the fireplace in the hotel lounge for hours. Fish was supposedly planning to spend time with his good friend Corliss Williamson. I don't want to be too judgmental—everyone's emotions are extremely fragile in the wake of our disappointment—but it would have been more appropriate for all of us to fly home together, a team to the very end. Once in LA we could go our separate ways.

There is still work to be done. I am still the coach of the Los Angeles Lakers. For how much longer, I do not know. On the plane Mitch brought up the annual exit interviews with the players. "You will want to go through with the meetings as you usually would, right?" he asked. Right. I feel it is the only proper way to offer the players honest feedback from myself and the other coaches. Whatever happens to this regime, these players will carry on with the rest of their careers. They should know what they did well, and where they need to improve. The meetings will start tomorrow, with the exception of Rick Fox. Fox asked if he could meet when we landed because he was scheduled to take an evening flight to New York. Shaq also came by. He and Mitch divvied up the shares of playoff money. At around two, after touching down at LAX, I met with Fox in his chauffeured car for maybe ten minutes. When I emerged, the parking lot was deserted. Everyone had already gone their separate ways. Jeanie drove up to take me home.

JUNE 17
Los Angeles

I went to the office as usual this morning. Only there were no video sessions, no postmortems, no need to rehash the obvious. The sooner we left Detroit behind us, the better. The focus was on the future. For months the staff kidded me about my plans. "Oh, you're going back to New York after this year," Frank said one day, assuming I would coach the Knicks. "It's all set up for you." Behind the kidding was genuine concern. My fate will largely determine theirs. Now, with a meeting scheduled with Dr. Buss for tomorrow afternoon, my fate is about to become known. "I'm ninety-five percent sure of retiring," I told them. They went right for the part that offered them hope: "What's the five percent?" The 5 percent, I explained, was if Kobe and Shaq and Dr. Buss asked me to come back. They know the odds on that one as well as I do. Everyone broke up just before the first exit interviews were about to start. "See you Monday," I said. The interviews went well. Mitch and I saw the kids—Cook, Kareem, and Luke; Slava, Jamal Sampson, who played only sparingly this year, and Devean. I was tough on Dev, as always. He is not fully utilizing his talent. "If you had continued your work on concentration and focus," I told him, "you might have been able to reclaim your season."

When the meetings concluded, I stopped by Jeanie's office before heading home. She immediately shut the door behind me. "Go to Mitch," she said, "or call up my dad and tell them that you can coach Kobe. Tell them that you guys worked together great in the last three months, and that it's no longer an issue. Look at how well you did at the end of the season." I wondered why this conversation couldn't wait till the evening. "Okay, Jeanie," I said, "what happened?" She told me John Black, the Lakers' PR guy, mentioned to her that the organization wasn't going to ask me to return. At first I took it as a clear message from management, Black knowing that Jeanie would relay the information to me. But then I realized that maybe Jeanie pried it out of him when he was walking around the office.

Either way, Jeanie was in tears. I held her on my lap for ten minutes. I wanted so much to hold her longer, to tell her what she wanted to hear but I couldn't. She wasn't just pleading for my job. She was pleading for our relationship. Jeanie was worried way back in the fall when the *Times* revealed details of the contract talks, upsetting her father, who figured I was negotiating through the newspaper. "Get it done," she said. Jeanie was worried even more in February when the negotiations broke down. If I lose this job, she figures, she loses me. I'll go back to the lake in Montana and never be heard from again. After a few more minutes, I left her office. The tears were gone for now. I meet with her dad tomorrow.

JUNE 18
Los Angeles

This was one day I will certainly never forget. In the morning I met with Kobe. In the afternoon I saw Dr. Buss. By the evening I no longer had a job. I was not surprised in the least, yet the end of any journey is always jarring. Once again I will need time to reflect. Kobe arrived in El Segundo with his agent, Rob Pelinka. Before the formal exit interview with Mitch, who was still meeting with Fish, I invited them into my office. I couldn't help but think of my meeting with Kobe back in February on the day after the All-Star game, when I was trying to salvage a relationship and a season. There was great tension, yet in a sense Jeanie was right. Kobe and I did work well together—for four months, that is. This time the same tension between us wasn't there. We both knew I would never coach him again.

While waiting for Mitch, we discussed Kobe's upcoming court appearance in Eagle County.

"Is the trial going to interfere with your free agency?" I asked.

"I don't know," he said. "The date hasn't been set yet."

"If it's set in July, will you be able to work around this?"

"Yeah, I'd have meetings on the weekends."

"How long will the trial last?"

"Anywhere from one to three weeks."

"Is there still a chance that there won't be a trial?"

"Yeah, there's a chance but either way, it doesn't matter. The outcome will be the same."

Just then Mitch came in. The chat was over. It was time for the official meeting. Mitch, Kobe, and I moved to the conference room.

I started by casually asking Kobe who called him on his cell moments before we left the locker room for Game 5. It was Brian Shaw, he said, a former teammate and part of our organization. "He told me to get after Gary, to make sure he was fired up." The advice, it turned out, was sound, but answering the call wasn't appropriate.

I then told Kobe how pleased I was with his ability to put aside our conflicts after the meeting in February, and make a strong commitment to the rest of the season. Mitch didn't waste the opportunity to praise Kobe's remarkable performances. The next subject was his decision to become a free agent, which killed a minute or two. I then got down to the questions I really wanted to ask.

"Will my presence or absence have anything to do with your desire to play for the Lakers?" I asked.

He looked puzzled. I rephrased the question. "Would my being with the Lakers or retiring have any influence on your desire to remain with the Lakers?"

I was affording Kobe an opportunity to bring himself back into the group, to see if he felt I was an essential part of his return to the Lakers. Perhaps I was dreaming but at least I wanted him to have the chance to say, "For all I've complained about the triangle and tried to do things on my own outside the structure of the offense, I really think I need the discipline that the system provides. I think I will be best as a player if you're here with the team, and I want this team to be the best it can be."

Of course, that's not what he said. That's not remotely what he said. He said I should make up my mind about my future independently of his decision.

"I'm going to retire," I said.

He raised his eyebrows. For the first time in the entire conversation, I thought I detected a little emotion.

"Really?" he asked.

I nodded. The next subject was Shaquille. "Will Shaq's presence on this team color your decision to come back or not?" I asked him.

"Yes, it does," he said.

"I meant what I said the other night after the game, that the two of you could coexist and play well together," I went on.

"There's no doubt about that," he said. "I've done that for eight years with him, but I'm tired of being a sidekick." His sentiment came as no surprise, obviously. In the last few years the entire city of Los Angeles has heard many times from many "sources" that Kobe was no longer willing to play a subservient role to Shaquille. But to hear it in the words of the only source that matters, to hear Kobe say "sidekick," really struck me. I told Kobe I hoped he would find happiness in basketball and in his life, and that his family would remain intact after everything that had transpired in the last year. The meeting was over.

So how do I sum up these five years with Kobe Bryant? How do I make sense of our inability to get along? I've never had trou-

ble coaching superstars before. Why was this relationship so difficult? Those answers will have to come another time. I do know
that there were many occasions this year when I felt like there was
a psychological war going on between us. Amazingly we came to
a truce, even to a higher level of trust. I made him the team's quarterback before the Houston series, and he proved worthy of the
new responsibility. Ultimately though, I don't believe we developed enough trust between us to win a championship. We needed
to be in total sync at all times and we weren't. I understand why
the Lakers treat Kobe as their most valuable asset. The kid will be
twenty-six in August. His ability to take over a game, to make an
impossible play, is unmatched. Yet it needs to be remembered that
Kobe is still an employee, and that he needs direction and guidance
in a way that helps him mature into the kind of adult we hope he
can be. Kobe is missing out by not finding a way to become part
of a system that involves giving to something larger than himself.
He could have been the heir apparent to MJ and maybe won as
many championships. He may still win a championship or two, but
the boyish hero image has been replaced by that of a callous gun
for hire.

Shaquille was supposed to be next, but his agent called Mitch to
say he wouldn't be coming. Last year Shaq got in a lot of trouble
for skipping his exit interview, which I thought was very disrespectful toward the coaching staff. I don't blame him for skipping
it this time, not after Mitch made it clear in a press conference yesterday that Shaq could be traded. Conversely Mitch said that there
was no possibility the Lakers would consider a sign-and-trade with
Kobe. The message was unmistakable: this is now Kobe Bryant's
team. With Karl not scheduled, the last meeting was with Gary. "I

wasn't Gary Payton," he said. "I didn't play like Gary Payton." I tried to assure him how valuable he had been during the injuries to Shaq, Kobe, and Karl, but he wasn't appeased. "You told me you wanted to take Kobe off the ball, and it ended up that Kobe took *me* off the ball. I'm a penetrator and a disher. I felt like I was playing a role I wasn't used to playing." I told Gary next year will be much easier, and then broke off the meeting. I was running late to my lunch with Dr. Buss. I spent a few minutes with Todd, my agent, who gave some last-minute instructions: don't offer your resignation first.

The drive from El Segundo to Jerry's house near the Marina takes ten minutes. I called Jeanie and said I would call back right after the meeting. I parked and rang the bell. Jerry and I exchanged small talk for almost an hour before the subject finally came up. "Phil," he said, "we're going in a different direction." *A different direction.*

"I suppose so," I said. "That seems logical."

Just like that, it was official: I would no longer coach the Los Angeles Lakers. Jerry soon launched into a description of how the Lakers had been assembled with the idea of winning championships the past five years, demonstrating with his hand the building of a mountain, but now it was time for the team to scale back, his hand fluttering down. I couldn't believe it. This was the exact same gesture Mitch used only a few hours earlier to describe the same change in philosophy. There obviously had been a plan in place for a long time, one that did not include me as part of it. He then offered me a position in the organization, which would include scouting and consulting.

At this point Jerry asked me to go to the phone with him to call Mitch. He told Mitch about our conversation, suggesting that a joint press statement would be in order to announce my retirement. The statement would include the offer of executive vice president, which Mitch must have questioned because Jerry had to remind him of something the two discussed previously. He handed the phone to me. I told Mitch I would go home and call him in fifteen minutes to work out the details of the release with him and John Black. Jerry walked me to the door, telling me he would never forget our first meeting in this house five years ago, when I was the one designated to take the team in a different direction. "I never heard of a coach who set such high goals for himself," Jerry said.

"The whole experience was a great pleasure for me," I said. "I've had the time of my life coaching this team, and with Jeanie." We made plans to talk about the offer by the end of the month.

I called Todd and asked him to meet me at my house and I called Jeanie to give her a full report. She was sad, if not surprised. There will be plenty to say later. In the car everything made sense. The finality of it all was a bit unsettling, but I knew this day was coming from that afternoon in late January when I told Mitch I wouldn't coach this team next year if Kobe Bryant was still on the roster. I've been around this organization long enough. I knew, somewhere inside me, that Mitch would probably tell Dr. Buss, and that it would lead to the end of my tenure here, and I knew that was exactly what I wanted to happen. I was putting myself in a position that was totally untenable to them, and it wasn't just because of my relationship with Kobe, although that was a big part of it. When I met Dr. Buss last spring in Hawaii, I was leaning toward retirement. But he was persuasive, and I wanted to give him another championship, maybe two. Yet as the season wore on, my earlier hesitation resurfaced. The toll from the road trips, the nights with too little sleep, the fissures on this dysfunctional team, were heavier than ever. I will be sixty a year from September and don't need this. Dr. Buss must have sensed my reservations. So then why, in today's meeting, didn't he give me an opportunity to walk away first? Why didn't he say: "Phil, what are your plans?" The answer is because he can't possibly imagine anyone ever voluntarily leaving his Los Angeles Lakers, the number-one franchise on the planet. It reminds me of a story about a guy who can't understand why his girlfriend would ever break up with him.

When I arrived home I went over the press release very carefully with Todd. There was the requisite praise—"the greatest coach ever"—and the mention of future employment, though when I uttered the words, "executive vice president," Mitch said, "of what?" Just what I was thinking. Of what? Finally, when we got it all straight, I told Mitch and John Black to release it. Just before hanging up, Mitch said, "Phil, I just want to let you know that we have not talked to any other coaches." This statement was totally unnecessary. I would expect Mitch to talk to other coaches. That's the role of a general manager, especially in this uncertain environment. What Mitch did not understand was that I didn't care if he talked to anyone else.

No matter. I wasn't about to hang around the house pondering these petty developments. Jeanie, the kids, and I needed to hurry to make it to the Greek Theatre in Hollywood to see *A Prairie Home Companion,* the popular radio program hosted by Garrison Keillor. My kids were very excited. They grew up listening to the show before dinner on Saturday nights when I coached the CBA team in Albany, New York, a lifetime ago. On the way I called my other three children and left them messages about my "retirement." When we arrived at the Greek, there were two TV trucks. While

Jeanie sprinted away, I did a quick interview, and then found our seats. The night was cool and beautiful, the music alternating between country, blues, and gospel. We were having a wonderful time. One gospel singer performed a spiritual hymn I recognized from my years in the church pew. I sang along with a joy that choked me up. When I turned to look at Jeanie, she smiled at me through her tears. "You okay?" I asked her. "You want to go?" She nodded, and we left, hearing Keillor sing "Good Night, Ladies," as we headed for the exit.

JUNE 22
Los Angeles

I met with the coaching staff on Monday as planned. We talked about the coup behind closed doors and made arrangements for a dinner later in the week. There was a message on my desk that Shaq had called. He had also left a message on my machine over the weekend. I had tried him back several times but his voice mail was full. Just as well. What would I have said to him? He would have asked if it was true the Lakers were trying to trade him, and I couldn't tell him anything. I would either betray the organization or Shaquille. In the intervening days, however, no longer privy to the inside dope, that conflict has passed. This afternoon I tried again from my car. He answered.

"Where you at?" he said.

I told him.

"I'm not far from there," he said. "Let's meet in five minutes."

We selected the St. Regis. Shaq pulled up in his Superman SUV.

We went inside, and enjoyed some iced tea, water, and candid conversation. Shaq and I have always been honest with each other, painfully honest at times. "I just wanted to get a hold of you," he said, "before all this broke apart. We had a great run."

I told him I was sorry he was putting his house up for sale. "I don't understand why it had to come to this," he said. "Guys were injured in the Finals, and we lost, but that doesn't mean the thing was broken. The club seemed to be making money. What was the big deal?" He said the reports in the papers have exaggerated the amount he's been seeking for a contract extension. Shaq admitted that he was getting older, but remained confident he can win more championships. "Make it happen for yourself," I said. "You've got a lot of ball left." We discussed possible destinations: Dallas, New Orleans, Orlando. I asked about the Knicks. No interest. Tough place for kids to grow up, he said.

The subject changed to one that could not be avoided, Kobe Bryant. "You gave the kid a lot of room the last couple of years," he said. "You stayed off his back and let him try to work things out for himself. I just don't understand why he didn't recognize that. I don't understand why he was unhappy, but Kobe wants more than he'll probably ever find to make him happy." I only listened. The days of mediating between the two of them feel long gone. Shaq and I soon started to say our good-byes, but I am sure he and I will stay in touch for the rest of my life. I was tough on him in these five years, sometimes too tough. His exchange with Tex in the Detroit series might have been because I had pushed him too hard. But he gave everything for me and for the Lakers when it really mattered. I took this job for the opportunity to coach him, and he made it an experience I will cherish forever. In an environment that often becomes too serious, Shaq always made me laugh. As we left the hotel Shaq turned to the maître d'. "This meeting never happened," he said.

JUNE 24
Los Angeles

We met this evening at a restaurant in Manhattan Beach, the men who have been with me through good times and bad times for much of the last decade, my assistant coaches and their wives. I've been worrying about them quite a bit over the last week. About Jim Cleamons, who hopes to land the coaching job at Ohio State. About Frank Hamblen, who hopes to stay on with the new regime if Rudy Tomjanovich gets the job. About Kurt Rambis, who hopes to stay in Los Angeles. He has a child who will attend UCLA in the fall, one in high school, and one in junior high. I don't worry about Tex. He claims he won't work next season. I don't believe it.

I ordered a couple of bottles of champagne and began with a toast. I thanked each of their wives for their understanding through the years. I asked for a lot from this group, maybe too much, and I know that could not have been easy on their families. I toasted each coach individually: Jim for working so diligently with the young players and the guards; Kurt for his unwaveringly upbeat attitude, humor, and leadership; Frank for his centered approach and ability to state the obvious; and finally, Tex for reminding us that the basketball gods have no favorites, that they always weigh the balance of each performance night in and night out. "And always remember," I said in closing, "that Shaq has his ear to the wall." There were laughs and there were tears. Everyone went home and promised to stay in touch.

JUNE 30
Los Angeles

I placed two important calls today, to Mitch and Dr. Buss. Mitch was first. I had hoped to see him yesterday when I moved out of my office, but his door was closed the entire time. I wasn't sure whether he was busy in meetings or phone calls, or if he was simply trying to avoid me. Either way I felt uncomfortable walking out with saying good-bye. Since Mitch replaced Jerry West in 2000, the two of us had spent countless hours discussing the team's personnel. Our ability to work well together was an integral part of the overall success. But I understand why the door might have been closed. By relaying my complaints about Kobe to Dr. Buss, Mitch played a role in the Lakers' decision to suspend contract negotiations, which led, of course, to the end of my tenure. I don't harbor any animosity toward Mitch, although in my phone conversation with him today, I told him I was disappointed he wasn't more supportive. Mitch said he was sorry he didn't have a chance to talk to me yesterday, that he was overloaded with Shaq's situation and the search for a new coach. He hoped we might have dinner before I left for Montana.

At nine A.M. promptly, I called Dr. Buss in Venice. For nearly two weeks I have been pondering his generous offer to stay in the organization. The idea of scouting and mentoring greatly appeals to me and it would certainly make Jeanie very happy. Nonetheless I told him I would decline. "Your positions are different than my positions," I told him. "If you want me to be an executive, I don't see how I can endorse them." I certainly could not endorse the decision to trade Shaquille. I acknowledge that his skills and athleticism are declining, and that his market value will never be better, but this is still Shaquille O'Neal, the most dominant big man in the game today, maybe ever. Nobody can replace him. Dr. Buss brought up the issue of Shaq's character, criticizing him for delaying his toe surgery in 2002. I felt a need to respond, to suggest that on the issue of character, Kobe was certainly no saint, either. "It's not that I'm enamored with Kobe's character," he said. "But he is twenty-six in August. The seven years ahead are the prime years of his career." Of course, neither of us brought up the possibility of those prime years being spent in prison. "Besides," Dr. Buss added, "aren't all superstars like that?"

"No," I told him, "not all of them."

He said choosing Kobe over Shaq was also to satisfy his constituents, the fans. "I have to serve the people who are loyal to me," he said. "My mail runs about 5–1 on Kobe to Shaq."

"Fine," I said, "but I don't know if Kobe is as attentive to his fans as maybe some of the people in the organization think he is. He's going to do what he wants to do, and believes he'll be adored by fans no matter where he goes, except maybe Denver."

Dr. Buss listened and was sympathetic. "I often felt sorry for you," he said, "because people always second-guessed your decisions. I understand entirely. I feel the same way about my ownership." We chatted for a few more minutes and made plans to reconnect in September after he returns from Italy. I like Jerry Buss and will miss working for him and our conversations about basketball and literature. He has been a tremendous owner, and Lakers fans should feel very grateful. But I did not want to endorse the *different direction* in which this organization is headed.

JULY 10
Los Angeles

Avoiding the latest twists and turns in the Lakers soap opera is impossible. I hear it from Jeanie. I hear it from my former coaches and players. Three weeks after the NBA Finals, this town remains consumed with the purple and gold: Will Shaq be traded? Will Kobe come back? I listen to it all with a strange, unfamiliar detachment. For five years, except for summers, this was my life. But now, with my bags packed, heading before dawn tomorrow morning to Montana, it is no longer my concern. When the draft was held two weeks ago, for several days, I didn't even know who the Lakers selected. I didn't know who the Bulls chose, or even who was the first overall pick. I have always been able to let go very easily. I'm the one now going in a different direction, to home, to a future that will sort itself out, one way or the other. I'm thinking about taking Interstate 15, which passes through Vegas, but I've never liked interstates. I prefer less crowded routes.

I feel at peace. That was the most revealing part of my conversation with Dr. Buss a few weeks ago. I slept great that night and have been sleeping great ever since. For so long there were intrusions, about players, about concepts, about what I could do to improve my basketball team. I have been happier without those intrusions. I look back at what we accomplished here—three titles in five years—and am very proud. I took this job because I believed the Lakers, with two incredible young stars, had underachieved. There is no doubt this team achieved a tremendous amount. Did I make mistakes? Of course. Are there statements I made and strategies I implemented that I would take back in a second? Absolutely. But winning in this profession is not as easy as outsiders might assume. Everybody wants credit, believing it is always about . . . them. In the end there is always some level of disappointment, of feeling disrespected.

When I was a free agent in 1996, after winning my fourth championship with the Bulls, Jerry Krause explained this business in perhaps the most honest terms I ever heard. "Don't feel so God damned privileged or good," he said. "You were paid to coach a team that could win championships and you just did what was expected of you. Some coaches have thirty-win teams and some have teams that can win sixty. You just did your job."

I countered. "I understand that," I said, "but was this team supposed to go 72–10 and win a championship?" I thought that was a good comeback, but there is truth in that story. I was given the opportunity to bring a championship to LA with a talented team. We were able to get three, and even with that measure of success it wasn't quite good enough.

In the weeks since I left the Lakers, many lies have been told. I was let go because I asked for too much money. False. Sure, I asked for a substantial raise, but I think three titles in four years should warrant a hike in pay, and I was eager to see if the Lakers truly wanted me back. Besides, the organization and I weren't far apart in February when the talks broke down. I am confident we could have come to an agreement. No, it wasn't about the money. Another story I've heard is that I was becoming stale, unable to motivate the players to believe in my system. False as well. After all, this team did make it to the NBA Finals. These lies are merely an attempt by critics to compensate for how the Lakers bungled my retirement. My exit could have been graceful, not clumsy. I felt like a leper the day I cleared out of my office.

So what now? Will I ever coach again? The way I feel today, it's highly doubtful. I do not want to deal with any more plane flights, hotels, or egos. But then again, I thought the very same thing in 1998 when I left the game for a year. I missed it. I missed the joy of the journey, of watching the guys I coached grow to become better players, and better men. The addiction to coaching is a powerful one, which is why so many come back over and over and over. I don't suspect I've got a serious case, but I am probably as susceptible to this drug as anyone else. I would never rule anything out. The real test will come in October when I won't be attending training camp. Will I miss the look on the faces of the rookies when they finally grasp a concept? Will I miss working with Tex, Jim, Frank, and Kurt, planning practices, designing sequences? Will I miss the games themselves, each one unique, with unexpected challenges and demands? Since the early 1960s, I've played or coached in more than two thousand games, and I can say safely there is nothing I've experienced outside of basketball that can match its intensity, its highs and lows, its feeling of fulfillment or failure. I can't imagine what my life would have been like without it.

What about Jeanie? She has long feared the end of my tenure with the Lakers would signify the end of my relationship with her. She's a fatalist. I am not. I remain as enamored with this beautiful woman as ever, believing we can have a future together, if perhaps much different than our past. The Lakers brought us together but they do not have to break us up.

It is almost dark. In a few hours I will put my bags in the car, and take off for Montana. I look forward to the journey.

July 12
Flathead Lake

I had been driving for almost two days, about 1,200 miles in all, easing again from one world into another. I was in the Benz this time, my top down, my mood up. In the hours before I left LA, the Lakers introduced their new coach, Rudy T., and went ahead with plans to trade Shaquille to Miami. I'm just relieved to leave everything behind and see the country. I decided to avoid Interstate 15.

A few hours ago I crossed Idaho into Montana. There was a sign indicating that Chief Joseph of the Nez Percé Indians took the same route with his tribe when retreating from the U.S. Cavalry in 1877. Lewis and Clark came through here first, from St. Louis to the Columbia River about two hundred years ago. They called it the Lost Trail Pass because they assumed they would never survive the journey. The Bitterroot Valley at the bottom of the pass was hit by a devastating forest fire four years ago. Charred trees remain, surrounded by new, verdant green vegetation. Morel mushrooms have sprouted, the kind mushroom hunters treasure. For me, too, there is once again a feeling of regeneration. "Unceasing change turns the wheel of life,"—the words come to me again— "and so reality is shown in all its many forms."

Just as I started up the pass, two bikers did a U-turn, and went right in front of me at high speed. I was reminded of the trip a year ago on my BMW bike and gave chase. One of the riders wasn't wearing a helmet, which looked odd, but this is a state that believes in personal freedom, even if it kills you.

I stopped at a gas station outside Missoula. Just as I was putting the gas cap back on, two teenage boys pulled up beside me in a pickup and checked out my car. One turned to me. "Are you Phil Jackson?" he asked.

"Yep," I responded, expecting a request for an autograph or cell phone photo.

The other kid piped in, "Hey, what happened to the Lakers?"

"We lost our way," I told them. "We just lost our way at the wrong time." I smiled, got in the car, and started the engine. I headed home.

EPILOGUE

SEPTEMBER 10, 2004
Vail, Colorado

I am once again on my traditional post-summer journey from Montana to Los Angeles, taking notice of every thought, every impulse, even, *especially,* the ones I wish would go away. Typically, refreshed after my annual escape into the mountains and streams near Flathead Lake, I experience a surge of excitement, anticipation, using this drive over miles and miles of empty road to ruminate about the game that has been my life, about how to motivate the young men who will soon assemble at training camp for the long adventure ahead. I think about the days and nights that we will share in our quest to become true warriors, to form a bond, to win a championship. There will be numerous sacrifices, but, if we play the game with passion and commitment, if we stay together no matter the forces against us, there will also be numerous rewards.

I'm experiencing different emotions on this trip. For the second time since the mid-1980s, I am not going back to a coaching job in the National Basketball Association. I am headed, instead, to a future of uncertainty. There is a sense of freedom, to be sure, freedom from planes and practices, from egos and tantrums, from the endless scrutiny that never seems to dissipate. Yet, there is also a strong, undeniable sense of apprehension. My diary chronicling the Lakers' turbulent season, which ended with our loss to the Pistons in the Finals, will be released next month. I wrote the book to convey the demands and challenges that emerge, both on and off the court, in an average basketball season. Of course, I was pretty certain that last season, with the additions of free agents Karl Malone and Gary Payton, with my lame-duck status, and, with the distractions posed by Kobe Bryant's case in Colorado, would be anything but average. In my entries, I tried to place as much emphasis as possible on the game itself, its purity, harmony. There is nothing quite like it when everything moves in its proper flow and rhythm.

Of course, I'm not naïve. I've been around long enough to know that the focus, at least in the papers and on the airwaves, will be on the tremendous adversity we went through, from the Kobe–Shaq feud in late October to the breakdown in my contract talks in February to our failure in June. We became the most riveting soap opera in sports. There always seemed to be a new plot twist to top the previous one. In recent weeks, I've endured my share of sleepless nights, wondering about how my perceptions will be received by the players, the organization, and, perhaps most importantly, the fans. Soon, at least, I will not have to wonder any longer.

The trip has already been more eventful that I could have imagined. When I was in Steamboat Springs, Colorado, to attend a high school reunion with six buddies, I learned that my house by the beach in Los Angeles had been robbed. The thieves got away with a television set, a computer, eight leather jackets, and some jewelry. Fortunately, concerned that the place might be a little exposed over the summer, I had put all my championship rings in a safe deposit box. The only irreplaceable item taken was an engraved watch given to me by Michael Jordan.

As I get closer to LA, any anxieties begin, thankfully, to lessen. I realize that whatever happens in the weeks and months ahead, I have been true to my convictions. I can't ask for anything else.

OCTOBER 15
Los Angeles

I was driving to San Diego a few days ago with Jeanie when she received an urgent call from John Black, the Lakers PR director. With excerpts of the book beginning to generate big news on television and in the papers, the Lakers decided they could stay silent no longer. They were about to issue a press release, claiming that the book contains "several inaccuracies." Hmmm, was there a typo I missed, a name I misspelled, a date I got wrong? I simply could not imagine what they were talking about. Neither could Jeanie, who tried to talk Black out it, arguing that I had not vilified the organization, and that pointing out "inaccuracies" without being specific would be meaningless. The Lakers, it seemed, were trying to damage the book's credibility, my credibility, without being held accountable. Jeanie argued to no avail. I suppose I can't blame the Lakers. They needed to protect themselves.

I am grateful, at least, that all the uproar over the book doesn't seem to have caused a rift in my relationship with Dr. Buss, which I have greatly valued. A few weeks ago, I called to let him know that I was not interested in accepting his offer to be a consultant, which he first extended back in June. I knew it would be a complete no-win situation for me. I did tell him, however, that he would soon be receiving a copy of the book before the press was given one. I felt he should be prepared for the inevitable barrage of questions from the reporters in training camp. I owed him that. He said he appreciated my gesture, and invited me to join him in his box for a game. Sure, I said, sometime in the spring.

NOVEMBER 17
Flathead Lake

After a solid, exhausting month of promoting the book, I'm back in Montana, ready to resume work on the new home. For the most part, the tour, which took me to Chicago and New York in addition to Los Angeles, went extremely well. I made an appearance on Leno, did a live interview with CNN's Wolf Blitzer, and was on dozens of TV and radio shows. The only difficult moments emerged when the interviewers kept pounding away at

Kobe's troubles in Colorado. I found myself, despite the criticism I had given him, becoming very protective, even defensive. I was no longer his coach or mentor. In fact, I was quite sure he was angry at me for the things I wrote about him in the book. Yet I still felt a great deal of compassion for this young man, for the difficulties he endured while awaiting trial, and for the challenges he will face in repairing his tarnished image. Even though the trial was called off, in the minds of many of his detractors, a verdict has still been rendered: guilty. Sadly, there seems to be nothing, at least for the time being, that Kobe can do about it.

He is not the only one who has received criticism. Several people close to the game have harped on about how I violated some unwritten code by exposing conversations and events that took place behind closed doors. Nonsense. There was no such thing as closed doors for the Lakers. Reporters used to tell me all the time that they couldn't wait for the locker room to open because players would routinely reveal what had just transpired in team meetings or in supposedly private conversations.

Meanwhile, there's recently been tension between myself and the Buss family. Last month, after a hectic day shuttling from one interview to the next, I attended *Bombay Dreams,* a Broadway musical with Jerry, Jeanie, and her brother, Jimmy. The play was excruciating enough, but that was only part of the problem. I was incredibly uncomfortable trying to squeeze into my seat. We went to dinner afterward at an Italian restaurant in Soho. Sitting there, I felt like a total outsider. It's no mystery why. While I've been on television and the bestseller list, the Laker organization, which is, after all, the family business, has had to deal with multiple questions, most obviously the wisdom of trading Shaquille.

DECEMBER 30
Los Angeles

This town was buzzing for days in anticipation of the Christmas Day match between Kobe and Shaq, staged at the Staples Center. Because if there's anything this town adores, it's conflict. The juicier, the nastier, the better. Yet in the hours leading up to the game, I didn't feel any excitement. For five years, from training camp through the playoffs, I hung around Shaq and Kobe almost every day. But now, spending Christmas in San Francisco with my ex-wife, June, and our kids, I was away from the action, and I liked it. I skipped the entire first half to play a board game, and watched only portions of the second. I had things to do, such as peeling white onions for dinner. I've made it a point, actually, to isolate myself as much as possible from the Lakers since the season started in early November. Of course, dating the owner's daughter makes that kind of, well, impossible. No wonder, then, as the year winds down, I'm looking forward to my eight-week sojourn to Australia and New Zealand. The Lakers and NBA basketball will be the furthest things from my mind.

JANUARY 27, 2005
Melbourne, Australia

For the past week, I've been near the court. The tennis court, that is, catching the action at the Australian Open. I love the game, the way it tests character and courage one shot after another. I've observed all the stars: Federer, Roddick, Agassi, Safin, Serena, etc. One former player, Pam Shriver, who is now a television analyst, asked if she could interview me in the stands on my first day. No harm there, I figured. I haven't been on the front page in months. Suddenly, however, out of nowhere, she asked me if I would be interested in coaching the Knicks. The Knicks? I thought they had a coach, a guy named Lenny Wilkens, a Hall of Famer in fact. Well, not anymore. Wilkens was gone, a fact that, not surprisingly, wasn't considered a high priority in the Australian papers. Even Down Under, apparently, there is no escape.

FEBRUARY 5
Perth, Australia

Definitely no escape. The other day, after fishing for herring and swimming in the Indian Ocean with Luc Longley, one of my former players with the Bulls, I turned on the computer to find an urgent e-mail message from Jeanie. Rudy Tomjanovich, my replacement, was rumored to be on the verge of quitting. I wasn't shocked. When I first heard in July that Rudy T. would take the job, I wondered if he could handle the demands, physically, because of his bladder cancer, and mentally, because of the intensity of coaching in Los Angeles. This was a long way from Houston. Soon, news of his resignation became official, and immediately the e-mails started to flood in, including one from John Black. The messages were all the same: Would you be interested in coaching the Lakers again?

Perhaps, but certainly not this season. The moment I learned that the opportunity might be available, I experienced two powerful, yet contradictory, emotions. One was attraction, the chance to again mold a group of individuals with different, often conflicting, needs into a single, cohesive unit capable of winning a championship. That's always been the lure of this job. I wondered, after our loss to the Pistons, whether perhaps it was me who had let them down instead of the other way around. Maybe I didn't discover the right way to motivate them. Maybe we should have tried another session of meditation. Who knows? In any case, returning to the bench would afford me a second chance.

My other immediate reaction was aversion. The old, familiar tensions, many linked to my arguments with Kobe, which had washed away in recent months, suddenly resurfaced. In many ways, leaving the Lakers probably saved my soul. I've always believed that you can lose your soul in some form or fashion when you chase the almighty dollar. If that is the case, then why would I want to put my soul in jeopardy again? Why would I want to deal with today's self-indulgent athletes, so different from the ones I knew in the '60s and '70s, even the '80s? And why would I want to spend so much time again with the members of the fourth estate? Do they really need to have access to me three or four times a day? No wonder I run out of things to say. Worse yet, no wonder, every so often, I say the wrong thing.

Besides, I'm enjoying the journey I'm on right now. I'm savoring this rare opportunity to travel on my own without the built-in restrictions of the NBA schedule. Luc is the perfect guy to hang out with, so sensitive and sociable. When I coached him in Chicago, I engaged in conversations with him that I never could have had with anyone else. He asked me about Jeanie. Before I left Los Angeles in January, I told her that I felt both of us should be free during this time apart to explore any social relationship that might arise without worrying that we would be betraying our trust in each other. "Who knows where I'll go when I get back?" I told her. Already, I'm convinced, it's made our relationship stronger.

One thing is certain: I will not allow this Laker soap opera to intrude on my travels. I'm pretty fortunate, actually, to be in the South Pacific, which is about as far away from Los Angeles as one can be, sheltering me from the hordes. I told Todd, my agent, as well as Jeanie, that there will be plenty of time in the months ahead to think about next year, about whether I want to coach the Lakers again. Whether I want to coach *period*. Right now, there is only one destination on my mind: New Zealand.

FEBRUARY 19
Auckland, New Zealand

Usually, around this time of year, I start to gear up for the play-offs, every game more intense, every move subject to scrutiny. Even the practices take on greater significance. Needless to say, my schedule has been a bit less rigid this February. I've seen so much of this beautiful country. I rode a motorcycle through the town of Greymouth, seeing miles and miles of coastline as breathtaking as anything in California. Hills, curves, mountains, one-lane bridges, you name it, this place has it. Of course, no matter how remote the location, how pristine the environment, once again it has been impossible to fully avoid the life I left behind. Last week, I received a call from Linda Rambis, Kurt's wife, who pressed me to make a decision one way or the other about the Lakers job so that Jeanie could tell her dad. With all due respect, I've been too busy swimming or snorkeling to think about the state of the Lakers. I called Jeanie after talking to Linda, and told her I would give more thought to the matter when I got back to LA in a few weeks. She understands. She told me about a recent conversation she had with Karl Malone, who has formally announced his retirement. "Don't make Phil come back and coach the Lakers," he told her. I'm sure there are others who share the same sentiment.

April 18
Los Angeles

During a recent game against the Rockets, I finally took Dr. Buss up on the long-standing offer to join him in his box. I was planning to be at Staples anyway, hanging out with members of 826 LA, an organization that helps students develop their writing skills. It sure felt strange to be in the arena, but not on the floor barking instructions, contemplating lineup adjustments. I've spent little time in my life as a "fan." It felt even stranger, though, to sit in the owner's box for two hours and exchange maybe a total of two sentences with Dr. Buss. There was a young girl between us, which is often the case, and, besides, I don't think he really wanted to be seen conferring with his ex-coach. I'm not surprised. Jerry likes to separate business from pleasure, even though there is always a message to everything he does. In this case, I'm pretty sure he wants me to know he's very interested in me coming back.

On the drive home, it dawns on me that the season is about to end, which means the long-delayed decision-making process is about to begin. Teams will be on the phone to Todd, trying to gauge my level of interest, and I'll have to engage in serious soul-searching. While I'm leaning toward two scenarios—taking the Lakers' job or staying retired for at least another year—I would be foolish not to take any meetings.

MAY 2
Los Angeles

I met recently here with Isiah Thomas, the head of basketball operations for the Knicks. There has been a lot of speculation in the press recently that Isiah and I would never be able to get along, that our egos would clash. As is the case with much speculation that's driven by the media, this is unfounded. I like Isiah a lot, and believe he is an astute observer of the game with his own vision of how to make the Knicks a contender again. Sure he and I were rivals in the late 1980s and early 1990s, but as you get older, you develop a deeper appreciation for the struggles you endured together. Instead of hating your rival, you learn to honor him. It is a vital component of the warrior mentality to respect your enemy, to realize that you cannot be great unless he is great.

Isiah was very gracious in our meeting, and though he did not make a formal offer, I got the feeling that the job is mine if I want it. Fact is, I don't. I know there are those who believe this move makes so much sense during this late, and perhaps final, stage of my basketball career. I started as a Knick, so, therefore, I should finish as a Knick. Yet, while I possess wonderful memories of playing in New York, of riding my bike to the Garden, of learning everything about the game and life from Red Holzman, I feel no urgent need to go to back to New York to fulfill some kind of destiny determined by others. So far, at least, I'm also not interested in the other possibilities that have come up. There have been no serious talks, and I don't expect any.

I'm waiting, instead, for a meeting that I'm sure will have a much greater bearing on my future—the one with Kobe. When I called after the season ended, he told me he was heading out of town for a few weeks, and would check in when he returns. I didn't get the sense that he was avoiding me, but he's clearly in no hurry, either.

May 18
Los Angeles

In a press conference two weeks ago, Dr. Buss downplayed the possibility of me coming back to the Lakers. Yes, I was on the list of potential hires, but he made it clear that there were others on the list, as well. This admission is threatening to Jeanie, who believes bringing me back is essential for stabilizing the franchise. She has stepped out of her normal role as Executive Vice President of Business Affairs to champion me as the logical successor. In the past, she had never taken an official stance in basketball matters.

I've made my own statements to the press lately, and some of them did not go over too well. Speaking at an event sponsored by the Positive Coaching Alliance, for which I am a spokesman, I left myself open to questions from the press, and believe me, they weren't interested in theories about positive reinforcement. I made the comment that the Lakers current roster was "not appealing at all," and there were players who, frankly, had not earned their lunch money this season. One writer jumped all over that one, interpreting it as a sign that I had serious reservations about taking the job. In fact, the exact opposite was the case. I was becoming engaged again in the state of the franchise, thinking like the coach I was before and might become again.

There are compelling arguments on both sides. On the one hand, there is something I refer to as the greater good for the greater number of people. Wherever I go, I'm approached by fans, some practically begging for my return. They don't even ask for a championship, only a team that plays with passion. With all the success the Lakers have enjoyed in recent years, watching a team struggling to play .500 has been a miserable experience for their loyal supporters. People think I would never take on a team that has no legitimate chance to win a championship. This is one of the major misconceptions about me. Success can be measured in many different ways. For one team, it might mean fifty wins, or forty. Either way, I would find the challenge just as invigorating.

On the other hand, I'm concerned about how going back to coaching, especially this team, might harm my health, physical and mental. My therapist consistently warns me that I'm still in denial, that I have failed to treat the end of my tenure last June as a truly traumatic event, and that it might take a year to eighteen months to fully recover. I see his point, but don't necessarily agree. I haven't felt pain or anger or rejection since then. Only relief.

MAY 31
Flathead Lake

Here, removed from the constant distractions in Los Angeles, I'm able to ponder on a more spiritual level the possibilities for the future. Already, I've reached one very important conclusion: I do not need to meet with Kobe to make up my mind. For months, I assumed, if there were any chance of me going back to the Lakers, he and I needed to see if we could bury the past and build a future. If we couldn't work things out off the court, how could we possibly get along on the court? Yet, I realize now, by making our chat such an integral part of the decision-making process, all it did was push him away. He's been blamed for enough already in this town without having to play the role of villain once again if, after our meeting, I were to decide not to accept the position. His reluctance to get together is, actually, a sign of a new maturity. He has decided to relinquish any desire to control the situation, letting the organization control it. I am proud of him, and more optimistic than ever that he will reach his true potential both as a basketball player and a man. Since the book came out, people have focused too much on the fact I called Kobe uncoachable. They skipped over another point I made, that Kobe was the floor general of a team that went to the Finals last year, and will surely be the floor general for years to come.

I've also dispensed with another longtime assumption, that my health would be endangered by a return to the NBA. "Dad, you're so much more relaxed," my son Ben and daughter Brooke told me the other day. Maybe so, but I now realize that returning to the vigorous work schedule required in the NBA would activate me in a way that I can't activate myself no matter how extensive a workout program I go through. Can coaching be an agonizing experience? Yes. Do I have to deal with children on occasion? Of course. Will there be more sleepless nights because of outrageous calls from officials? No doubt. But do I love this game? Absolutely.

Nonetheless, I have yet to make a final decision. I suppose I'm waiting for some kind of divine intervention, a magical moment where everything becomes clear. I'm heading back to LA in the morning. Maybe it will come there. It better come soon. I told Mitch I would give him an answer by the end of the week.

June 15

Los Angeles

I went back to work today. I met with Mitch about the draft, held one-on-ones with several players, and did some interviews from my office. I was once again coaching the Los Angeles Lakers. Why did this happen? Why, nearly one year after I was replaced by Rudy Tomjanovich, after what I truly believed was my last season, am I ready to try this again?

The answer, I've come to realize in recent days, has to do with how I define who I am. I have always believed in a world of endless possibilities for renewal, of opportunities for rebirth and reconciliation. I simply do not want to contemplate a world in which such possibilities don't exist. Believe me, I tried the other way. I tried to tell myself, Jeanie, Todd, and others close to me that

I wouldn't take this job. I even said it out loud. I suppose I wanted to see how I really felt once I allowed that idea to sink in. I did not feel good. For the first time in my life, it seemed I was running away from my destiny.

I have no illusions. The honeymoon period is wonderful now, but I know there are going to be moments when I'll question my sanity for jumping back into this most intense environment. Maybe it will be after getting blown out in Cleveland. Or maybe after somebody forgets a defensive assignment on the last possession. Or maybe after another one of those endless flights, or nights when sleep doesn't come. I know it will happen, but when it does, I will remind myself how I felt at the press conference yesterday at Staples, when for the first time in a long time, everything was right again.

Soon, after the draft, I will be head back to Montana for a few weeks of rest. I will check on the progress of the house, and prepare myself, physically and spiritually, for the adventure ahead. I'm turning sixty in September. I can't assume that I will be able to do my job with the exact same energy that I possessed with the Bulls, or even during my first years in Los Angeles. Every year, the demands and challenges of coaching in the NBA grow, and I want to make sure that I am ready for them. Next season will not be easy. There will be no Shaquille, and we have a lot of holes to plug to put ourselves on the same level with the elite teams in the Western Conference. Nonetheless, I can't wait for training camp to begin.

I can't wait to teach the fundamentals of the triangle offense, to explore the concepts and movements that make basketball the greatest game ever.

I can't wait to hear the sound from the crowd after a victory, the sound of a community that believes once again.

Most of all, I can't wait to bring twelve individuals into a circle before practice begins, to look in their eyes, and know we are a team of One.

I can't wait for next season.

FOR THE BEST IN PAPERBACKS, LOOK FOR THE 🐧

In every corner of the world, on every subject under the sun, Penguin represents quality and variety—the very best in publishing today.

For complete information about books available from Penguin—including Penguin Classics, Penguin Compass, and Puffins—and how to order them, write to us at the appropriate address below. Please note that for copyright reasons the selection of books varies from country to country.

In the United States: Please write to *Penguin Group (USA), P.O. Box 12289 Dept. B, Newark, New Jersey 07101-5289* or call 1-800-788-6262.

In the United Kingdom: Please write to *Dept. EP, Penguin Books Ltd, Bath Road, Harmondsworth, West Drayton, Middlesex UB7 0DA*.

In Canada: Please write to *Penguin Books Canada Ltd, 90 Eglinton Avenue East, Suite 700, Toronto, Ontario M4P 2Y3*.

In Australia: Please write to *Penguin Books Australia Ltd, P.O. Box 257, Ringwood, Victoria 3134*.

In New Zealand: Please write to *Penguin Books (NZ) Ltd, Private Bag 102902, North Shore Mail Centre, Auckland 10*.

In India: Please write to *Penguin Books India Pvt Ltd, 11 Panchsheel Shopping Centre, Panchsheel Park, New Delhi 110 017*.

In the Netherlands: Please write to *Penguin Books Netherlands bv, Postbus 3507, NL-1001 AH Amsterdam*.

In Germany: Please write to *Penguin Books Deutschland GmbH, Metzlerstrasse 26, 60594 Frankfurt am Main*.

In Spain: Please write to *Penguin Books S. A., Bravo Murillo 19, 1° B, 28015 Madrid*.

In Italy: Please write to *Penguin Italia s.r.l., Via Benedetto Croce 2, 20094 Corsico, Milano*.

In France: Please write to *Penguin France, Le Carré Wilson, 62 rue Benjamin Baillaud, 31500 Toulouse*.

In Japan: Please write to *Penguin Books Japan Ltd, Kaneko Building, 2-3-25 Koraku, Bunkyo-Ku, Tokyo 112*.

In South Africa: Please write to *Penguin Books South Africa (Pty) Ltd, Private Bag X14, Parkview, 2122 Johannesburg*.